W9-BFN-566

STUDENT LIFE AND EXAMS
Stresses and Coping Strategies

Daniel C. Albas
Cheryl Mills Albas

University of Manitoba

**KENDALL/HUNT
PUBLISHING COMPANY**
Dubuque, Iowa

To Our Students

Copyright © 1984 by Kendall/Hunt Publishing Company

Library of Congress Catalog Card Number: 84–81102

ISBN 0–8403–3362–5

Printed in the United States of America
10   9   8   7   6   5   4   3

Contents

Appendix A. Methodology, 158

Preface

In this monograph we aim to reach a sociological understanding of university examinations. To this end exams (as we shall call them throughout the book) are placed in an historical and social structural context and their impact on students is thoroughly analyzed. The major focus of the work is on the sources of exam related stress students face and how they go about coping. The monograph is organized in a manner which allows us to follow students through the "Study Phase" of activity into the "Examination Situation" itself and finally to their eventual reintegration with the everyday world of routines.

This work is intended to be of interest to academic social scientists, to practicing teachers at all levels and of course to students themselves. Anyone who has ever been a student will find him/herself described over and over again throughout the book as the largely unconscious, taken-for-granted exam related aspects of the world are brought to light and made comprehensible. It is hoped that all readers will gain insight into their fundamentally social nature as they discover that many problems they believed were personal are actually widely shared. In the process, the sociological theories, propositions, and concepts introduced along the way are meant not only to sensitize readers to the sociological aspect of exams but also to provide a better understanding of the sources of role strain students face and thereby the possibility of allowing them to develop more effective coping and study strategies. The concepts are defined in a clear, down to earth manner to reach the student population while for fellow scholars, the frequent definition of what might be regarded as the "obvious", is not so much in the interest of telling them what they already know as in recognizing the considerable diversity of definition and perspective which exists in the discipline. It is hoped that teachers at all levels will come to a more complete understanding of examinations, how they aid in "tying society together" and their profound effects on the lives of students.

The attempt to reach disparate audiences creates inherent difficulties for the authors because of the necessity to straddle different levels of sophistication and professional terminology. We attempt to walk the tightrope between levels and to avoid making the presentation too simplistic for one audience or too complicated for the other. In spite of these difficulties it is our sincere hope that both audiences will find the book rewarding to read.

Even though we include an appendix which details the research procedure, readers need to be alerted at the outset to some of its most important points. Firstly, the monograph is based on empirical data gathered over an eleven year period, and consists of recorded observations made by ourselves in study areas, examination halls and other places, interviews with students, and exam logs kept by students throughout their examination experiences. The use of exam logs allowed us to "get inside" the students' perspective to understand the situation as they view it. For this reason, throughout the monograph we use the students own words (and grammar most of the time) to bring a reality and subtle insight to the description of the exam experience. We also insert these quotations rather abruptly at times with the quotation marks as their only identification. It is hoped that readers will accept this mode of presentation in the spirit intended.

Secondly, the methodological strategy employed in analysing the data is one of triangulation in which different approaches to the topic (e.g., participant observation, quasi-experimental controls, critical comments of the students themselves to early drafts of the study, unobtrusive measures, and incorporation of other pertinent research findings) are followed in such a way as to have the strength of one approach compensate for the weakness of another. Quantitative measures are utilized, but minimally so. However it should not be inferred that the study is impressionistic. We have attempted to make it rigorously rational and factually founded.

Briefly, the outline of the book is as follows. Chapter 1 sets examinations in their historical context and establishes their centrality to contemporary society in both the macro world of public affairs and the micro world of face-to-face relations. Chapters II and III present a theoretical scheme for making sense of the ways in which students cope with examination stress. Chapters IV through IX empirically describe the stresses students experience and the ways in which they cope. We also attempt to interpret these stresses and coping strategies in terms of the conceptualizations presented in Chapter II and III. In chapter X we provide a critical assessment of the case against examinations and conclude with practical study recommendations for students.

Briefly, then, the promise of the sociological perspective is that it increases and enriches our understanding of the world and of ourselves. It encourages us to examine the ongoing forces at work in close-up, face-to-face "micro-world" encounters and considers systematically the vast behind-the-scenes network of the "macro-world". As Berger says: "The fascination of sociology lies in the fact that its perspective makes us see in a new light the very world in which we have lived our lives." With this work we hope that we have, to some extent, achieved such a goal.

Acknowledgments

This work could not have been completed without the co-operation and insight of hundreds of students who were willing to share their exam-related experiences with us. To them we express our deep appreciation.

We are deeply indebted to the following people who helped to make this project a reality. Dr. K. W. McCluskey provided feedback on the earliest formulations of the study. Professors E. D. Boldt, L. W. Roberts, G. Baureiss, S. Moon, J. Goldstein and L. Driedger, University of Manitoba provided critical comments on various drafts of the monograph. Professors Robert Stebbins, University of Calgary and Wilfred Martin, Memorial University carried out painstaking reviews of the entire work. Professor Rodney Clifton, University of Manitoba was a source of insightful comments and encouragement throughout the project. Finally, we express special thanks to Professor D. L. Rennie, University of Manitoba. His insights, constant valuable criticisms, and unending encouragement lightened our burden throughout and added immeasurably to the completed product. Of course, the authors accept responsibility for all of the shortcomings of this work.

We are also grateful to the University of Manitoba for providing financial assistance in the form of a research grant to aid in preparation of the manuscript.

Chapter I

Introduction

The Centrality of Exams to Student Life

To understand fully the nature of student life, one must realize just how much of it revolves directly or indirectly around the exam. All students, from primary schoolchild to Ph.D candidate, are faced with having to participate in this most trying of student rites. Exams are occasions where the institution not only controls the body—by subjecting it to minute and detailed scrutiny—but also penetrates the mind with its tests. The purpose of these probes is to expose the amount of "knowledge" possessed by individuals, or perhaps the relative lack thereof. Also exams are used to determine how well individuals have been able to bear their manifold responsibilities. Certainly the educational institution gives considerable weight to test scores.

For many students, one of the central features of a course is the nature of its evaluation procedure. Indeed, first classes usually start off with students wanting to know how they will be evaluated. Almost invariably, a substantial portion of the evaluation rests on examinations. Students soon become more specific and want to know the number of exams required as well as their format (essay, short answer, or objective type questions) and relative weight (percentage of final grade). Students also want to know the relative emphasis that will be placed on lecture material and assigned readings. In a sense, everything revolves around the exam. As one student put it: "As soon as I know the exam dates, I write them on my calendar. My life from then on centres around them."

Not only does the first significant interaction between professor and students revolve around the topic of exams, but the impending examination rite also serves as a background for every class encounter. Students continually evaluate what professors say in class in terms of its potential relevance for exams. Thus, at a point where discussion seems to meander, a frustrated student will frequently raise a hand and inquire, "Is this going to be on the exam?" Indeed, one common source of complaints against professors is that "they tend to wander" from core test material.

Interpenetration of the Micro and Macro Worlds

It is clear that people live in what may be conceived of as two worlds: a micro world of face-to-face relationships and a macro world of institutions which structure face to face relationships and even determine whether they take place. The exam is one of the micro worlds within which students live. It was stated above that the exam is central—and so it is as far as being of focal importance and that around which student life largely revolves. And yet it is also true to say that the exam is a part of the macro world as well. It is clearly a mechanism by which the micro world penetrates and is penetrated by the macro world.

Exam behaviour has consequences which extend far beyond the boundaries of the situation within which students are enmeshed for only a short period of time. Students who prepare for and enter the world of the exam carry with them many unstated values and assumptions acquired from the larger social context. Since such values and assumptions play a significant part in students' exam behaviour it is useful to make them explicit because, as Scheflen (1972:134) notes, "a society is maintained by carrying over basic images and values from one transaction to another." An understanding of the images and values of each life transaction is necessary for understanding subsequent ones.

If we are to understand the exam we must look at the continual, reciprocal interpenetration of the micro world of face-to-face interactions and the vast, behind the scenes structures of the macro world which results in experiences that "make sense" to the interactants. Exams would have little meaning if there were not a larger competitive, achievement-emphasizing society which values higher education and elaborates an occupational structure to accept the graduates of these trying occasions. Because both professors and students are socialized to the norms and values of the larger world, these norms and values aid in the maintenance of the occupational structure and reinforce some of its most central values, for example, achievement and competition. However, these values have not always existed, but rather have gradually developed as a part of the various social changes that resulted from the industrial revolution. For one thing, increasing division of labour resulted in a separation of household and economic pursuits. As the economy became more complex, a system of mass education arose to train people in the newly required skills. There was a simultaneous decline in traditional family functions including the importance of family connections for securing jobs. A new respect for professional competence and merit emerged and concern for the evils of nepotism increased. The new emphasis on achievement and competition as criteria of qualification for desired professional and administrative positions meant that a new technique for assessing occupational qualifications, acceptable to both the contestants and the larger society, had to be developed. In Britain during the 1850's considerable effort was expended to extol the merits of standardized public examinations. Among the points stressed in XIXth Century England were that public examinations would motivate students to study harder, force teachers to "keep on their toes," and increase general standards; all of which would benefit the society's values and economic standing. By the

2

year 1900, formal exams were accepted and subject "only to cultivation" (Roach, 1971).[1]

Because the members of a society, for the most part, do not themselves originate values like competitive achievement but rather confront them ready-made as aspects of their culture, such values tend to be fragile. As Berger and Kelner (1964:4) put it there is "an ever-present glimmer as to their social manufacture and relativity." These values therefore must be continually enacted and thus validated. While such validation must be undertaken by individuals themselves, it must also be expressed by others in routine face-to-face situations (where others demonstrate that they also hold the same values). In this manner values are objectified and become part of reality. Consequently, society at large backs up, supports and preserves the exam, and the exam supports and preserves the larger social order.

Exams provide a social arena where cultural values of achievement and competition are regularly acted out. Exams not only shape the identities of the actors, but also provide living testimony to the current relevance and applicability of these values. In the event that exam occasions of some sort did not exist, or if the interactants refused to countenance the values of competition and achievement, exams would soon lose not only their moral vigour but also their reality. When asked what exams meant to her, one student replied: "Exams mean work, no sleep, and above all the goal to do well."

The goal of achievement is actualized through intense, concentrated effort under severe time restrictions where writing and thinking are the main involvements. The fact that these main involvements have been internalized is reflected by students who noted: "During an exam the right thing is to be working hard . . . Wasting time during exams is horrible." The existence and the compelling quality of this norm is clearly evident in the fact that some students taking an exam feel a distinctive need to be seen engaged in work when an invigilator passes by.

Exams are perhaps one of the purest embodiments of inner worldly asceticism which, in the Western world, is known as the Protestant Ethic. Exams have the structural characteristics of their religious origins where the one-to-one relationship between man and God is now substituted for by the more secular relationship between professor and student. They also involve intense disciplined effort. And, as we know, academically related thinking is painful; so we avoid it whenever possible. However, well-designed exams literally force one to think and, in the words of one student, are "brain-wracking experiences."

---

1. Prior to this period examinations were not completely unknown. Indeed, as an extension in many ways of the traditional system of disputations, exams enjoyed a high degree of confidence as well as respect. Disputations included a written examination (in English) plus an oral defense of the thesis (in Latin). The tradition facilitated the ability of universities to develop a monopoly over school examinations, a tradition which continues as one of the university's major function.

The achievement theme motivates and regulates performance, and also has a direct bearing on the self identities of the participants. After all, exams are a type of student trademark—a part of their identity. For example, one student noted the implication of performance for self-concept by stating: "Exams are a necessary symbol by which one can prove to himself and others that he really is a student who is learning." Another added: "To be identified as a 'good' student one must do well in evaluations, which usually consist of exams." Thus, one must write exams not only as a part of one's role, but also as a means of achieving an identity—that of "good student." In a similar vein, another individual noted that " 'A' students are rewarded by a feeling of confidence and can legitimately play their role of achiever." In other words, exams play a fundamental role in the student's socialization and development of self concept. Along with the emphasis on individual achievement comes a strong element of competition: "Exams bring with them a keen competitiveness for grades. If a person in front of you is madly writing, you feel an acute sense of nervous panic; you get the feeling that he really knows his material so you also start to write madly." Exams, then, are stituations wherein the participants routinely embody and give living testimony to certain values, thereby invigorating and validating them.

Another related way in which the micro and macro worlds meet and interpenetrate is in the sorting and selecting functions of exams. Exams are the usual means of sorting students into those considered to be promising achievers and those who are not. More importantly, exams determine who can continue in the role of student. As Hurn (1978:73) suggests, this sorting process has consequences for future adult status: "educational qualifications both symbolize higher status and are instrumentally important in achieving such status." In short, exams may be linked to the process of social stratification and the distribution of differential rewards such as power, privilege and status, which must be effectively legitimized for purposes of social stability. To prevent dissatisfaction and potential unrest, members of society must be convinced of the worthiness of individuals occupying certain highly rewarded posts. This legitimation is especially difficult in a democratic society which stresses that all persons have a right to the opportunity to attain highly rewarded positions. Furthermore, attainment is ideally based on merit rather than on the inheritance of a favourable social legacy. Indeed, in Britain during the years 1850–1900, arguments favouring standardized testing were frequently based on the fact that exams served to moderate feelings of social discontent. A system of open competition or formal exams among all social ranks would, in the words of one educational reformer, "do more to attach the lower and middle classes of society to the institutions of their society than any other measure of reform" (Roach, 1971:29). During a period when ideas of Marxian class consciousness and revolution abounded, this sort of reasoning had tremendous impact. From this perspective, the evaluation of students by the educational system takes on increased importance.

4

The most convincing form of evaluation has traditionally been found in the examination, where the school goes to elaborate lengths to ensure that students (regardless of external system characteristics such as race, creed, or sex) are treated equally. In an effort to insure that students are on an equal footing, the logic of experimental design is implicitly employed. All students write the exam in the same area, frequently a gymnasium, where they are exposed to the same stimuli of temperature, lighting, and extraneous noise (from heating pipes, etc.). Possibilities of maturational effects are also controlled, since all write the exam at the same time and none have the opportunity to study longer or to ask others what the questions were. All students have the same amount of time to write the exam and, very importantly, everyone must answer the same questions. In other words, the exam situation is structured to insure that the results represent the efforts of the individual student: it highlights the importance of achievement versus ascription.[2] While parental social class can, of course, influence school performance, "parents can by no means be said to control its outcome" (Hurn, 1978:89). It is the academic institution—in a sense the occupational processing centre—which mediates between class origin and class destination (cf. Beriter, 1977).

Differential performance, at least in terms of pass or fail, is linked to differential rewards in adult life; so the social organization of exams helps to insure that each student is treated equally. In Hurn's (1978:65) words: "The legitimators of inequality . . . require equality of opportunity." Of course, it is also possible to take a Marxian view and suggest that exams perpetuate the myth of equality of opportunity because students tend to perform very much in accordance with their relatively ranked privileged origins (Hurn, 1978). Roach (1971) asserts that upper class Victorians were quite ready to live with a system of public examinations. The feeling was that the more expensive educations of the upper classes would afford them a distinct advantage in any contest.[3] In any case, as exam acts are repeated, they tend to reinvigorate the

2. Kwong(1983:97–8) presents an extreme illustration of the lengths to which a society is willing to go to insure equality among students. In modern day China exams are set by a central committee composed of university and high school faculty from across the country. "To ensure confidentiality and secrecy these committee members remain isolated in a pleasant resort for about five months after the examination questions are set until the examination date . . . examinations are not held in the students' schools but at centers established in the city and county seats . . . each candidate is assigned a number and no name appears on the examination paper. . . . They trust that 'before the system of grades, everyone is equal' and that a fair system of selection has been instituted."

3. Roach (1971) states that an unintended benefit of public examinations was to demonstrate that successful women participants were capable of handling the strains associated with preparing for and writing exams. Parents were usually reluctant to allow their daughters to sit for the exams fearing that the young females might overwork themselves, suffer mental breakdowns, and that open competition might compromise their reputations. Special arrangements were adopted to overcome this view. The invigilator had to be a married man and, at all times, would be accompanied by two lady members of the examination committee. Also, writers (competitors) names were concealed and numbers were used for identification in order to prevent the stigma of aggressiveness when the results were published.

5

values, beliefs, dogma, and authority structures of the larger society, the school, and the very classroom situation within which they occur. The larger social organization maintains the programming of the exam and the program maintains the social organization (Scheflen, 1972). Or, "the education process is above all the means by which society perpetually recreates the conditions of its very existence" (Durkheim, 1956:123).

To this point our discussion has revolved around the importance of exams in student life and how exams and society interpenetrate each other. Our next task is to attempt to make sociological sense of exams by employing appropriate theoretical perspectives.

Chapter II

Making Sociological Sense of the Exam

The exam is a sociological phenomenon in its own right since it is an occasion which both brings people together and, on the other hand, disperses them. In addition, because of its structural components and social psychological overtones, it generates considerable stress in students. Accordingly it seems a worthwhile sociological endeavour to set out those concepts and theoretical perspectives which may be used to explain the origins of stress in the exam situation and the reasons for the stress-coping mechanisms exhibited by students. In what follows we develop the structural concepts of role, position, role set, and status set as well as aligning actions such as motive talk and fritters within the symbolic interactional frame of reference. We will also endeavour to show how these two theoretical perspectives complement each other in making sociological sense of the exam. This monograph is, however, not merely theoretical. It is an empirical study (the methodology of which is described in the appendix) in which the theoretical orientation of a wide spectrum of authors are tested and modified and new propositions are offered.

Conceptual Orientations: The Structural and Symbolic Interactional Approaches

A. The Structural Approach

i) Positions, Roles, and Norms

The structural approach generally stresses the role of factors which exist independently of individuals and which constrain them to act, think, and feel in particular ways. Role theory, as a facet of the structural approach, assumes that a society, organization, or group is composed of a network of interdependent positions defined by reciprocal ties to other positions. These ties may be conceptualized as expected behaviour on the part of people occupying these positions (i.e., their roles). Furthermore these expectations are in terms of norms which define the rights and duties actors may legitimately demand of each other. In sum, normative expectations cluster together to form a role, and roles cluster together to form a position. Since positions and their roles establish where and what people are in social terms, they provide answers to the question of who we are and give us a sense of social identity.[1]

ii) Role Sets and Role Sectors

A person who assumes the identity of student is implicated in a variety of prescribed performances with a number of interdependent "role others." Merton (1957a) conceptualizes this multiplicity of expectations as a "role set" (i.e., the entire complement of roles to which a person is linked by virtue of occupying a given social position). For example, a student relates to an array of role others—professors, librarians, administrators, counsellors, and fellow students—each relationship with its own cluster of norms constitutes a role sector. In the student-professor role sector, a subset of the student role set, students are expected to relate to professors one way while class is in progress, another way when speaking to them after class, and in quite another when writing an exam.

iii) Status Sets, Position, and Identity

In assuming the identity of student, one immediately "inherits" a set of norms (interpreted as duties) requiring the devotion of some portion of time to studying.[2] However, any given individual is not only a student but, at different times and places, possibly also a son or daughter, parent, wage earner, friend, member of a religious community, and so on. Merton (1957a) refers to the various social positions individuals occupy as their "status set". These identities have their basis in different social worlds and, figuratively speaking, can be visualized as a series of circles which come together and intersect in

1. Indeed, Park (1950:249) states that not only is everyone "always and everywhere, more or less consciously, playing a role . . . but that . . . it is in these roles that we know each other. It is in these roles that we know ourselves." Also, when asked to respond as quickly as possible to the question, "Who am I?" (Kuhn and McPortland, 1954) people tend to describe themselves by listing their social identities (e.g., male or female, husband or wife, student, doctor, lawyer, or whatever). In interactional terms identities are established when the announcements people make about themselves are congruent with the placements others make of them.
2. In the student-professor role set the duties of the student are the rights of the professor and vice-versa. Students have the right to expect reasonable amount of reading material, competent lectures, and fair exams from professors (professors' duties). Professors have the right to expect that students will study, take exams, and attend classes (students' duties).

single individuals (Simmel, 1969).[3] Any change in the demands of one "circle" (social world) will necessitate adjustments in the others.

A major weakness of the structural approach is that roles and norms are frequently viewed as more "fixed" than they really are. In a sense, they are reified in that structuralists often lose sight of the essentially human side of actors who must cope creatively with everpresent conflicts and ambiguities as they go about enacting their roles.

B. The Symbolic Interactional Approach

i) Motive Talk

According to symbolic interactional theory, individuals, in the process of interaction, take each others' roles and jointly fit their acts into evolving activity systems. Thus, social organization is a product of "joint action" (Blumer, 1969). Structural features such as norms and roles—to the extent they are taken into account by interactionists as creating definitions of situations— are visualized as loose frameworks within which interaction occurs rather than as rigid determinants of action. Actors are regarded as beset by competing and conflicting norms as well as norms that are frequently absent or too general or diffuse to provide step by step guidelines for behaviour. This results in continual problems of interpretation and selection of some courses of action over others, which, in turn, demand various forms of "motive talk" (Mills, 1940: Scott and Lyman, 1968: Bernstein, 1976) to smooth over interactions and clarify identities. Mills (1940) introduced the concept "motive talk" to refer to conversations, whether with self or with others, where an effort is made to justify the selection of one course of action over another. In turn, "motive talk" provides the foundation for Scott and Lyman's (1968:46) notion of "accounts" which are statements made by a social actor to "explain unanticipated or untoward behaviour—whether the behaviour is his own or that of others, and whether the proximate cause for the statement arises from the actor himself or someone else." In essence, they provide a tentative catalogue of types of accounts people typically give when their actions are called into question and the probability of having these accounts honoured. Bernstein (1976) draws

3. When persons belong to many groups, each of which has considerable autonomy from the other and from the larger society, there is less likelihood of anyone else sharing the same intersection or combination of circles. Also, smaller segments of an individual's experience are involved in any one such relationship, facilitating easier mental movement out of it (and the ability to view it in a more detached manner—from the perspective of one's other "circles"). The consequence is conscious appraisal and freedom of action. On the other hand, individuals can also be viewed at the centre of a series of concentric circles. The Jonestown suicides are a contemporary example illustrating the loss of freedom of action and individuality which come from the concentric circle arrangement. Each member's set of affiliations (family, friends, work, religion) were subsumed and tightly integrated into an over-arching community. Thus, when the fateful order came, individuals had no independent groups to serve as points of reference against which to judge their actions and were consequently highly susceptible to influence from the group leader.

on the Scott and Lyman tradition for his concept of "fritters", justifications students give to themselves and others for not studying in response to felt pressures to do so, and which are limited to open, never-ending tasks like studying.

ii) Norm "Looseness" And "Tightness" as a Variable Constraint on Motive Talk

The norms regulating relationships can themselves be seen to vary on a continuum of "looseness to tightness" (Boldt, 1978; Turner, 1962). Roles are "loose" to the degree that their guidelines take the form of general proposals for action, thus allowing players considerable interpretation, or room for negotiation as to how they will implement them. The structural stability which comes from adherence to the norms which go into making up these "loose" roles is ideally motivated by internalized standards—what Festinger (1953) and Merton (1959) term attitudinal conformity. Conversely, at the "tight" end of the role continuum, more emphasis is placed on the imposed and received (versus proposed and interpreted) nature of role expectations and on behavioural (versus attitudinal) conformity. That is to say, conformity is motivated more by external rewards (or conversely, fear of punishment) than by internalized standards. Tight roles are also subject to more direct surveillance by others (Boldt, 1978; Coser, 1961).

The relative "tightness" or "looseness" of roles varies not only for different positions but also for various role sectors. While the study role tends to be "loose" and allows considerable room for interpretation and negotiation, the exam writing role leaves little room for improvisation (Albas and Albas, 1981). Likewise, demands within the same role sector may vary over time; the study role may be comparatively "loose" when exam dates are in the distant future, but as they approach, negotiation possibilities decrease (i.e., friendship and athletic roles must be sacrificed).

iii) The Occasion[4]

Other symbolic interactionists look beyond the "work" participants do to accomplish interactions and focus on their attempts to achieve and maintain "face" (i.e., a favourable image of themselves). Since "events may occur within the interaction which contradict, discredit, or otherwise throw doubt upon the actor's projection of himself", engineering desired impressions is always prob-

---

4. A social situation can be defined as "an environment of mutual monitoring possibilities" (Goffman, 1963:135). A social situation comes into existence when two or more persons become conscious of being in each other's presence and it can usually be identified by subtle changes in demeanor as they orient to each other. The persons who find themselves in such a situation are referred to as a gathering. Gatherings may be characterized by nonfocused interaction, for example, in elevators where individuals may glean information from others and even adjust themselves to others without indulging in verbal exchange. If interactants join in a state of talk, the gathering is characterized by focused interaction. In turn, the situation is frequently contained by a wider social affair, the *occasion* which provides a structuring context for situations that emerge, dissolve, and re-emerge.

lematic. There is concern not only with the embarrassment produced by disruptions in performances, but also with the "preventive practices" used "defensively by the actor himself; and protectively when the audience strives to save the definition of the situation projected by the other" (Goffman, 1959:7).

Our perspective draws upon Goffman's concepts, but differs from his approach in three major ways. First, Goffman does not directly consult his actors and ask for their interpretation of their acts and situations; he appears to take an "omniscient" stance and assume that his interpretations are valid irrespective of the participants' view of things. Second, Goffman almost totally neglects the emotional side of the life of people. His actors "play their role with minimal manifestations of love, hate or other emotions" (Manis and Meltzer, 1978:49). Third, Goffman limits himself to expressive action in face-to-face contexts and neglects both the instrumental aspect of action and the larger social structures. We hope, by including these dimensions, to make an additional contribution to the study of social occasions, of which the exam will be considered an example par excellence.

iv) The Case for Using Both Approaches

While the strength of symbolic interactionism comes from its capacity to focus on the dynamic and processual character of society, it comes at the expense of not being able to explain effectively the stabilities of social life. However, since the strengths of one framework reside in the weakness of the other, it is possible to view them—not as competing or mutually exclusive—but as complementary and mutually reinforcing. Thus, the strength of symbolic interactionism lies in its focus on negotiation, but the parameters within which it occurs are conditioned by structural factors. This information suggests that while the structural approach may be useful for investigating "tight" roles, the interactional approach may be most useful for investigating "loose" roles. Stokes and Hewitt (1976) actually attempt to synthesize both perspectives by suggesting that actors are simultaneously influenced by the larger culture (structural) and the immediate interactional situation. They feel that when expectations conflict, the tendency is to yield to situational demands.[5] However, actions are still aligned with culture, because actors feel the need to justify or excuse their course of action. Since "motive talk" pays homage to and thereby invigorates cultural ideals they can be maintained in spite of pervasive deviance.

Handel (1979:855) provides a more concrete suggestion for integrating both approaches. He states that structural theory can be used to identify the major sources of role strain and the institutionalized mechanisms employed to articulate roles. However, "the question of how the actor copes with conflicting expectations is not addressed in middle-range structural theory, although it is implied as a conceptual problem." This, he suggests, is precisely

---

5. This tends to hold primarily in situations characterized by "loose" roles.

the strength of interactionism. In accordance with Handel's suggestion we focus on how actors experience and cope with the changing demands of their student role set and the implications of this for their entire status set. The integration of symbolic interactional and structural frameworks, then, allows for a more complete understanding of the effects of exams on students and how students respond.

Chapter III

Uncertainty, Stress, and Coping Mechanisms

In the last chapter we noted the complexities of social life and how individuals are located in multiple statuses each of which is linked to a role set. Role demands compete and may even conflict with each other and so produce role strains. For any individual, strain levels above the optimum result in distress which we may describe as simply stress. In situations of role strain, stress is caused by the uncertainty of the outcome and the anxiety caused by the uncertainty. In effect we can translate anxiety into stress. This is clearly a structural explanation of stress.

It is also possible to locate the source of stress within the personalities of actors due to their inadequate or noncongruent socialization for focal roles. In this chapter we describe in detail the nature of role strain associated with inadequate socialization to roles, role conflict, role competition, role overload as well as the mechanisms individuals employ to cope with stress so induced.

1. Sources of Uncertainty and Stress

An important source of stress is role strain, that is, difficulties people face in meeting their role requirements. Since role relationships establish what and where actors are in social terms, anything which interferes with their performance will be experienced as stressful because their identity is being questioned. As we mentioned earlier, interactional roles have their basis in norms, and norms themselves may be described as ideal (i.e., those formally taught) or real (i.e., how people actually behave). If people were able to achieve "ideal" levels of role performance, uncertainty and anxiety would be greatly reduced. The fact is, of course, that this is rarely the case for there are pervasive discrepancies between "ideal" and "real" performances throughout all human endeavours.

A. Inadequate Socialization to the Position

One of the major structural sources of role strain is inadequate socialization to the position. The achievement of role demands is facilitated to the degree that individuals, through the process of socialization, internalize the appropriate norms. Socialization is facilitated to the degree that norms are unambiguous and the role is highly observable and when deviance does occur sanctions are quick to follow. Such "tight" roles can be contrasted with "loose" roles which allow for much more interpretation and negotiation so there is always some ambiguity as to whether or not their demands have been fulfilled. This ambiguity is further accentuated by the fact that "loose" roles tend to be highly insulated from observability. Thus, role strain is more likely to occur under the more uncertain conditions associated with loose roles.

B. Personality—Role Conflict

A second source of role strain comes from personality—role conflict. Individuals are not simply mirror images of the normative expectations of the roles they play; each individual has a unique set of need dispositions or spontaneous tendencies to action, that is, to act in one way as opposed to another. These facts always raise the issue of the degree of congruence between each individual's personality and the institutionalized requirements of the role. To the extent that personality is incongruent with the institutionalized demands of the role, strain will result. For example, a highly introverted person ("true" personality) who finds that the only employment available is as a commission sales person—where success is contingent upon being highly extroverted (role personality)—will, at least initially, experience role strain. However, in the process of becoming socialized to the role, such persons may adapt so that "true" personality and role personality become more congruent.

C. Role Conflict

A third source of role strain emerges when individuals are exposed to role conflict where the expectations of the different roles they play are discrepant, such that meeting the demands of one automatically means violating another. Role conflict can be subclassified as i) inter-role conflict which occurs when two or more positions (each of which has its respective role sets) conflict with each other. To illustrate, when a policeman discovers a crime in progress and finds that the "criminal" is her brother, institutionalized role expectations associated with the family role set conflict with those of the occupational role set; or ii) intra-role conflict which arises within a single role set. For example, if a student has his friend sitting beside him during an exam and the friend is trying to copy from his paper, he is faced with intra-role conflict; does he conform to his role as student and report the offence to the invigilator or does he serve in the role of friend and allow the cheating to continue? One cannot do both. Role conflict also occurs in the workplace when workers must choose whether to honour the work restriction norms of the informal subculture or to live up to the productivity levels demanded by employers.

14

D. Role Competition—Role Overload

Another pervasive source of strain comes from the fact that in our pluralistic society, role sets impose obligations on individuals which compete for their time and energy. While society institutionalizes hierarchies of priority, individuals frequently face difficulty in distributing their efforts accordingly, especially when lower ranked roles are more attractive and more immediately observable than the higher ranked ones. Guilt and anxiety result when individuals internalize the institutional priorities but find their actions at odds with them. This form of strain differs from role conflict, in that there is nothing inherently contradictory in devoting more time and energy to some roles rather than to others (even though the latter may be higher ranked)—it is just that they cut into the time and energy available for more focal roles. With judicious scheduling, one ought to be able to meet the obligations of all these roles. Role competition becomes role overload when the demands of a role (or roles) become so immense that, even with careful planning, there is simply not enough time or energy to serve the entire status set. Problems of role competition are especially associated with open, never-ending roles. For example, a politician's work is never done. More private roles (e.g., family, recreation) do not necessarily conflict with public functions, but merely compete with them, so, with judicious scheduling, a happy balance can usually be achieved. However, as elections approach, the politician role tends to become all consuming, and there is insufficient time to meet the demands of other roles. In such cases, role competition becomes role overload. As we have seen, then, uncertainty is inherent in the exam occasion. To the extent that sources of role strain lead students to neglect their study roles, the uncertainty and anxiety already inherent in the situation are magnified. The result is that students must develop coping strategies if they are to survive.

2. Uncertainty and Stress: Coping Mechanisms

Uncertainty causes anxiety which, in turn, can interfere with task performance and thereby create a need for coping strategies. Lofland (1976), using a symbolic interactional approach, suggests that a comprehensive way to visualize how people cope with uncertainty is to locate coping strategies on a fourfold classification system in which "Most Proximate Audience" is dichotomized as being either "Self" or "Others" and "Prevailing Activity" is dichotomized as "Words" or "Actions". Accordingly, a given coping strategy may be located in cell three of the fourfold table (see Figure 1) if it involves words directed to others. Words directed to self would fall in cell 1, etc.

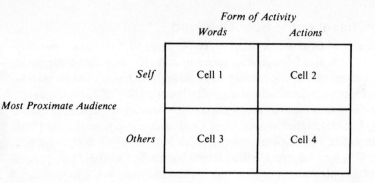

Figure 1 Coping Strategies: Audience and Form of Activity

A. Actions Directed to Others

A classic study related to the theme of stress, uncertainty and anxiety is Malinowski's (1954) ethnography on the Trobriand Islanders which highlights the difference in the behaviour of fishermen when they fished in the safety of the inner lagoons as compared to when they fished on the high seas. Success when fishing in lagoons was guaranteed because the fish were easily located and caught—there were few risks and no dangers to bodies and "selves". On the other hand, considerable physical danger was involved in fishing on the high seas and there was always the possibility of fishermen returning empty-handed (which could endanger their identities). Under such conditions of uncertainty, the fishermen would gather together and engage in joint magical acts (Cell 4) prior to their departure. The implication is that as stress increases (i.e., exams approach) so does interaction which in turn increases cohesion, thereby reducing stress. Research on wartime soldiers (Mandelbaum, 1952: Marshall, 1951) also supports this contention.

Several laboratory-type studies demonstrate that merely being in the presence of others who are undergoing the same trying experience reduces self-reported anxiety levels—especially for subjects who are first born or only children (Wrightsman, 1975; MacDonald, 1970). Bovard (1959) and Back and Bogdonoff (1964) also indicate that individuals subjected to stress show less severe physiological disturbances if they are simply placed in the presence of others (no verbal interaction) undergoing the same ordeal. Hence, as exams become imminent we might expect students to want to be physically close to others sharing their predicament even though they do not engage in focused interaction.

B. Actions Directed to Self

Gmelch (1971) extends Malinowski's argument to the area of professional baseball and focuses on the self-oriented acts of magic (Cell 2) players engage in to manage anxiety. He notes that positions and activities associated with baseball vary in terms of the degree of uncertainty, much as do the activities of fishermen. Outfielders (like fishermen in the lagoons) have almost complete control over their activities and commit few errors, while pitchers (like fishermen on the ocean) are considerably more vulnerable. As Malinowski would have predicted, Gmelch found few elements of magic associated with outfielding and many magical rites among pitchers. For example, practices like "tugging the cap between pitches, touching the rosin bag after each bad pitch or smoothing the dirt on the mound before each new batter", were in wide evidence (Gmelch, 1971:40). The most elaborate magical practices are associated with batting—the position of highest uncertainty. During a successful streak many players wear exactly the same clothes (including undergarments) in exactly the same manner, or always tag second base on the way to the outfield. One player experiencing a "good streak" was asked if he ever neglected his ritual, he responded "Never, I wouldn't dare. It would destroy my confidence to hit."

Gmelch (1971) also extends Malinowski's work by classifying magical practices as i) rituals—which prescribe actions to be taken; ii) taboos—which proscribe certain actions (i.e., crossing bats brings bad luck), and iii) fetishes—objects which come to be endowed with supernormal powers (i.e., "good luck" charms). Given that exam writing is the most uncertain activity associated with student life, we would expect to find all of these forms of magical practices.

C. Words Directed to Others

Schachter (1959) carried out the first experimental study on the powerful effects of anxiety. He created high and low anxiety conditions by informing some of his female subjects that they were about to receive a series of "painful" electric shocks and others that they would receive shocks so light they would resemble "a tickle". While the experimental equipment was supposedly being set up subjects were given the choice of either waiting alone or with others who were also about to be shocked. Twenty of the thirty-two subjects in the high anxiety condition (i.e., painful shock) chose to wait with other subjects, while only ten of the thirty subjects in the low anxiety category (i.e., light shock) chose this option. Thus he empirically verified the old adage that "misery loves company."

Schachter then turned to the question of why other persons become so attractive to people under stress. He first drew on Festinger's (1954:17) social comparison theory that "there exists in the human organism a drive to evaluate his opinions and abilities." The major motive behind these evaluations is accuracy. When individuals are uncertain about their opinions or abilities they are motivated to compare themselves to others who provide the most accurate information and so reduce feelings of uncertainty. Schachter tested this proposition by exposing all of his subjects to a high anxiety condition and then allowing half of them a choice as to whether they waited alone or with others who were to share the same "shocking" experience. The other half of the group were given the choice of waiting alone or with others who were about to see their faculty advisors. Since the first condition provides the most accurate basis for comparison it should have, he argued, the greatest effect on the desire to affiliate. Indeed, 60% of the subjects chose to wait with others who were to go through the same experience; while in the second condition all of the subjects chose to wait alone. Thus Schachter (1959:24) not only offers support for social comparison theory but concludes: "Misery doesn't love just any kind of company, it loves only miserable company." Students ought to be most uncertain as to their eventual outcome as they enter or emerge from the exam room so at these points they will likely seek out others to engage in the social comparison process.

Symbolic interactionists (i.e., McCall and Simmons, 1978: Goffman, 1967) offer a role identity support explanation for the increased desire to affiliate under conditions of stress and anxiety. They view the building of human identities as a continual process intrinsic to every social encounter where each individual has a unique identity which emerges from the variety of social roles enacted. Such an imaginative view of self is idealized and incorporates standards of conduct that are difficult to achieve even under the most favourable of conditions. Diffuse tension is produced because role-performances are never consistently perfect. Thus, in every interaction, individuals must prove to themselves and to others that they have not lost "their touch." Any condition which threatens a role identity (i.e., exams) should increase the desire to seek out others who will support a cherished image of self. As Goffman (1967:84–85) notes: "While it may be true that the individual has a unique self all his own, evidence of this possession is thoroughly a product of joint ceremonial labour . . . the individual must rely on others to complete the picture of him of which he himself is allowed to paint only certain parts." These "painted parts" are a result of impression management, where individuals attempt to control and manage appearance, manner, and setting so that others will "play along" thereby offering support to cherished aspects of self.

If the self-enhancement motive is basic to interaction, then we can question Festinger's contention that people will be motivated solely by accuracy in their search for evaluations of abilities and opinions. That is, persons attempting to enhance a sense of self may well be motivated to avoid accuracy of comparison. Indeed, Goffman (1967:16–18) suggests that individuals make use of a variety of practices such as avoiding interaction with others who, through accurate feedback, may discredit their "self". Furthermore, once an individual hazards an encounter, he will "suppress any show of feeling until he has found out the kind of line that others will be ready to support for him."[1] Under potentially threatening or uncertain conditions, any claim regarding self will be made with "belittling modesty" or "with strong qualifications" and "hedging". In this way, individuals will have prepared a self that will not be discredited by exposure, personal failure, or unanticipated acts of others. Once in an encounter, they will attempt to avoid discrediting topics and, if this is not possible, they will, as a last resort, "make a gracious withdrawal" before the threats become imminent. In Goffman's view social interaction is governed by an elaborate set of rules which facilitate the maintenance of face[2]—but frequently preclude honest interaction.

Given these competing explanations, we felt it would be useful to test the relative strengths of accuracy versus self-enhancement motives under high anxiety conditions which are highly ego-involving (a central feature of Goffman's model of interaction). At the same time, we wanted a situation that would offer individuals an opportunity to compare their skills, opinions and emotions to those of others like themselves. Pre and post exam gatherings provide such a situation. Exams generate considerable anxiety, are ego-involving events (because individuals' performances are viewed as a reflection of their intelligence), and have important consequences for later career aspirations (i.e., professional schools or the immediate job market). Universities also have an institutional policy which requires each class to have a wide distribution of grades—by definition, there exists a wide variety of comparison others.

D. Words Directed to Self

According to Lofland's classification scheme, individuals can also reduce anxiety by directing words to self. Indeed, Mills' (1940) notion of "motive talk" refers to conversations individuals have with themselves, or others, in problematic situations in order to attempt to justify the selection of one course of action over another. As Mills (1940:905) states: "Men live in immediate acts of experience and their attentions are directed outside themselves until acts are in some way frustrated. It is then that awareness of self and motives occur." We would expect that students who know they ought to be studying and yet do not do so would engage in "fritters" and other forms of motive-talk as a means of moderating their guilt. To this point, then, we have taken a theoretical look at role strain and coping strategies. The next step is to see

1. While both Schachter and symbolic interactionists stress the importance of social support and, by implication, identity support, the latter is more central to the symbolic interactional thesis and has received considerably more conceptual development. Indeed, self-enhancement is a pivotal point for both Goffman's and McCall and Simmons' models of social interaction. Thus, it seems appropriate to identify the role-identity support motive with the symbolic interactional tradition. Also, at certain points the role identity support motive comes into conflict with the social comparison motive stressed by Schachter.

2. Thus there is a need for aligning actions, "accounts", role bargains, and other balancing mechanisms.

how students experience these strains and the actual strategies they use to cope.

The discussion of stress and coping will be conceptualized as occurring in four distinct phases, as follows: Phase 1, Early Pre-Exam (Ch. IV–VI), Phase 2, Immediate Pre-Exam (Ch. VII), Phase 3, The Exam Act Proper (Ch. VIII), Phase 4, Post Exam (Ch. IX).

Chapter IV

Phase I: Early Pre-Exam

Although studying is a vital part of the student role set, most of it tends to be done solo. As a result, one is not directly tied to complementary role-others in face-to-face situations. Nevertheless, studying as a normative activity is at the very foundation of the student role set and basic to other role relations. The most direct role-other pertinent to the studying role is the symbolic presence of the professor. Students report they attempt not only to understand the material from the professors' perspectives, but also continually try to outguess them concerning which questions might be asked on the exam. Thus, even though students may be alone, they are in continual symbolic communication with their professors and, in the process, the role identities of both parties are simultaneously reinforced. When students neglect their studying, their identities—as well as those of the professors—become problematic. What kind of professor is it who can't motivate students to study? The studious role, then, can be viewed as a sub-role of the more basic professor-student role since the professor is used as a continual reference-other even when not in the immediate situation.

The Study Role: Sources of Role Strain and Ways of Coping

Although studying is crucial to the role set, most students face considerable difficulty in motivating themselves to meet this portion of their role. While they agree that they ought to keep up with their readings and assignments throughout the year, data from interviews and exam logs indicate that only 15–20% of students could be described as meeting the ideal. The remaining 80–85% experience varying degrees of role strain. Indeed, since studying is so central to the student role, and since such a large proportion of the students find it somehow difficult or unpleasant, non-studying requires an explanation. We will attempt to explain why students neglect studying by focusing simultaneously on structural and interactional theories. As we noted earlier, structural theory allows for the identification of the major sources of role strain while interactional theory allows us to describe how students experience and cope with it. The major sources of role strain may be classified as (1) inadequate socialization for the "loose" role of university student; (2) personality-role conflict; (3) role conflict; and (4) role competition.

A. Inadequate Socialization to the Role

In the first place, many university students may be inadequately socialized to the "looseness" of their new role. At university they are given considerable freedom to organize their time on a daily basis, and are only held accountable for it at some future date when exams and term papers are required. Initially, students are provided with a course outline which gives a list of topics to be discussed, a corresponding list of required and recommended readings, the due dates for assignments, and the dates of the examinations. Students are expected to be sufficiently socialized to attend classes, complete readings and assignments, and be properly prepared for their exams.

The absence of direct surveillance provides quite a contrast with most high schools and community colleges, where the scenario includes shorter, more frequent, and less open-ended assignments along with more direct surveillance by the teaching staff. Incidentally, these structural variations suit the different tasks graduates will eventually perform. For example, since unskilled manual workers and lower authority personnel (i.e., "tight" occupational roles) have their work closely supervised, they must be trained to accept instructions and be at least reasonably respectful to those who give them. Conversely, persons who occupy positions of higher authority, or elite positions (i.e., "loose" occupational roles), must develop self-discipline, tolerance for ambiguity, and a flexible attitude towards change and innovation. Essentially, this form of anticipatory socialization prepares university students for future obligations. Having fewer but more highly weighted exams and term assignments trains students to tolerate ambiguity and preserve poise under stress conditions, a most important attribute for any elite position. Those who best reflect these characteristics have a competitive advantage when applying for admission to graduate school and the professions (i.e., medicine, law, architecture, etc.). Hence, undergraduate university education implicitly shapes the character of students by making them "more fit" for their post graduate academic careers and, ultimately, for occupational demands.

Inadequately socialized individuals will, however, experience difficulties in meeting these "open-ended", "loose", requirements. The following typical comments sum up the situation succinctly: "Coming out of high school, I wasn't really prepared for all the work I had to do, or should have done. I came here not knowing that I would have to work as hard as I should have. . . . I knew others who worked, and wondered how they could do so much studying. I always found something better to do and wondered why they couldn't. I thought that you either knew the answer or you didn't; so why put so much time into studying?" The lack of socialization to the ideal norms of the university setting is also a source of role ambiguity. Many students are only vaguely aware of the cause and effect relation between studying and performance, preferring instead to perpetuate the notion of the "genius myth" which, in essence, states

22

that some people are so "naturally bright" that they don't have to study.[1] Attitudes toward studying developed in junior and senior high school also provide a partial explanation as to why students do not study as much as they ought to: "Studying and good marks become unpopular at around grade seven . . . and . . . persist into the upper reaches of high school." As a result, many students come to university with the habit of studying "just enough so I know I won't fail"—or "doing just a few hours of reading to provide me with enough information to pass." While studying is "more acceptable in university . . . habits acquired earlier are hard to change." This is especially so when they are combined with the shift from a comparatively tight social system like the high school to a loose one such as a university.

The combination of a loose social system with the extreme low observability of the study role is highly conducive to "frittering"—i.e. "when there is work to be done, students fritter away time" (Bernstein, 1976:375). In contrast to the individual quoted earlier, most students know and feel that they ought to study: "For myself, I know I should study but I just keep putting it off until the last minute." When students' actions are not in accordance with internalized norms they feel guilty and attempt to justify their actions, at least to themselves. In fact, as we saw earlier, Bernstein (1976:376) defines a fritter as "a justification a student gives to himself for not doing student work in response to felt pressures to work."[2] A student, who had never heard of Bernstein, referred to the tendency among fellow students to procrastinate as being especially productive of a disease termed "excusitis"—a mental condition

1. A closely related folk concept is that some students possess a photographic memory and need only listen attentively during lectures to automatically perform effectively on exams. This concept may be a carryover from the high school setting where exam questions are largely drawn from classroom lectures. However, in the university setting, most students are responsible for at least one textbook and at least one book of assigned readings; the corresponding requirements require analytical skills as well as memory capacity. Hence, students who experience initial difficulty in adjustment to university life may be suffering from inadequate socialization to their new role.

2. Bernstein (1976) conceptualizes fritters as types of "accounts" (Scott and Lyman, 1968) used by students to justify procrastination of studying. Since fritters are rather standardized and readily honoured by others they become part of student culture. Support from others alleviates much of the guilt and provides partial explanation as to why students neglect their study role. Bernstein draws much conceptual inspiration from Matza's (1964) work on delinquents. The comparison is apt because students who neglect their studies frequently use comparable terms to describe their acts—"deviant", "delinquent", or "misdemeanor." Both groups experience guilt even though delinquents are usually involved in "crimes of commission" while students engage in "crimes of omission." It is not surprising, then, that both groups develop neutralization techniques to free themselves from the moral constraints which accompany their "deviant" acts. "Fritters" also fit with Stokes and Hewitt's (1976) concept of aligning actions. Although there are discrepancies between cultural ideals and the amount of time and effort students actually invest in studying, to the extent that they justify the discrepancy they are aligning their actions with culture.

which induces one to use any excuse to stay away from studying.[3] One of the most frequent justifications for not studying until the last moment before the test is the appeal to a faulty memory: "Yeah, but if I study for the test now I'll just forget it all . . . and I'll end up having to cram for it anyway." Bernstein actually classifies fritters into four general types: task based, valuative based, social relations based, and person based. Although he did not record the presence of the appeal to a faulty memory as a fritter (which is surprising considering its pervasiveness), it is best subsumed under the category "person based." However there is one glaring weakness to the faulty memory fritter; while the forgetting process sets in quickly—especially for material that does not cohere—relearning is much easier and faster the second time around, which means not all material is "lost" (Ebbinghaus, 1913; Sprinthall and Sprinthall, 1981). Also, relearning the material results in individuals gaining a more intimate grasp of it—an especially important factor in answering questions which demand analytical insight. Furthermore, highly arousing, stimulus intense events like exams favour the performance of dominant "overlearned" responses and hinder performance of inadequately learned tasks (Zajonc, 1965; Yerkes and Dodson, 1908). Hence, studying long in advance and then relearning the material not only results in greater command of the subject area but also favours performance in high stimulus conditions. Consequently, there is greater protection from nightmare events like "exam blank-outs" and an increased probability of truly outstanding performance. Indeed, Zajonc (1965:274) advises the student "to study all alone, preferably in an isolated cubicle [low stimulus intensity while learning] and to arrange to take his exams in the company of many other students, on stage, and in the presence of a large audience. The results of his examination would be beyond his wildest expectations, provided, of course, he had learned his material quite thoroughly."

B. Incompatibility of Personality and Study Role

Many students have an aversion to studying and will do almost anything to avoid it, even if it means engaging in activities they otherwise detest: "In lieu of studying I find time for sewing, cleaning windows (a task I hate), and doing other jobs that have been put off." "I have never been a neat person, yet as the pressures for studying increase (coming exams), I find myself clean-

3. Students also attempt to minimize guilt by selecting the environments they spend time in: "I stay far away from any kind of studying atmosphere . . . particularly libraries, where the reminders of studying are strongest. . . . Instead I go to where the action is" (i.e., gyms, cafeterias, radio rooms, etc.).

ing out drawers and cupboards that have remained stagnant for months".[4] "Procrastinating is an art with me. I can almost always find something to do if it means getting out of studying . . . and when I finally do sit down to study, my mind frequently wanders off into . . . more satisfying topics such as hockey or hunting."

This aversion to the study role suggests the importance of personality as an intervening variable which mediates between study role obligations and actual role performance. If inadequate socialization to the student role can be classified as the first source of role strain (which explains why so many students renege on their study commitments), a second, related source is goodness of fit between the pattern of personality traits required by the study role (role personality) and the student's "true" personality. That is to say, people vary considerably in their capacity for sustained and concentrated work, and highly extroverted students experience more strain than introverted ones when they must withdraw from significant others to engage in serious study (usually a solitary activity). The effect of such "closeting" seems to have a real impact: "As I seclude myself to study I begin to feel more and more alone, and yet more and more in need of companionship."[5] "While I know that studying long in advance increases one's knowledge of a subject, just the thought of studying makes me worry." These students indicate that studying makes the exam experience more immediate and results in "a general feeling of insecurity regarding just about everything—not just academic marks." By avoiding studying and "in the end cramming, I reduce the amount of time spent worrying— besides, when I really cram I don't have time to panic." Whatever guilt they may experience from the delay in studying is neutralized by appealing to the ever popular "I work best under pressure" fritter (words directed to self).[6]

There is some empirical support for the notion that discrepancies between student role (role personality) demands and actual role performance

4. These acts directed to self fit best under Bernstein's (1976) classification of task related fritters and the more precise sub-classification of "preparation related fritters." Although activities like sewing, washing windows, etc. do not fit directly into this category, many students also report experiences where they discover the desk top needs cleaning; and then decide that "while I'm at it, I might as well clean the whole desk," and so it goes. These latter fritters reduce guilt because they are viewed as being directly related to task completion (studying).

5. Schachter's review of empirical literature reveals that isolation heightens a state of uneasiness, especially in persons who are highly extroverted (a characteristic of many first born children). His conclusions fit some of our students very aptly since "one of the consequences of isolation appears to be a psychological state which in its extreme form resembles a full-blown anxiety attack" (1959:12).

6. Once again, Bernstein did not note the presence of this fritter which can be subsumed under the category "person-based." A possible reason for these oversights is that he was focusing on how students deal with short time delays rather than the days, weeks and months with which the present study concerns itself. For example, in the category of "task-based fritters" he includes "time-symmetry" ones where students do not begin to work immediately but wait for the hour, half hour or quarter hour to arrive. The longest period of time he mentions involves the "great-divide" fritter where students finally decide its too late in the day to start on anything new and so they feel justified in putting off studying until "tomorrow."

are greater for extroverts than for introverts (true personality). Furneaux (1957) notes that university students who show high extroversion on personality inventories do not perform as well in classroom examinations as those who score high on introversion. These differences in performance are not evident in high school and only become apparent when students enter university. He suggests that stricter supervision in the high school setting "checks" the "socializing" tendencies of the extrovert. This explanation is congruent with our earlier discussion of the differences in the organization of instruction between the two settings.[7]

A related personality characteristic bearing on study habits is the rate of accumulation of inhibition as work proceeds (Eysenck, 1960). That is, the length of time students study before they experience satiation or the feeling that "my brain just won't take it any more." One individual who has a high satiation threshold reported that after "a good study period I wish I could write the exam right away, just so I wouldn't have to force myself to study more." He was also concerned with the moral implications for identity and noted (words directed to self) that he was not lazy and would work hard at almost anything he got involved in—except studying. This suggests a basic incompatibility between personality (rapid build-up of reactive inhibition) and studying. Entwhistle and Entwhistle (1970) also noted that extroverts scored lower on university exams and built up reactive inhibition earlier than introverts. Furthermore, students with below-average scores on extroversion had higher scores on study methods and academic achievement motivation scales.

However well-demonstrated the relationship between personality type and studying behaviour may be, persons need not be hopeless victims of personality. Indeed, it need not determine behaviour in any simple, direct way; rather it shapes individuals' sensitivities to the environment and their impulsive tendencies to act in one way rather than another. Personality is a composite of values, attitudes and overt behavior surrounding and reinforcing a "self" component. The self consists of an impulsive, dynamic and not wholly predictable component called the "I"; and also a more disciplined, socialized and predictable component called the "Me" (Mead, 1934). The "Me" consists of the cumulated norms of society as perceived by the individual and internalized by him or her. Accordingly, the behavior of an individual in a partic-

7. Differences in the performance of extroverts and introverts may also not be as apparent in high school settings because there is less need to engage in intensive study to obtain comparable grades: "In high school you could know your material just "so-so" and come out with a super mark but here (university) you have to know your material extremely well to pull off an A. It's difficult because we're not used to studying the material until we know it completely."

ular situation is always the resultant of the "I" and "Me" vectors of the self acting together and is always problematic.[8]

Symbolic interactionists view action as a continual development wherein the "I" and "me" represent phases in a process of minding. The "I" designates the subject and the "me" designates the object phases of the process. Acts begin in the form of an "I" (unorganized , spontaneous dispositions) and soon come to be viewed from the organized perspective of social others ("me"). The "I", then, represents the initiation of an act before it comes under social guidance. The act's final direction is contingent upon interplay between the "I" as impulse and the acting-back-upon the act by the "me".[9] The spontaneous, propulsive nature of the "I" insures that we can never entirely predict how the act will end. Conversely, any strengthening of the "me" forces allows individuals to exercise greater control over their predispositions. For example, persons who have a personality make-up which impulsively leads them away from studying may still engage in it: they simply will have a more difficult time. The situation can be improved by increasing the "strength" of the "me" by identifying with groups that stress the value of mastering areas of knowledge. We discovered that students who aspired to graduate or professional school had less difficulty than others in disciplining their impulses. This identification, then, provides them with a clear purpose for studying and makes it consistent with their evolving conception of self. For these students, graduate or professional schools serve as reference groups.[10]

Hopkins, Malleson and Sarnoff (1958) also noted that students who chose a subject area as a means to enter an occupation, and felt confident their performance would allow them to enter it, were more likely to score high on examinations. Likewise, Stinchcomb's (1964) study revealed that when high school students perceived a link between current student activities and future

8. The "generalized other" refers to the influence of "society" upon individuals, especially in terms of their perception of its expectations of them in particular situations. The "generalized other" may also refer to other more specific and limited groups of people (i.e., medical or legal practitioners, Christians, students, etc.).

9. This process is more readily observable in children who have not yet fully internalized language. For example, a small child who reaches out to touch the dials of the family television set (a forbidden object)—and then reprimands him/herself with a slap on the fingers and a vocalized "no-no"—is reflecting a struggle between the "I" (impulsive) and "me" (social) aspects of self. In adults, this type of conversation typically occurs subvocally.

10. Reference groups may be conceived of as generalized others considered significant to an individual. The concept was coined when it became evident that some people did not identify with the perspectives of the groups to which they belonged (membership groups) or even adopted perspectives of groups they were not members of (as in the case of some of our students). The distinction is meant to accentuate the fact that membership groups are not necessarily reference groups. Reference groups can be subclassified according to the normative and comparison functions they serve. For example, students who identify with the professions are provided with a moral code (normative function) which stresses the value of hard work and mastery of a subject area. The reference group also provides a standard or comparison point in the form of minimum grade point average for admittance to the profession. This comparison function of groups was described earlier in relation to Festinger's social comparison motive.

occupational positions they were more likely to accept the school's emphasis on hard work and good grades. Marks' (1977) energy producing theory of role performance is also consistent with these findings. His central proposition is that: "Abundant energy is found for anything to which we are highly committed . . . we find little energy for anything to which we are uncommitted, and doing these things leaves us feeling spent, drained or exhausted." Thus students who commit themselves to an occupation are more likely to find the energy necessary for studying and, in turn, are more likely to achieve higher grades than students who lack such identification. In this case, the greater congruence between self conception and student role duties, the more likely one is to embrace the study role. Conversely, students who suffer incongruities in this respect are more prone to "rapidly decelerating feelings of energy." As Marks (1977:932) states: "Many of my under-committed students report that when they sit down to study, they not only feel little energy but often feel suddenly overwhelmed by the need to sleep." Our students support these observations. One person reported feeling unaccountably "groggy" the moment he approached the study desk and felt the need to "take a brisk walk to freshen up." Upon returning, however, he "felt a bit tired" and decided "to take a nap." The feeling of fatigue persisted after the nap and the response was then to "go out for a cup of coffee to wake up." After all these acts directed to self the decision was "to get up early tomorrow morning . . . when I'll be able to work better." Bernstein (1976) classifies such behaviours as "biological necessity fritters."

C. Role Conflict: The Student Subculture

Given that so many students share common problems of adjustment to the study role and at the same time have considerable opportunity to interact with others like themselves, the ground is laid for the emergence of a subculture whose expectations are at variance with those of the formal university community (Cohen, 1955).[11] Since the expectations are more compatible with students' personal dispositions, the resultant norms justify spending less free time studying and even disparaging students who do. Thus students who wish to maintain a positive sense of self in the eyes of this subculture will be prepared to restrict the time spent on study: "Having to study continuously is considered 'uncool' and makes you something of a social misfit." Those who violate the informal code are sanctioned by exclusion and labelled as a "keener",

11. Cohen's work with delinquent boys provides the basis for a theory of subculture. He states that a new frame of reference for evaluating objects (including oneself) will tend to emerge when: (1) a number of individuals in a setting share common problems of adjustment (e.g., difficulties in studying); (2) there are opportunities for interaction (e.g., outside formal lecture periods; and (3) they effectively communicate to each other that the problem is shared (versus being limited to a few isolated individuals). In the process, a new frame of reference, which serves as a new measuring rod for evaluating achievement and success, can be forged. When this occurs the student who finds it difficult to study may now not only receive social support for studying less but even gain some measure of status.

"bookworm", "four-eyes", "grind", "goody-goody", "sissy", "suck", "buff", and "brown-noser."[12] These words directed to specific others reduce problems of adjustment by reducing feelings of guilt and dissonance which come from neglecting the study role: "It's rewarding to put down the studious types. It takes attention off our own misdemeanours[13] and even makes the hard working student look bad." Thus, role strain is reduced by providing each other with social support and, at the same time, introducing a new frame of reference which, through the exchange of social rewards and punishments, provides some sense of reality.

Students also partially control the situation within which they are enmeshed by constructing pressures to reduce studying output. Since every class is expected to have a normal distribution of grades, the curve facilitates the achievement of the lower passing grades such as D's or C's.[14] If a class underperforms together, the grades as a whole will tend to be scaled upward. These norms also allow students to increase their control over the environment and, at the same time, lessen their dependence on professorial expectations.[15] Some students do not experience personality non-congruence with the study role and do not find studying painful; they may in fact even enjoy it. Due to subcultural pressures, however, they are encouraged to study less if they want to be members in good standing of their peer group. These students experience role conflict—a discrepancy in expectations between the informal membership grouping and the formal demands of the student role (such that compliance with one violates the expectations of the other).[16] On the other hand, a closer inspection of the norms of the informal student body, also reveals a stigma attached to the complete neglect of the study role—especially if the result is a failing grade. Students who fail are often labelled "grubs", and steteotyped as being either lazy, dumb, or both.

12. Hard-working students are not always called uncomplimentary names. Sometimes they are viewed compassionately as unfortunate creatures incapable of appreciating the finer things of life: "Their social life is so bad that studying is the most interesting thing they have to do."

13. There is an ambivalent aspect to the subcultural norm that downplays studying and scholastic achievement—note the word "misdemeanour" used to describe the acts of omission.

14. Many professors take pride in reporting that, although the administration demands a wide distribution of grades, they have never had to actually "force a curve." Little do they realize they may, in some measure, be "profiting" from student work restriction norms!

15. In pluralistic societies such as our own, individuals participate in a vast variety of more or less autonomous social worlds (i.e., Simmel's intersecting versus concentric circles). Consequently, problems of articulating the demands of these worlds (roles) must be resolved. Merton (1957a:iii) makes an attempt at "identifying the social mechanisms which serve to articulate the expectations of those in a role-set so that the occupant of a status is confronted with less conflict than would obtain if these mechanisms were not at work." One such mechanism is the development of subcultures which provide social support and modify the demands of those in positions of power.

16. Since these discrepant expectations emanate from the same role set (i.e., professor-student and informal student-student roles) we can technically classify the situation as one of intra-role conflict.

Epithets such as "grub" are not usually employed in face-to-face encounters with the offending individuals but are used to describe group members not present or non-group members. Failing students who sense their relations with others are strained gradually find themselves moving to the margin of their group: "I dread failing because it's so embarassing when your friends ask you how you did on the test. It makes you feel like you just stunk up the place. It's also painful because they don't know how to act towards you. They'd prefer not having to see you . . . and when they do talk to you, you know they're just trying to be nice. You both act differently toward each other. I think it would be a lot easier for everyone if they just openly said what they thought—'You're a 'grub', you're 'stupid', or 'how could you fail a test like that?' "

A failing grade will result in stigma, but so will one significantly lower than the group one "hangs around with." In other words, "in order to relate equally, one needs equal grades." Even though students negatively sanction what they consider "excessive studying", they admire persons who can obtain high grades seemingly without having to put forth much effort. Consequently, the "genius" myth perpetuates itself.[17] Such a system of rewards and sanctions is certainly conducive to deception. That is, students who wish to lay claim to being highly intelligent may invest some considerable time in study, yet conceal the fact from their peers.[18] Many such "in-the-closet-studiers" report that they study either early in the morning or late at night—in this manner they are able to use the social organization of sleep (Schwartz, 1970) as a means whereby they segregate conflicting audiences into different space and time slots.

Merton identifies this insulation from observability as another basic social mechanism that "allows for role behaviour which is at odds with the expectations of some in a role-set to proceed without undue stress." Occasionally, these types of students indicate that, as exams approach, they participate with their non-studying friends in "worried acts of hysteria" and join in the emerg-

17. It is interesting to note the pervasiveness and tenacity of the genius myth despite the fact that persons who have made the greatest contributions to learning stress the importance of hard work (with statements to the effect that it is "98% perspiration and 2% inspiration"). A major reason for its persistence seems to be its function as an effective "fritter" which helps to relieve the guilt of those persons who do not study. Indeed, the myth is most popular among non-studiers. They also point out that someone who works very little but does well on tests anyway displays greater intellectual potential than someone who studies a lot for the same grade. While the statement may have some truth to it, a system that places a premium on effortless success would also be conducive to the production of clever loafers. And one is left to ponder their overall contribution to society.

18. Bushnell (1962:507) points to a similar informal organization among Vassar students. The ideal Vassar girl is one who consistently receives high grades and yet reserves enough time and energy to maintain her other social identities. Bushnell also points to the use of impression management on the part of those who "have to work quite hard to maintain an impressive grade-point ratio." They will devote a "considerable effort to presenting an appearance of competency and freedom from academic harassment."

ing chorus built around the theme "I'm going to outfail you."[19] They not only stress the importance of compartmentalizing their lives, but also of managing their presentations of self when with friends so as not to give off any discrediting information (Goffman, 1959). If the act is successful and in a "particularly difficult exam . . . you pull off a 95% . . ." the rewards are apparent because "your friends hold you in awe and regard you as a genius." Consequently, behaviour at odds with claimed identity and the informal peer code can proceed without undue stress. However, should friends learn of the "secret", the person will "probably lose them all."

Given the advantages that accrue from the control of studying (as well as the status given for obtaining high grades without seemingly having to study very much), it is not surprising to find that students are wary—if not actually suspicious—of each other's studying behavior.[20] "Some (students) become deceitful . . . saying they only studied a little when, in reality, they've studied for days. Some even talk their friends into sluffing off so they can feel mentally superior." An extreme example comes from a group of students who were competing for admission to medical school. A study group of friends gathered together and were preparing—on an individual basis—for an upcoming organic chemistry exam. They were approached by a classmate (who was not a group

19. Merton (1959) defines such behaviour as "doctrinal conformity." Individuals bear verbal witness to group norms but, when insulated from observability, act in other ways. Coser (1961:31) adds that "doctrinal or ritual conformity . . . takes place only under conditions of observability" and identifies it as another basic social mechanism which offers individuals some measure of freedom to articulate conflicting roles. Doctrinal conformity conceals a lack of attitudinal conformity to a conflicting audience. Thus, a person can maintain membership in significant groups and yet not act in ways injurious to one's other identities (i.e., intelligent and hardworking).

20. Becker, et al., (1968), in their participant observational study of a midwestern university, do not discuss students' suspicions of each other's studying behaviours and report only the presence of weak pressures to "restrict production" (i.e., "occasionally" there are epithets like "brown-noser" or "damned average raisers"). They indicate this is quite a contrast to findings of their earlier study (Becker, et al., 1961) of medical students and Orth's (1963) study of freshmen students at Harvard Business School. The major reason for the difference seems to lie in the general university setting; students from the same class have "little in common outside the classroom" and "little opportunity for interaction"—conditions necessary for building and maintaining an effective subculture. In the midwestern university, most of the students free time appeared to be absorbed by other members of their fraternities and sororities who seldom attended the same classes at the same time or shared similar professors. Since fraternities do not play a significant role in the universities we studied, students would presumably have more freedom to interact with others in their classes and thereby develop and maintain work-restriction norms. Indeed, as Becker et al. would predict, the most visible effects of informal group control occurred in an off-campus class comprised of 48 students, 22 of whom were student psychiatric nurses. Most of the student nurses lived together in the nuring school residence. They ate together, took classes together, and spent much of their recreational time together. Under conditions of such high visibility to each other, there were few opportunities to withdraw to study without the others becoming aware of the fact. These living conditions also made the group a very potent source of rewards and punishments. We would expect that one half of these students would receive a grade of C+ or better. In fact, two received "F's" and sixteen of them received grades of D and C. One person received a grade of B and three persons received "A's". Of those students who received grades of A or B, three lived in their own homes away from the residence and one who did live in residence was a virtual social isolate.

member) and told: "Professor X let me know today that we're supposed to know Alcohols." This was a section the professor had earlier explicitly stated would not be covered on the exam. As one of the members of the goup later reported: "We suspected the statement was a lie. The exam was the next evening and we thought this student (who we knew would get an A anyway) was trying to divert us from our last minute cramming so our marks would suffer . . . thereby increasing his chances for admittance to medical school. We questioned the professor the next morning and he confirmed our suspicions." This information suggests another interpretation of Coleman's (1961)[21] explanation for the growing polarization between students and the larger society. He viewed the conflict as the manifestation of the youth culture which emerged with industrialization. As the division of labour increased, there was a corresponding separation between the economy and the family. With increasing economic complexity the need grew for educational institutions to train individuals to fit new occupational positions; achievement was emphasized and individuals were evaluated by their worth according to universalistic standards, rather than on the basis of family position. Adolescents were required to spend much of their time in formal education organizations which were unable to satisfy all of their socioemotional needs and so they were forced inward toward "their own age group, a small society" with "only a few threads of connection with the outside adult society" (Coleman, 1961:3).

While there is some merit in this macro view, a more situation specific explanation for the emergence of student norms which conflict with the official school goals can be found in the basic incompatibility between role and true personality, as well as in the various forms of role-competition. These explanations seem especially relevant because older students who have strong connections to the "responsible" adult side of life, also experience similar sources of strain and occasionally act in ways that lend support to informal student norms. This pattern of conflict between the informal organization and the formal organization is widely distributed and has been described in Roethlisberger and Dickson's (1939) classic view of the industrial workplace as composed of socially integrated, responsible representatives of the larger society. Like workers, students have a set of "primary" relations from which professors or supervisory personnel are precluded. Out of these relations flow a set of norms which tacitly prohibit friendly, informal relations with professors; individuals who engage in such relationships are suspected of "sucking" or "brown-nosing." Also there are work related norms where "rate busters", those workers whose production exceeds the group's work norm, are negatively sanctioned. Since the workers in the industrial setting were working on a piece rate, greater productivity meant higher pay. However, there were suspicions that if "too much" work was produced management might simply raise

21. Coleman's study of high school students was the first to document the presence of a student subculture in conflict with official school goals.

the required number of units and keep the pay constant. Likewise, students seem to fear that if everyone works hard, it may simply mean a raise in the curve to maintain a more or less normal distribution. Furthermore, workers, like students, had norms regulating "underwork" and violators were termed "chiselers." While such norms are to some extent in conflict with official organization ideals, they are in another sense compatible because they encourage at least a moderate rate of performance.

The university population is, however, also composed of a rather substantial core (15–20%) of highly motivated, hard working, committed individuals. These students seek out "fellow believers" of the same orientation for instrumental and expressive support. In interaction with each other they frequently evolve a flattering view of themselves as a type of "academic elite." Their feelings about non-studiers are mixed. On the one hand, many "studiers" are covertly happy because non-studiers reduce the competition for scarce grades and ultimately positions in graduate or professional schools. On the other hand, non-studiers are viewed with some measure of disdain and even contempt—as immature, irresponsible, lazy, dumb, and especially around exam time, as "bellyachers", and "bitchers."

Occasionally, hard working students not only form friendship groups but will divide into "teams" that compete with other "teams" from the same class. This competitive aspect motivates study and makes it effective. For example, if one member is experiencing difficulty and asks for assistance from others, the ensuing discussion may well lead to information on study strategies or the sources professors use for their lecture material. However, at times the groups may become almost overly competitive, as illustrated by students in a chemistry class. The whole class was having great difficulty in taking down and understanding the professor's notes. The assigned text for the course was of little assistance. By chance one member of the group was searching through the library and happened to come upon the source book for most of the professor's lectures. The group told no one else of this discovery and took turns borrowing the book from the library every time it came due so that no one else could share their advantage.

D. Role Competition

Another reason why students do not study as much as they could (besides inadequate socialization, lack of congruence between role and true personality, and the emergence of a subculture that discourages "too much" studying) is that they occupy a variety of social positions and so many roles compete for attention. Students are not merely students but persons with multiple identities, each of which vies for some measure of satisfaction: "I am going to school, working, playing volleyball, trying to train a puppy, and supporting myself all at the same time." The outcome of these multiple role demands can be formally conceptualized as "role competition", activities that compete for a person's time and energy, thereby cutting into the time needed for performance of a given focal role.[22] Thus, individuals are placed in a situation where they must choose one role over another, and the emergent "role identity hierarchies" establish which roles have priority (McCall and Simmons, 1978). In the case of students their friendship roles offer the greatest competition to studying: "It's very seldom I'm not faced with a decision of either a night out with friends or a night in with the books." And, for a substantial portion of the academic year, their sociable roles take priority: "School is important to me, but having friends and a good social life is more important." Choosing to spend time with friends over books is easy, because, in socializing, students experience "instant gratification through talking and laughing"—a much more rewarding experience than "spending time with non-living things like books." These emergent relationships generate their own moral demands and serve to reduce further the time available for study: "I feel I should fulfill my responsibilities to others. . . . I'm more ready to neglect my schoolwork because it's a responsibility that's directly my own. I feel I can compensate for it somehow on my own time, without having it interfere with the time I owe others."

Postponing exam preparation then can no longer be considered mere coincidence but rather a systematic response to a vast number of alternative responsibilities (i.e., friends, family, job, and extracurricular activities). These responsibilities not only vary in terms of their desirability and rewards but also in their degree of observability by role others (Merton, 1957a; Coser, 1961), and since all of them (except studying) involve high-observability, role-others are soon aware if a duty is neglected: "If I don't clean the floor, cook a meal, do the dishes or laundry, I'm quickly open to public scrutiny." When students stop socializing with their friends during "spare" periods, they are soon missed and often told: "You're never around anymore." And if they belong to a group which sanctions too early a start of studying, there is always the danger of being classified as "one of those" or being accused of "brown-nosing it, eh?" The same logic applies in part-time job situations and most extra-curricular activities.

Conditions are quite the opposite when it comes to fulfilling the study role: "If I postpone test preparations, I'm the only one to know." Such low

22. Though referred to in Ch.III, since many of the following distinctions have not been explicitly noted in current sociological literature, they bear repeating. Role competition differs from role conflict. In cases of role competition, expectations for roles are not inherently incompatible as they are in role conflict where, for example, people simultaneously belong to groups that restrict study output and to groups that stress its value (i.e., parents, professional schools). In the latter situation, students who meet the expectations of one group necessarily violate those of the other. Role competition also differs from role overload (where there is insufficient time to honour all of one's role commitments). Theoretically, individuals have sufficient time and energy to service all of their relevant roles. Activities like reading the newspaper, becoming physically fit, working on a hobby, or even going out to the bar do not violate expectations of the student role—they merely consume time. As long as deadlines (i.e., exams or papers) are far enough in the future, people can—by employing judicious scheduling—have sufficient time and energy to honour all of their roles.

observability allows for considerable freedom to pursue other interests and, with "an all out last ditch effort", it's still possible to meet the minimal demands of an academic role set: "By postponing study I'm able to satisfy all my roles without too much stress. Instead of studying throughout the year, I meet my social obligations and enjoy life until I feel overwhelmed by guilt. Then I cram like hell. This way I only suffer for a few days at a time."[23] Students of this sort feel compelled to justify "slacking off" by evoking "valuative-based fritters", especially "higher good-work-avoidance strategies" (Bernstein, 1976). A particularly effective excuse used to reduce guilt is to appeal to various acts of allegiance that one owes to others. Not only does the student appear altruistic, but the student role is placed in a larger perspective of values where its importance, by comparison to other roles, can easily be diminished:[24] "One half of me says people are important, but the other half says schoolwork is important. However, I easily deduce that people must be worth more than anything, including work."

Students also feel compelled to justify the importance of "enjoying life" which, incidentally, leaves little time for study. "Enjoying life" is a moral mandate, almost a duty, for young people in our society: "When you're young, you're supposed to have fun, make friends, and generally not take life too seriously"; "University years are supposed to be the best years of our lives because we don't yet have the responsibilities of adult life . . . so we should enjoy life while we can." However, when students delay exam preparation until the "bitter end" and then feverishly attempt to learn masses of information, the result is but a fragmentary grasp of the material. Consequently, they must reconcile themselves to having less than perfect marks and certainly less than a full command of the subject area. Indeed, in an effort to reduce dissonance, many students abandon all hope of achieving a high grade point average and simply emphasize "getting by": "So long as I pass, that's all I care." This state of affairs is justified by other valuative fritters, especially existential ones: "the decision to work or not work is cast as having no lasting practical or existential effect on the course of one's life" (Bernstein, 1976). One frequent rationalization is that there are only so many openings in graduate and professional schools: "Even if [by studying] I made myself continually miserable, my chances of getting in would be 'ify' to say the least." "So long as I graduate, what the hell sort of difference would it make to my life if I got a 'C' instead of a 'B'." While some individuals originally experience problems of fit between personality and student role, the discrepancy is reduced by lowering aspirations and thereby effectively reducing felt pressures to work. In this situation,

23. Insulation from observability is one of Merton's (1957a) central mechanisms for the articulation of competing roles. Indeed, as Coser (1961:39) states: "The determination of who can hide from whom may be as essential to the workings of a social system as determination of who has power over whom."

24. This aspect of Bernstein's valuative fritters overlaps with Scott and Lyman's (1968) account which justifies untoward acts by "appeals to group loyalties."

the main problem is to find courses and professors who do not demand too much work in return for "that passing grade." Actually, students must attain an overall average of at least 2.5 (out of 4) in order to graduate. While this means they must put forth effort in some of their courses, they soon learn that requirements can vary considerably among professors teaching the same course.

Conclusion

In this chapter we attempted, by focusing simultaneously on structural and interactional theories and balancing the weaknesses of one against the strengths of the other, to explain why students neglect their study role.[25] While structural theory provides the framework which allows for the identification of the major sources of role strain, interactional theory provides the background for an examination of how students experience strain and the strategies they actively employ to cope. Perhaps a major implication of this chapter is the realization that individual study biographies are played out against a structural background which provides many competing, attractive alternatives for students' time and energies. Since many of these alternative roles are also more highly visible than the study role it is possible to see how individuals might be encouraged to service one at the expense of others. Furthermore, variations among individual biographies (i.e., conflict between characteristics demanded by the study role and characteristics of individuals) combined with potential inadequate socialization to the "loose" study role also present obstacles to adequate performance.

Traditionally, students have been able to employ "fritters", "accounts", and other forms of "motive talk" to justify negotiations within the study role. It may well be that "debunking" some of the "fritters", and notions like the "genius myth" will aid in a clearer understanding (for both students and teachers) of what the study role entails. The next step in our investigation is to see how students actually succeed in negotiating their way out of competing role identities as exam dates draw nearer and role competition blossoms into role overload.

25. Some persons might view this analysis as a subtle form of "blaming the victim" (Ryan, 1971); i.e., if text books and professors were more interesting and relevant all students would live up to ideal role expectations. While "interesting" textbooks and professors do have some impact on study behaviour (i.e., some students do study more), the majority of them still do not meet the "ideal" requirements of their role. In fact, they may simply feel more guilty and actually apologize to the professor for their poor performance, indicating that it does not reflect their real interest in either the subject matter or the class itself.

Chapter V

Phase I: Early Pre-Exam (Continued)

Studying and Status Sets

In the last chapter we delineated sources of uncertainty and stress which students face and the strategies they employ to cope. The aim of the present chapter is to show how students deal with the role overload and the psycho-physical symptoms that result from the demands of their other positions as family members, employees, and members of religious groups, as well as friends. There is also an emphasis on the increasing importance of studying. We begin with an inspection of rates of use of popular study areas around the university.

A. Studying: Movement from a "Loose" Role to a "Tight" One

As we noted earlier, at the beginning of the school year the study role is a relatively "loose" one and not highly visible. However, as structural theory predicts, when exams approach the study role becomes more observable and students are forced to negotiate their way out of all forms of role competition and find a new sense of self-discipline. This self-discipline is evident in the increasing number of students who use public study areas, particularly libraries. We noted variations in library use by gauging the number of revolutions of turnstiles in the central library on campus.

An examination of Graph 1 indicates that the number of students using the library increased from September to October and peaked at the end of November, which corresponds to the last full week of classes for the term and the point in time when many half-credit classes would have had final in-class tests. Many full credit classes also have mid-term exams at this time. The pattern is even more pronounced during the second term when library usage increased from January to February and soared to its peak in March, when students were preparing for final exams in both half and full credit courses. The two most prominent points on the graph correspond to the dates of the final examinations.

Graph I: Turnstile Statistics: Entrances to Library by Month

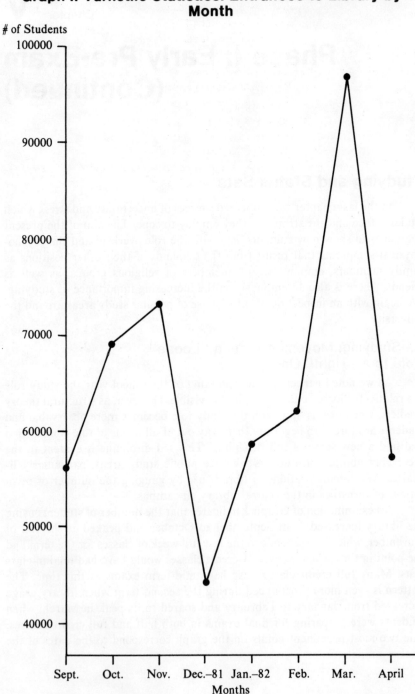

# of Students

100000

90000

80000

70000

60000

50000

40000

Sept. Oct. Nov. Dec.–81 Jan.–82 Feb. Mar. April

Months

An examination of weekly library use provides a more detailed picture of student study patterns (See Graph II).

Library usage increases gradually by the week and peaks during mid-October, just about the time of the first set of exams. Exam periods tend to be followed by dips in library use as students recuperate and then begin to prepare themselves for the next evaluation period. Note that this November peak period is followed by a more protracted dip and finally by another peak which corresponds to preparations for final exams in half-courses between November 30–December 6). Finally, there is a progressive decline in library use as more students finish their exams and begin the Christmas vacation period.

The second term begins on a high note, with considerably more students using the library than during the first week of the fall term (i.e., 8300 for the week of September 8–13 vs. 12,000 for the week of January 4–10). Library usage continues its upward climb and reaches its first peak at the end of January—corresponding to many first exams of the new term—followed by the usual "rest" period and another peak just before mid-term break when many more tests tend to be scheduled. Once again, the peak is followed by an even more pronounced rest period. While the mid-term break (February 15–21 or thereabouts) is euphemistically called "study week" it is widely defined as "spring break" and walls in the university are usually plastered with advertisements for various ski resorts. However, when students return they use the library even more frequently than before the break. The library now is quickly filled to capacity and remains that way up to and including the last week of classes (ending April 8th, since April 9 was Good Friday and the university was closed) when many in-class final exams are held. Since this last week had only four working days we can account for the slight drop in usage from the previous week. As students finish their exams during April, library use drops dramatically.

Studying is but one activity associated with libraries; for students also search out source materials for writing research papers. To ensure that the variations in turnstile revolutions reflect actual increases in studying, we checked to see whether they corresponded to the number of students using public rooms which are devoted entirely to study activities. To this end, every Friday at 3:30 P.M. we recorded the number of students in the "Coloured Room", one of the most popular study areas on campus. The room is quite large and when comfortably full holds about 150 students. There are study carrels along the walls and large library tables in the centre. The students who regularly occupy these tables tend to spread out their books over quite an area so that only two to four persons can occupy a table at any given time.

An examination of Graph III indicates that variations in the use of the Coloured Room correspond closely to variations in library turnstile counts.

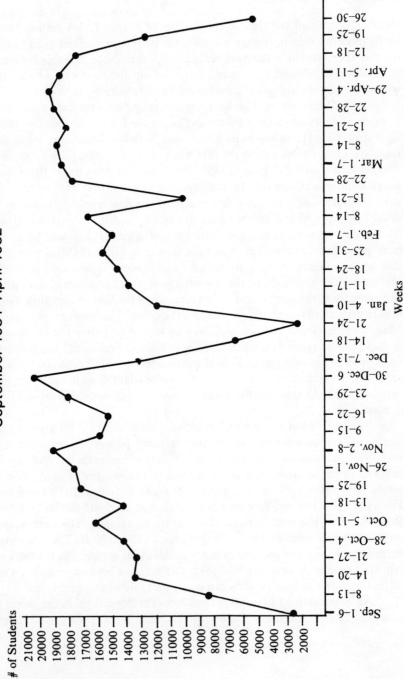

Graph II: Turnstile Entrances to Library by Week
September 1981 – April 1982

# of Students

Weeks

Graph III: Use of Coloured Room Study Area by Week

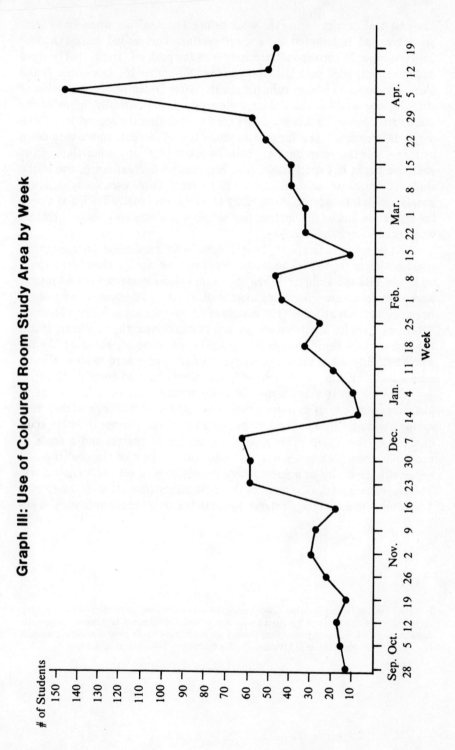

The first peak occurs during the week before Thanksgiving when many tests are given and is followed by a short decline. The second peak (October 26–November 2) corresponds precisely with the peak on Graph II. The third and more protracted peak lasts three weeks (November 16– December 7) and also corresponds to library turnstile counts. After December 7 the number of students who study in the Coloured Room drops dramatically. Many of the same variations as for library usage are found during the second term. The major difference is that a far greater proportion of students (more than twice as many) use the room during "finals" week than at any other time of the year. We ought to expect these more pronounced fluctuations in use of the study room because, unlike libraries which have multiple uses, study areas are simply meant for studying. Also, 3:30 P.M. Fridays is usually defined as a time for relaxation and as our information suggests students only make sacrifices when exams force them to do so.

As we see from Graph II, those students, who, a few weeks prior to exams, could not force themselves to study, somehow now change their "frittering" ways and find the ability: "When the exam notices come out, I find myself slowly but deliberately becoming more methodical . . . studying can no longer be put off as it has all year." The major reason for the change is fear of failure: "Nature strives for minimum energy. But exams combat the very heart of this law because they instill enough fear and anxiety to motivate a student like me, who's basically not a keener, to study;" "I find it very hard to sit down and read a textbook, but the thought of failure scares me into doing it."[1]

Not all students are motivated solely through fear of failure or status loss; some view exams in a more optimistic light as a challenge to their reasoning abilities: "I do not seek to pass the exam but attempt to attain standards I set for myself. This gives me a feeling of control and a sense of accomplishment." Others stress the competitive aspect of the challenge: "I personally see exams as a game where the object is to get the highest mark. The player (student) who receives the most points (marks) wins the game." The competitive challenge extends to obtaining tangible rewards such as en-

1. Kelman's (1961) classification—compliance, identification, and internalization—designates varying degrees of conviction associated with acts of social influence. Compliance—where students study merely to avoid punishment (failure)— would rank as the most superficial response. Festinger (1953) and Merton (1959) classify this reaction as behavioural conformity.

trance into graduate or professional school, getting on the Dean's Honour List, or earning a scholarship.[2]

Another reason for studying mentioned with some frequency is a sense of loyalty to parents or professors. Students are loath to "let down" people they admire.[3] Sometimes, students who do not perform as well as they would have liked actually approach the professor to offer an apology, indicating their grade does not reflect their interest in the lectures or the subject matter.

A most interesting feature is that some students will work just as hard in a subject for almost the opposite reason: "When professors announce an upcoming exam I feel an instant hatred towards them. I then make them a type of enemy I must beat or they will have the joy of conquering me."[4]

Now that some of the major reasons for studying have been outlined, we will take a look at what happens when students begin to devote more time to it. Remember, studying has consequences not only for the students' competitive roles and activities, but also for their entire status set: "The effect studying for exams has on my life is phenomenal. It seems to become an issue in each and every relationship I have." Given the fact that such a large number of students delay their preparation until the last possible minute, earlier problems of role competition now become accentuated into problems of role overload: "As role obligations increase, sooner or later a time barrier is confronted which forces the actor to honor some roles at the expense of honouring others." (Sieber, 1974:567). However, since "each claim [role] presses its rights in complete and pitiless indifference to other interests and duties, no matter

2. When students study because studying is a standard they have set for themselves, they are practising what Kelman (1961) terms internalization and what Festinger (1953) and Merton (1959) call attitudinal conformity. Not only is the activity consistent with their inner values, but much of the reward comes from factors intrinsically linked to the act. While studying to win a scholarship might be termed a form of compliance or behavioural conformity (to the extent that the rewards lie in the competitive aspect of the challenge), it can also be classified as internalization. Specifically, students are viewed as having internalized the value of competition and are acting in a manner consistent with it.

3. This reason for studying ranks between compliance and internalization in Kelman's (1961) scheme and is classified as identification. Students accept influence because they like or admire the person exerting it. Unlike the case with internalization, students do not find studying to be intrinsically satisfying; they study only because they do not want to let down the person (group) they identify with. The reasons for studying become especially apparent when exams are no longer required (i.e., after graduation). Students who internalize the value of studying will probably continue in a life-long search for "knowledge", while those who practice compliance will probably end the "quest."

4. This mode of adaptation is somewhat of an anomaly. When persons form negative relationships with individuals or groups and behave in ways opposite to social expectations, the referent-others are classified as negative reference groups and the behaviour is termed anti-conformity (Hollander and Willis, 1964). However, in the present situation, students form negative relationships with professors but act precisely in accordance with their expectations.

whether they be in harmony or in utter incompatibility with it" (Simmel, 1969:121), it is not always easy to withdraw, even temporarily, from other role involvements. Thus, the stage is set for what Marks (1977:923) calls, "a sociological version of the Hobbesian War of all against all. Each group in an individual's set of affiliations becomes the potential enemy of every other group, all warring for the individual's scarce time and energy." Given these potential problems of role overload and role conflict, students must "juggle the multitudinous commitments and demands of positions and relationships so as to negotiate a 'safe' and 'meaningful' passage" through the exam period (McCall and Simmons, 1978:231). This frequently demands directing acts and particularly words (i.e., "aligning actions")[5] to many role others to negotiate new agendas that will allow sufficient study time and yet maintain the relationships in some serviceable order. In this manner, students can manage their situations without undue strain.

Students also receive some degree of institutional support in their efforts. Since exams reflect so many central values in our society, they are ranked high in terms of society's hierarchy of role obligations.[6] Hence, in a role overload situation, conflict between "studying for an upcoming exam" and some other role obligation, the former is often given priority: "When someone asks me for a date, the answer (words directed to others) 'I would like to, but I have to study for an exam,' is usually acceptable. Let's admit it, who in their right mind would want to bear responsibility for a student's failure?" To the extent that such a hierarchy of role obligations is widely shared, the justification of "having to study" greatly facilitates withdrawal from alternate involvements.

B. The Family and the Student Studying for Exams

The family, as a group and social institution, affects and is affected by exams in different ways, depending on the social position of the student as a family member. Exams most frequently involve students who are children in their families of orientation but may also affect students who are parents in their families of procreation. In families of procreation, there are more demands on students who are wives and mothers than upon those who are husbands and fathers.

---

5. Stokes and Hewitt (1976) use "aligning actions" as a bridging concept to synthesize symbolic interactional and structural explanations. Aligning actions refer to the various rationalizations, justifications and excuses actors use to smooth over divergencies encountered at interpersonal (interactional) and cultural (structural) levels. When students go to the extra effort of justifying (via fritters) the discrepancy between the time and effort actually expended in study and cultural ideals, they pay honour to and invigorate them. The concept of aligning actions is another way of making evident the interpenetrations of the micro and macro worlds.

6. Merton (1957a) states that culturally shared agreements concerning role priorities offer another social mechanism for the articulation of roles, and, that in our society, "family and job obligations" are among the highest ranked.

Although the family and educational systems are separate institutions, the parents and teachers who represent them are both concerned with transmitting the society's values. Consequently, students who live in families of orientation usually find their parents' expectations congruent with their own role expectations. Indeed, parents often act as professional role senders: "My parents understand that studying must be done and totally encourage it. It makes me smile; when they know I have a test the only thing they ask me is why I'm not studying." The general effect of an upcoming exam is to raise the social status of the student within the family. Parents and siblings reorient their activities to focus on the student and modify their behaviour to make the home a place conducive to study. Several students report that their "parents go out of their way and even out of the house so that it will be quiet." Out of the approximately three hundred exam logs collected, only one student, who was failing and who came from a lower class background, reported a lack of support from a parent. In this case, the mother was supportive but the father was not: "I feel like he does not like me going to school. He gives me the feeling that he thinks I should be out working. . . . He usually sits in front of the T.V. with the volume too high, even when he knows I've got an exam to study for." This sort of attitude is the exception, however, since most parents support their children's studying. Most parents also side with students when they demand "peace and quiet" from siblings: "When I ask for quiet to listen to T.V. or records, the request is not readily respected. However, an appeal for quiet so I can study for an exam is the ultimate 'silencer' "; "In our house, studying for an exam has priority over other activities. For example, my little sister can't have her Friday night party because I must study at home in peace." Since family members are so interdependent, it is easy to see how this sort of thing might cause hostility between siblings. Parents, however, tend to become more understanding and often excuse students who are studying from chores and family activities. Many students also report an increase in socioemotional support around exam time: "My family becomes an institution of comfort, a place where I can justifiably moan and groan about all the work and studying I have to do." "The attention I normally seek is finally found and is now as easy to get as snow in Winnipeg." Some individuals also report taking advantage of the situation by "squeezing out more sympathy and understanding than I really deserve . . . it's a great way of escaping responsibilities of all kinds."[7] In the intitial phase of intense studying, several students living away from home report that "all of a sudden pictures of family, friends, and pets

---

7. The exam preparation role has some similarities to the sick role (Parsons, 1951) in that: 1) individuals are excused from the performance of their usual tasks; 2) others provide greater emotional support; and 3) just as sick people have a duty to do their best to get well, so students have a duty to study to the best of their abilities.

are looked at more frequently," or that "homesickness becomes stronger and depression becomes deeper." Interestingly, as they become more fully involved in the study role, the frequency of writing letters home decreases: "Normally I write to my parents once a week. However, during the examination period, I can only write every second or third week." The resulting guilt is minimized by some form of "motive talk": "Though I know they (parents) impatiently await my letters, I nevertheless feel that spending more time on studying would probably be their advice to me." While parental expectations are usually compatible with those of the school, they are occasionally perceived as excessive, "composed of guilt trips, cries of 'where did we go wrong', and cruel threats only a parent can get away with." These parental pressures complicate the situation: "I do not like to be nagged at about studying. . . . When I am it sets me off. The result is . . . a series of high pitched arguments with my parents, a condition hardly conducive to concentrated study."

A further source of pressure emerges when parents attempt to encourage achievement by promoting competition between their offspring and others in the class; students are pushed to "outdo" their classmates. In this sense, the student is removed from the position of an individual, and becomes instead a "representative of the family." Indeed, "success on exams is often used to describe how good a daughter (or son) one is. The information will sometimes be passed on to a complete stranger." Consequently, students may equate how well they do on exams with how well they are liked: "I sometimes get the feeling that my parents think my final marks are the main reason for my existence." Excessive pressures for achievement are, however, almost always backed up with elaborate means of "social" and "physical" support. Some parents, especially mothers, will read over a student's notes and then quiz them on the facts.[8] The granting of such role privileges including physical amenities like pots of tea or coffee makes the duties of the student role easier to bear. Parents also provide comfort for students: "I realize my family is praying and hoping for me." "If I don't do as well as expected, my family is still there for support . . . telling me 'you'll do better next time'."

Divorced parents may prove to be a source of role overload for students. A daughter of newly divorced parents reports that she had to be careful to apportion some of her "precious study time" to her parents because "each is sensitive about the time and attention given to them by my brother and myself." She managed the strain by "making shorter visits to each, and making extensive use of the phone." The substitution of voice-to-voice visiting for face-to-face encounters allowed her to maintain her relationships in a serviceable order and yet not cut too extensively into study time. Reducing the amount of time and effort spent on activities that compete for increasingly limited study time is one way to overcome the problems of role overload, for example,

8. Some students report that the parent may develop an interest in the subject and consider going to the university herself.

decreasing the number of letters home. Indeed, this strategy is used so often that it may be formalized with the term "role contraction."[9]

For married students, especially mothers with children, the picture becomes even more complex. The family is now more a source of role strain than support; "a greedy institution who with its demands almost devours" the mother (Coser and Coser, 1979). Even though she may be employed outside the home as well as going to school, the major burdens of housekeeping and child-rearing still rest with her. In cases of conflict between family and other roles, she is "normatively required to give priority to her family" (Coser and Coser, 1979:379). This is quite a contrast to the majority of students who experience their student role as a master status while other identities are reduced to auxiliary positions (Hughes, 1945).

Preschool children provide the greatest source of competition with the student role: "My little son is four years old and an only child. Therefore, as long as exams are far away, I try to keep my studying down during his waking hours." This mother goes on to describe an episode that dramatizes the movement of the child from a source of role competition to one of role overload. As exams approached, time became more and more scarce (role overload), and she was forced to honour one role at the expense of another: "As the deadline (exam) approached, I couldn't wait until eight P.M. to start in at my books." As a result, she modified her role schedule by making an early dinner and arranging with her husband to care for the child. This delegation of one's role to another is one way of coping with the problem of role overload. She also removed herself physically from her husband's and son's presence, thereby employing the strategy of role compartmentalization. After a couple of hours of study, however, the student reported that her "compartment" was invaded by her major competing role-other: "I heard my door open and shut very quietly. When I turned around there stood my son with the saddest, big, blue eyes. He then said, 'poor old empty me.' I asked him what he meant and he said, 'I miss you, mom.' At that moment my heart felt like it was breaking; it was as if he was being neglected. I gathered him up in my arms, closed my books, and took him out to play." Here we have an episode where, because of time pressures, mother and student roles shift from role competition to role overload and, as Coser and Coser (1979) predict, the identity of mother takes precedence. As she went on to point out, however, this mother switched identities because "the exam was still three evenings away." When the child employed the same tactic the night before the exam, the mother "couldn't give in, regardless of how sad he looked."

Although the mother's student identity took precedence for a time, she clearly experienced a considerable amount of guilt, which often happens

9. Role contraction is defined as the performance of minimal tasks necessary to sustain a relationship. Role contraction differs from the related strategy "role withdrawal"—where individuals (temporarily or permanently) withdraw from relationships which may cause problems.

whenever one violates internalized normative standards. One way to cope with the increased role strain is to employ some form of motive talk, thereby directing words to self, which leads to redefining the painful situation in terms that are socially and personally acceptable. The mother here notes: "this course and its more distant rewards will only benefit my child in later years." Other mothers, perhaps less convinced of the direct utilitarian benefits of a university education, frequently point out that devoting time to study in the present will enable them to pass the course, which, in turn, will put them in a better frame of mind and allow them to become better mothers in the long run. Another frequent response is: "I only have one chance at this exam, but I'll always be a mother, mate, or friend."

Husbands and housework are often treated in a similar manner: "Once I begin studying intensely, all other 'unnecessary;' activities—spending time with husband and children, entertaining, and housework—are left largely unattended [role withdrawal],[10] while necessary activities like meals, and care of children are simply covered as quickly as possible" (role concentration). In the process, acts and words directed to others in the form of role bargains and appeals for understanding are made: "I make deals. For example, if you are good (children) or cooperative (husband) so I can study, then I'll give you a treat (kids) or devote my time and self to you (husband) when I'm finished." The sexual dimension of the husband-wife relationship is also affected. "I usually don't indulge in sexual relations with my husband because studying makes me tense. Husbands seem to understand this; at least mine says he does." "As the exam date draws nearer, I find myself taking my text to bed with me at night to get a little more reading done. As a result I'm not open to my husband's intimate advances . . . but I promise that after exams I can splurge." Others withdraw from conjugal intimacies because of fatigue: "I'm usually too tired for more than a quick kiss and a hurried goodnight." These students offer a modicum of support for Freud's notion of a scarcity of energy. Looking at it from Marks' (1977:921) perspective: "civilizations and lovers are enemies who jealously compete with one another for the individual's libido or energy . . . people do not have enough energy to be both good civilization-builders and lovers." On the other hand, all interaction is open to negotiation and, should a husband be especially helpful and supportive, the nature of the interaction may be altered: "I become all consumed with the task at hand, forgetting about my husband's plights and concerns. However, when he prepares the meals and cleans up after . . . I feel guilty and think I should reward him in other ways—sexually, or granting other favours such as a massage."

By employing appeals to role taking ("Just put yourself in my place") and making various compensatory promises for future behaviour ("I'll really

10. Role withdrawal can be considered as a type of role set contraction. In role withdrawal the number of role others we relate to is reduced whereas in role contraction we continue to play roles, but we pare down performance to its bare essentials.

study now, and I'll make up for it after"), the student is able to juggle various role requirements and still keep the relationship to others in a serviceable order. Sometimes though, regardless of how skilled a negotiator one might be, impasses do occur and competing roles cannot be articulated. In this situation, the dispositions of the actors are sorely tried. As the wife of an otherwise "most understanding husband" notes: "A dinner party was held at my husband's place of employment for all the staff members and their spouses. It was pretty much compulsory for him to be there and, to keep his married status in the eyes of his co-workers, he wanted desperately for me to go along. . . . However, it was the night before my final biology exam [role overload]. I knew how important it was for my marks to study hard, but I also knew how important it was to my husband that I accompany him."[11] In the end, her student identity prevailed, but the problem remained. "I might as well have gone with him for all the studying I accomplished. Sure, I was at my desk, but the conflict seemed to be a locked door to my being able to master the material."[12] When her husband returned home, she learned that "he was the only one at the dinner without his wife." She attempted to alleviate the stress by telling him, "just as soon as I'm finished with exams, we'll have all those people over for a dinner party here" [compensatory strategy].

Occasionally, there are even more extreme forms of residual conflict. One student, who is also a wife and mother, reports her husband was most reluctant to "let her" attend evening classes. Finally he "went along" with her wishes but "stipulated" that she must not let classwork interfere in any way with her home-based expressive and instrumental functions. She was expected to keep up her "pleasant disposition", continue with her household duties and entertain their many guests. She indicates that around exam time "life can become a living hell" because the "stipulation" which "permitted" her to enter university prevents her from employing the usual role bargains and strategies. Consequently, role withdrawal, contraction, delegation, and various other aligning actions are out of the question—yet she is still expected to wear a smile. Such cases highlight the importance of considering the underlying structure of relations within which actors are implicated. To the extent that this structure is "tight", interpersonal negotiations will be circumscribed.

11. This situation is technically one of role overload because the strain comes from insufficient time to meet the requirements of both roles. Role overload is distinguished from role conflict since, if more time were available, honouring the demands of one role would not necessarily violate the expectations of the other.

12. Merton (1957a:118) suggests that these types of situations produce "residual conflict". That is, the social mechanisms for the articulation of roles are not sufficient to reduce the incompatibility of expectations below the level required for effective role performance (i.e., studying). He draws an analogy to mechanical systems and suggests that "this is not unlike the case of engines which cannot fully utilize heat energy. If the analogy lacks force, it may nevertheless have the merit of excluding the utopian figment of a perfectly effective social system." In effect, Merton sees residual conflict as endemic to social systems, so actors are continually faced with practical problems of role adjustment.

On the other hand, some married students point out that exams tend to "loosen" typical role relationships within the family. Husbands and children often agree to assume the "roles of cook, laundress, shopper, and housekeeper" so the mother can study. In fact, exams provide a legitimate stimulus which puts family relationships in a state of flux. After all, once the exam is over, the mother can press to make these modifications to her typical role lasting ones. At the same time she assumes the new role of "instructor" for house-related activities and starts directing proceedings: "That should not have been put in the dryer" and "Check prices before buying."

Since joint effort often generates a sense of cooperativeness and closeness, one result of exams can be a reinvigorated family life. Several mothers report a greater sense of identification with their student children, and vice versa. As mothers come to realize how difficult it is to obtain top grades, they quit "continually hounding" their children for higher marks. A sense of equality emerges as "they study, mom studies." "My daughter has been the most understanding of all. I snapped at her just before I came here to write the exam because she spilled ice cubes all over the kitchen floor . . . she snapped back . . . she had an exam today, too. We looked at each other, grinned, laughed to relieve the tension, both of us said 'sorry', cleaned up the mess together, and then stuck our noses back into our books." Such experiences, she continues, "serve to bring us closer together." Wives also report receiving and very much appreciating empathic acts of kindness from their husbands. "A thoughtful act on the part of my husband is the reassurance he gives me that I'll do well and that he still loves me." The increased support at exam time often makes the student who is also a wife and mother feel a more "valued person."[13]

The student who is a wife and mother also belongs to a family of orientation. And the family of orientation is usually supportive—they tend to visit less frequently to reduce the overload problem, and often invite the daughter and her family for meals: "To help give me some time to relax, my mother phones and asks us all over for a meal. This . . . relieves the pressure a bit." Another student who lives some distance from her parents reports she always receives phone calls and well wishes on the day of the exam. In these instances, exams perform somewhat similar functions as regular, ritual occasions like birthdays or Christmas, because they intensify family interaction and serve as bonds to both the nuclear family and extended kin.

Wives are also expected to serve as "kin keepers" to parents who may be in need. One student discusses her obligations to her mother, a widow living alone. Prior to becoming a student, "I drove my mother where and when she wanted to go. However, there are many times when I should be studying and

13. On the other hand, the almost complete take-over and successful execution of household duties by the husband and older children may "create feelings of less self-worth. . . . I now realize that my family could do without my continual assistance."

she calls, making even a trip to the store for milk sound urgent. At first I would drop everything and do her bidding, but it got to the point where I could not get in enough study time" (role overload). The student did not know "how to tell her without hurting her." Her husband suggested she ought to convey the information in a matter-of-fact manner, "showing her (mother) exactly how much I had to study and how much material I had to learn." The suggestion is consistent with another mechanism Merton (1957a) identifies for role articulation; that is, making conflicting demands observable to members of the various role sets who are causing the problem so that, in some measure, it also becomes their problem In the present case, the outcome "was fantastic; mother understood completely and wondered why I hadn't told her before. My response was only a smile, and I think that was the best answer I could have given."

Since students who are also husbands and fathers tend to have fewer household and childrearing responsibilities; "distracting" family obligations impinge less on them than on their female counterparts. Their wives are almost always supportive in both the emotional and instrumental (e.g., typing assignments) spheres: "As far as my wife is concerned . . . well she is one understanding person . . . she understands how much this degree means to me." However, there are occasional exceptions: "As I start studying for exams, my wife wants to go out to escape the . . . boredom of having a silent husband. This leaves me more to worry about . . . ranging from concerns over the survival of my marriage to having to make supper." When wives work outside of the home, husbands face similar role problems as those of their female student counterparts. Interestingly, both sexes employ very similar coping strategies. In the sexual domain, for example, males also report a decline in libido: "Sex even becomes a problem. I find that in order to make love, you should feel good and there ought to be practically no worries. . . . Exam time is not a good time as there is no concentration; no ready willingness to give of yourself. . . . So I try to avoid the topic." The decline in willingness (by both men and women) to engage in sexual interaction is perhaps not so much due to a scarcity of physical energy ("burned up" in studying as Freud might suggest) as it is to the fact that people are "planning animals" and things take on meaning in relation to plans (McCall and Simmons, 1978:58). Plans tend to centre round the problematic and so exam related stimuli move to the foreground while stimuli associated with competing identities (i.e., mate-lover) temporarily receed to the background. To the extent that mate-lover roles only receed and not totally disappear, they leave some mark on behaviours associated with the competing student identity. In the case of sexual interaction the act is reduced to its bare essentials with time and elaborations contracted. One wife, a non-student describes her student husband as follows: "With exams a change comes over my mate's sexual behaviour. He isn't interested in holding hands, or in hugging and kissing. He neglects the small things that mean so much to me. He becomes more aggressive, overriding my wishes and neglecting me in the process."

As we noted, students' positions within families of orientation or procreation result in varied forms of interaction, especially at exam time. The degree of strain students experience varies with the number and complexity as well as relative tightness of their family related roles. In families of procreation, women with pre-school children tend to experience most strain and make most use of coping strategies. On the other hand, students in their families of orientation tend not only to have less compelling and fewer role demands but parents often provide study-conducive environments and may even pressure students to study.

C. The Workplace and the Student Studying for Exams

Students are not only members of families; many are also members of the labour force—on either a part-time or full-time basis. Since work roles rank high in our society's hierarchy of role obligations, they are another source of competition for the student's time and energies. In turn, exams have consequences for the work role. The following comment is typical of students with part-time jobs: "As exams approach, I become more tense on the job and . . . feel . . . I should be studying instead of working." The experience of role overload affects both disposition and performance, particularly in the realm of interpersonal relations, and many working students respond to the strain by requesting a few days off (role withdrawal).[14] It appears that at least for part-time employees most supervisors recognize the precedence of the student identity and grant their requests. Exams apparently offer something of an exception to Marks' (1977:932) general proposition that ". . . scarce time and energy excuses typically will not be honored within work activities, but they will often be honored outside the occupational arena." The exception, however, may be more apparent than real, in that such excuses are largely made by and granted to part-time employees-who also tend to be full-time students with studying considered their major "work role." Despite the overall priority granted student role obligations, many students experience guilt and anxiety in asking supervisors "for such favours", probably because the overload problems could have been avoided by earlier exam preparation.

Part-time students who are full-time employees also have an effect on the work place. For example, many students report that their supervisors are aware of upcoming exams and attempt to alter demands and schedules to facilitate studying. As one police officer reports: "My supervisor, the corporal in charge, told me to take the day off to study. He suggested that shifts could be rearranged and I could put in an extra day at the end of the week." One secretary noted: "My boss's behaviour changed—he gave me less dictation

14. Many students actually quit their part-time jobs just before the end of the academic year and then look for full-time employment for the summer.

and stopped asking me to make the usual phone calls and do other chores I normally do for him." Even though the supervisor in this instance did not verbalize his sentiments, the result was more time to review notes.

Students also note that colleagues, especially if they have been students themselves, often alter their schedules to provide more study time. "At work my colleagues are willing to take over some of my duties so I will have more free time for studying. However, there is always an unmentioned agreement that I will repay them in the future . . . or that I'm being 'paid back' for helping them in the past." Such exchanges are appreciated because they provide study time without causing undue disruption on the job. These role bargains also help reduce financial strain and, most important, give students the sense that they are "earning" their incomes. The exchanges also reduce guilt feelings which, in turn, serve to facilitate involvement in the study role. The secretary quoted earlier also noted that when her supervisor altered his work demands, "this created a sense of guilt." As exchange theorists (Homans, 1961, 1974; Blau, 1964) would predict, she felt that the special concessions she received lowered her contribution to the job, and that she was in no position to readily "repay."

Another office worker, who took his notes to work, felt self-conscious when fellow workers who were aware of the upcoming exam stopped by his desk: "I could feel their eyes searching for my class notes . . . and it made me feel guilty because I was studying on company time!" Clearly part-time students who sense insufficient time to honour both occupational and student identities frequently do not entirely abandon one in favour of the other (role withdrawal), but attempt instead to juggle and make simultaneous compromises in both roles.[15] A few particularly fortunate students have jobs which actually assist in exam preparation (rather than providing a source of role competition or overload): "My job did not interfere with studying at all; as a matter of fact it helped. . . . I worked at the hockey arena and some mornings I had to open up at six (A.M.). There was usually nothing to do at that time so I would get quite a bit of studying done . . . and I was getting paid for it."

In sum, students who are also members of the work force face competing demands from both roles, especially at exam time when the student role is at its "tightest." Since the student's identity ranks high in our society's hierarchy

15. Occasionally exams have the opposite effect. The following comment was made by an employee working in an office with several other persons who were also taking the same university class (and so would be aware of the upcoming exam): "I was not feeling very well but I went to work just the same so people wouldn't think I just took the day off to study for the exam—or—so that they might not think that I was studying too hard and that was my reason for being sick." Although this instance is an exception to the rule, it is one time when an exam actually increased work performance—or at least the person's presence at work.

of identities, employers and fellow employees frequently are willing and may even go out of their way to engage in various role bargains which alleviate role strain and allow students more time to study.

D. Religion and the Student Studying for Exams

While studying also intrudes on students' role sets other than family and work, a temporary withdrawal from them is more generally accepted because these other roles are either ranked lower than work related roles in the overall value structure of the society, or are viewed as less pressing in their demands. This legitimized role hierarchy generally aids students in determining time allocations (Merton, 1957a). Nevertheless, in the event that the abandoned role ranks high in the student's own hierarchy of identities, a certain measure of strain will be encountered. As one student who is a member of an evangelical denomination points out: "I am a Christian and an active member of my church. I spend considerable time in church activities which I see as the duty of a good Christian. However, in trying to prepare myself for exams, I can no longer afford time for Church duties. I feel guilty about it because I would like to be both a good student and a good Christian." Typically, this student engages in "motive talk" to work through his sense of guilt by convincing himself that, while the exam role involved an "immediate deadline", the church role did not. The "motive talk" was also supplemented with a compensatory strategy: "I overcame many of my feelings of guilt by promising that I would be an even more devout church member after finishing my exams. In this way I'll make up for it." On the other hand, a cohesive religious community will often react to non-participation by its "faithful": "Church attendance ranks high on my community's list of priorities. When a member's attendance drops, it quickly becomes a matter of concern. Fellow members will usually pray for their 'backsliding brother' and he may even receive counseling. Exams, however, change everything—its almost as if he receives a temporary pass relieving him of his usual duties. It is not recommended, but it is at least understood by most. The student now receives prayer in order to help him with his exams rather than his soul." While some devout students do withdraw completely from their religious role-sets for a brief period many use some form of role contraction. Consequently, attendance may be limited to a single weekly service, and participation in extra-church involvements may also be curtailed. The only frequently mentioned exception was for "extra special" occasions, such as the weddings or funerals of close friends or relatives.

E. Friends and the Student Studying for Exams

Exam preparation affects and is affected not only by students' institutionalized ties but also by their informal relationships, particularly those involving friendship networks. Relations between student role and friendship role normally involve less role conflict than they do role competition. Friends frequently offer the student more attractive alternatives than studying. For example, "Though I often know I should be home doing some reading, when my friends call, I usually always go because I don't want to miss out on any of the fun. Why should they have all the fun while I stay home to study?" As exams approach, however, students are forced to choose priorities and the demands of friendship now change from being a source of role competition to one of role overload. One must be forsaken for the other. As one student notes: "Friendship and social life are very important to me, but so is passing my courses with decent grades. This requires considerable work, so as exams come around the corner my social life deteriorates. The result is usually a sense of guilt for neglecting either friends or schoolwork."

From a structural perspective it ought to be relatively easy to withdraw from friendship networks, since they rank lower than work-related ones in our society's hierarchy of role obligations and are informal and amenable to alteration. However, non-married students find these the most difficult roles from which to extricate themselves. Friends are part of a student's primary relations and a source of emotional support and satisfaction. Friends also may play a vital role in shaping our self-concept. Research in university settings indicates that friends play a crucial role in the development and maintenance of high levels of self-esteem (Manis, 1955). Given the direct and constant nature of friendship associations, it is no wonder that students are so responsive to their friends' views: "As I try to pry myself away from my friends to study, they become frustrated with me because they feel that's all I want to do . . . after a couple of times they start going out with other people. This makes for additional tension because not only do I think they are having just as good a time without me but I also wonder if they are talking about me . . . it sounds so sissy to say you can't go because you have to study . . . I also become paranoid, worrying that they might never call back, even once the exam is over."

To devote more time to study while neither compromising one's self nor alienating significant others requires considerable interactional skills. Students must be able to convey the need to study and also be capable of persuading others to go along with the alterations in schedule: "I had an upcoming exam to study for, but some of my friends asked me to go out for a couple of beers. I said, 'I'm sorry but I have to study for my sociology exam.' However, they persisted—'it'll only be for a couple of hours, what can it hurt?' So I said I'd meet them later for supper at the hotel. . . . After we finished eating, I hated to leave but I knew I had to. When they asked me again to go to the bar briefly with them 'just for a round', I finally forced the issue humorously by saying, 'Would you really want to see me go through another whole year of Introductory Sociology?' They sympathetically agreed they would not and so I was free to go." This student successfully engaged in the process of role negotiation. First, there was a compromise solution: she agreed to take time off from study to share a meal, thereby maintaining her identity as friend.

55

Second, by using an altercast,[16] which made the others' identities as friends more salient, she was able to persuade them that the student role was uppermost. By casting her associates in the role of "friend", she was able to activate normative expectations appropriate to that role; namely that friends should not cause suffering. Consequently, she effectively 'forced' them to release her so she could pursue her student duties.

As Merton (1957a) would predict, students who withdraw in order to study face their most difficult negotiations with those others who have never been students. Since the others have not been exposed to the pressures and strains of exam preparation, and may even hold different values and aspirations, they are less likely to empathize or take the role of the students: "My boyfriend (who has never attended university) feels neglected and slightly unwanted while I'm spending most of my free time studying in the library. . . . He won't believe me. . . . In high school we didn't have to work like this." Communication becomes difficult for those who lack a shared universe of experience, simply because implicit assumptions are not congruent. One result is faulty transmission and receipt of subtle messages. For example, with the arrival of exams the student identity becomes more prominent, divergencies in lifestyle and identity become more apparent, and the increased possibilities for inter-personal conflict may set the stage for re-evaluation of relationships: "My brother, who never went to university, had a girlfriend who was a student. As exams came she tried to give him hints that she needed time alone to study. He, not understanding, still tried to hang around with her, all the while feeling hurt by the coldness she generated." The lack of a shared universe of experience meant that the male was unable to appreciate his girlfriend's desire for compartmentalization of her student and lover roles. Her subtle attempts at altercasting failed, so she eventually forced to become more blunt and tell him to "hit the road. . . . This lead to their breakup."

On the other hand, effective communication is facilitated when both parties share similar experiences. Negotiations go much more smoothly at critical points like final exams when both parties may wish to withdraw temporarily from each other: "We make promises to each other that after the exam we will go out and have a great time in order to make up for not getting together for such a long while." Conversely, students experience role conflict if they belong to a group that negatively sanctions too early a start in exam preparations. One student noted that his group went out drinking together, but he was not included. When he inquired why, the response was: "We were going to ask you to come along, but then we figured you'd be studying." He goes on to note, "The way it was said sort of let me know there was some

16. Weinstein and Deutschberger (1963) introduced the concept "altercasting" as a counterpart process to Goffman's (1959) notion of "presentation of self". If the presentation of self refers to individuals' attempts to present a favourable "self" to others, altercasting refers to the processes through which an actor (ego) creates an identity or role which forces another (alter) to act in a way advantageous to Ego (the manipulator).

underlying resentment." In sum, it appears that friendship roles provide most students with their greatest source of role competition. Participation in friendship roles is highly gratifying and vitally important to feelings of self esteem. On the other hand, friendship roles are also highly observable which makes withdrawal from them difficult. However, negotiations are facilitated to the degree that friends are members of the same role sets and share similar problems.

Overall it appears that family, work, religious, and friendship role sets provide sources of role competition and overload for students studying for exams. While coping strategies may alleviate much of the strain, feelings of "residual conflict" persist. The next section deals with the psycho-physical symptoms of strain which students experience.

F. The Student Studying for Exams and Psycho-Physical Symptoms

Psycho-physical symptoms are an almost universal reaction to high levels of strain and tension.[17] Given the varied sources of role strain and the pressures of exam strain itself (e.g., "Am I studying the right thing?", "Will I have enough time to learn it . . . will I remember it?"), we might expect students to experience a variety of psycho-physical discomforts (Whyte, 1949;[18] Jackson, 1962; Kahn, et. al., 1964; Kerchoff and Back, 1968; Sarbin and Allen, 1969). Student records do often indicate "the sudden break out of pimples"; "a raw lower lip as a result of gnawing at it"; "ragged fingernails . . . from chewing on them"; "nightmares where I can't find the examination room or answer the questions"; "disturbed sleep patterns"; and "sudden mood alterations, where crying can quickly turn to laughter or vice versa." Students also report increases in other minor ailments such as eye strain, headaches, sore backs, stomach upset,[19] constipation, and diarrhea.

17. An important pre-condition in heart attacks is the presence of high cholesterol levels in the blood which, in turn, is linked to tensions associated with role conflict, role overload, and risk-taking (Jenkins, 1971). Students, before exams, should be prime candidates; and indeed, House (1974) found significantly higher levels of cholesterol in blood samples of medical students on the day before their examinations, and similar readings were found in accountants as the April 15 deadline for filing U.S. federal tax returns approached.

18. Whyte (1949) demonstrated that waitresses' outbursts of crying are related to strains built into their role set. That is to say, while cooks relate to other cooks, and kitchen supervisors relate to kitchen runners (supply men), waitresses are required to interact with other waitresses, supervisors, service pantry workers (or cooks), bartenders and between fifty and one hundred customers each day. The diversity and number of role others creates difficulties in role-articulation—especially when they refuse to cooperate; for example, customers demand rush orders so waitresses attempt to speed things up by shouting them to countermen, who don't appreciate being shouted at "by a woman" and retaliate by slowing down. The result of the strain is that waitresses, especially during rush hours, sometimes break down under the strain and cry.

19. Jackson (1962) found cases of upset stomach and general nervousness to be most frequent among people experiencing role conflict.

Many of these physical symptoms are precipitated or accentuated by the altered dietary habits adopted during exam periods. For example, increase in acne activity can be linked to "eating habits . . . which increase . . . especially in the direction of rich food."[20] Additional food consumption results "as an excuse to take a break from studying without having to feel guilty" or "as a reward for my daily and lengthy hours of study."[21] Even fingernails can substitute for food and serve as anxiety reducers: "I constantly nibble and eat while studying. When food runs out, my fingernails become an extra goodie." While some students respond to examination stresses by increasing food consumption, others react in the opposite manner and skip meals, "because, though my stomach frequently has an empty feeling, I don't seem to have an appetite." In more extreme cases, students cannot eat anything without becoming sick.

Insomnia may arise from the hyperactive state induced by attempting to cram months of work into a few days of concentrated effort. Students also report alterations in sleep rituals; many go to bed later than usual and study right up until the last moment before going to bed, a practice which leaves the mind "racing" and unreceptive to slumber. Furthermore, increasing coffee consumption "to keep alert . . . in order to cram in as much information as possible" does not "exactly help one get a good night's sleep." Cigarette smoking also increases dramatically as students attempt to "calm their nerves." The attempt to cope with higher stress levels by increasing consumption of "junk" food, coffee, and cigarettes frequently has unfortunate consequences. Instead of making students feel better, these products often cause upset stomach, insomnia, and "feeling sick from smoking too much." One might explain the persistence of these practices more in terms of their latent consequences than in their overtly expressed purposes. That is, students, as a group, define cigarettes as appropriate normative coping devices and, to the extent individ-

20. Sarbin and Allen (1969) also found that some individuals experiencing role strain resorted to food, while others reverted to sleep or tranquilizers.

21. This behaviour may be classified under Bernstein's (1976) person-based fritters. These "biological necessity" mixed with "rest-on-your-laurels" fritters usually offer fool proof justifications for work avoidance, because students have bodies which have needs which must be fulfilled. Besides, after working so hard, "you owe it to yourself."

uals share this understanding, social interaction and integration are facilitated.[22]

The various sources of role strain also affect "personality." Many students describe the loss of their otherwise, normal pleasant disposition ". . . because of the pressures I'm under, I become crabby, irritable, and highly prone to sudden spurts of anger." Certain students also become more selectively susceptible to "noises" of all types, and frequently vent their frustrations in this direction. The "offenders" include voices of people who talk while students are trying to study, sounds emitted during eating ("I will snap at my husband if he chews his food too loudly"), and even the flow of water into the toilet ("Do they really need to flush every time?"). They also report an increase in acts of "unkindness", even towards persons who are attempting to provide support. One person who "closeted" herself in the bedroom to study states: "My mother brought a pot of coffee to my room . . . only to receive a sarcastic remark about forgetting the sugar." Another individual notes, "My girlfriend tries her damndest to please me, but because of the state I'm in nothing works out right. . . . I argue over the most trivial of things, like whose turn it is to call." Yet another student received a phone call from her boyfriend, who invited her out for dinner to "get away from studying for an hour or so"; she responded with a loud "No! I'm not in the mood. . . . You really don't care if I pass or fail do you?" Like many others, she states that these outbursts "give a terrible guilt complex during and after exams." On occasion, individuals will actually purchase gifts to compensate for their "inexcusable behaviours": "I find myself buying roses for members of my family to compensate."

On the other hand many students appeal to exams to excuse their "almost heartless" attitude towards others: "Exam writing becomes a crutch (which encompasses) every type of account and justification imaginable." Since exam-related troubles are part of the background expectancies[23] of our society, students who engage in unbecoming behaviour can use the excuse of exam pressures. Not only will this excuse be interpreted as a way of accounting, but

22. Merton (1957b) distinguishes between manifest and latent functions. Manifest functions are the intended consequences of or purposes for which a social act is performed (i.e., smoking to relieve strain), while latent functions are the unknown and/or unintended consequences of a social act (i.e., mechanisms for the facilitation of social interaction). Latent functions are especially important in explaining the persistence of patterns of behaviour which appear to be irrational since they fail to meet their intended purposes (e.g., intensive smoking appears to increase rather than decrease strain). Merton uses the Hopi Indian rain dance to illustrate the distinction between manifest and latent functions. The manifest function of the practice is to bring rain, but it persists despite its lack of connection to the goal (i.e., raining). Therefore, the practice must serve the latent functions "of reinforcing the group identity by providing a periodic occasion on which the scattered members of a group assemble to engage in a common activity" (1957b:63). The practice persists, then, because it allows members to affirm and maintain the ongoing reality of the group, renew acquaintances, and generally revitalize the social component of identities.

23. Scott and Lyman (1968:53) describe background expectancies as "those sets of taken-for-granted ideas that permit the interactants to interpret remarks as accounts in the first place."

it will most likely be accepted as an adequate motive for the action and honoured because "everyone knows exams are trying events." Despite this licence for offensive behaviour, most students withdraw from their routine affiliations while they are studying, not only because other individuals occupy a less central role in the task at hand, but more importantly because students have no desire to "actively destroy relationships by doing things they would later regret."

Conclusion

If students adapt to the initial phases of exam preparation by becoming "semi-recluses", they become "social write-offs" during later phases. Much of the strain associated with neglect of other role identities is relieved by temporarily redefining the value or worth of what is lost. For example, one student notes: "As exams draw closer I question the wisdom of being involved in heterosexual relationships. Once I distance myself from them, I tend to feel that the work involved in maintaining them is more than they are worth." Or, more bluntly, "I no longer have time for distractions like friends or family" and "I now consider partying as childish and immature." In redefining the value of objects and activities previously sought out, students make it easier for themselves to embrace the studying role.

Connecting the exam preparation phase to the interpenetrations of the micro/macro world allows us to see how exams compel students to organize their lives in terms of values associated with the Protestant Ethic. Students become more ascetic and self-denying; "the role of partying, pubbing and having fun is greatly reduced" as they "abandon worldly desires" and develop the necessary self discipline to "shut themselves off from competing attractions by using bedroom doors, library booths, and study halls." Their attitude set may be likened to part of Weber's seventeenth century Protestant Puritan entrepreneurs. Both groups are involved in a risky "business" (i.e., Will I get the grade I need?). Much as the Puritan believed that asceticism and hard work were the only means to allay the anxiety associated with damnation, students, likewise fearing failure, defer gratification and study harder. In sum, the sudden surge in serious studying may be likened to the serious life-long dedication of the Puritans to their "calling." While the exam provides only a temporary "calling", its voice is urgent at the time, and because of its long-term consequences it may be viewed as a way-station to an ultimate vocation.

The major explanatory framework employed to account for variations in role strain, especially as they pertain to the ability to study, is structural . The individual's experience of role strain is systematically tied to the number, type, and intensity of ties with role others. As the demands of the student role become salient, cross-pressures emerge from the "pull" of other identities, for example, from child to mother; boss to employee; peer group to friend. Single, non-working students face their major source of role competition from friends, especially non-students, who do not understand the rigours and value of studying. The situation is aggravated even more if the individual involved is a boyfriend or girlfriend. On the other hand, students whose friends are other students (especially if all have similar reference groups) experience less strain and may even be encouraged by interacting with others who have congruent goals and interests. Individuals in the latter situation provide each other with a continual source of socioemotional and instrumental support. Membership in such a group also increases one's access to other types of valued information. Isolated students who lack access to these sources of information are at a considerable disadvantage.

While other social science studies have documented how people in various positions in the social structure react when confronted with urgent situations[24] (Killian, 1957), the present study focuses on the interactions themselves. By taking the role of students we have attempted to document the emergence of motives, negotiations, and compromises carried out by students with themselves and others. It appears that roles are considerably more open and fluid than pure structural perspectives would suggest. For example, in attempting to negotiate their way through the exam period, students were forced to modify usual role performances and adopt strategies such as withdrawal, or remaining and negotiating various forms of role contraction. This is especially so for mothers and wives who could not withdraw but restricted themselves to meeting only essential demands. Structural role descriptions were even modified in the workplace by temporary suspension of some rules, bosses demanding less work, and informal negotiations with fellow workers. None of these role adjustments were part of job descriptions but were forged and hammered out in the give and take of social interaction. This view of roles is considerably more open and fluid than those found in traditional "structural" studies of interaction.

To this point the discussion has revolved around how students' other statuses, that is, their membership in family, workplace, religious, and friendship groups affect and are in turn affected by studying. The next step is to examine the impact of studying on the student role set.

---

24. Killian (1957:46) studied the conflicting loyalties individuals experienced when a set of oil storage tanks exploded and partially wrecked their workplace and surrounding town. Workers had to choose which group to service: their family, friends, fellow employees, company, or community. He notes that "only the unattached person in the community was likely to be free of such conflicts." However, Killian failed to go beyond a structural analysis of role strain and study interactions themselves, probably because the critical nature of the situation involved meant that interactions would be so speeded up there would be little time to engage in motive talk or other forms of negotiation.

Chapter VI

Phase I: Early Pre-Exam (Continued)

Studying and the Student Role Set

In the last chapter we examined the impact of individuals' status sets on studying. The focus of this chapter is on withdrawal from other roles in the student's status set, and concentration on the role set related to the student status proper (i.e., student- student and student-professor interaction).

A. Studying and the Student-Student Role Sector

In some ways the tendency we noted in the last chapters for students to withdraw from other members of their status sets runs counter to the earlier contention that "misery loves company." However, closer inspection reveals support for Schachter's (1959) modification of the contention which states that "misery loves miserable company" (or, others who are sharing the same experience). Final exams, in particular, create similar experiences for students, and it is at this time that one can readily detect an opening of personal boundaries and a relaxation of conversational preserve.[1] One individual who, though only in first year university, strongly identified himself as a future law student and did most of his studying in the law library, reported: "Being that I was a 'non-law student', I was considered an outsider and, throughout the year, excluded from everyday interaction. However, several weeks before the scheduled final exams the situation changed . . . often law students who were taking a break from their studies introduced themselves to me and discussed the upcoming exams." Although law students served as a reference group for this particular individual, he was only able to become an actual part of the membership group when exams approached.

As exam time nears, students shift their affiliational interests to others who share the general student role set, and especially, as Schachter (1959) would predict, to those who will write the same exam. One part-time student, a married teacher, illustrates this change in focus: "My interaction with my husband steadily dwindles as the exam date approaches. Conversations with

---

1. Goffman (1971) conceptualizes conversational preserve as a territory of the self whereby a person or persons have a right to exert some control over who can summon them into a state of talk and when.

fellow teachers in the staff room also decline, because I now find idle talk or gossip uninteresting. However, I do seek out other staff members taking the same course. I also talk more, by phone, with other students."

As students experience exam-related anxieties, they become increasingly concerned with how they might fare and, because there are no objective scales (Festinger, 1954), they are forced to rely on social reality (i.e., seek out others to see how they compare). Consistent with Festinger's "accuracy hypothesis", students seek out others who will write the same exam because they provide the most meaningful base line for comparison. Other related social comparison factors which motivate students to affiliate stem from the uncertainties associated with studying: "My biggest worry is how do I know if I'm getting the same concepts from the readings as the professor?" Uncertainty escalates as students attempt to "second guess" test questions and gamble that they are on the same wave length as the professor. Before almost every test you can hear at least one student comment: "If he/she asks the three questions I've studied for, I'll ace it. If he/she doesn't, I'll probably fail."

Given the accumulation of stress associated with studying and the withdrawal from usual interactional orbits, Schachter (1959) and the symbolic interactionists (cf. McCall and Simmons, 1978) would predict an increased desire among students for socio-emotional support. Indeed, in the words of one student: "Your cares associated with the exam become central and you want empathy."[2]

Since students as a social category—especially those enrolled in the same class—are exposed to similar difficulties and demands, they soon realize that others share much the same role sets (i.e., schedules which provide less time for other role sets) and face the same workload for the upcoming exam. The base of common circumstances facilitates the empathetic process which, in turn, makes students who share the same structural characteristics more attractive objects for interaction:[3]

"Once I start preparing for an exam, I want to see other students in the same position as me. I don't want to be alone . . . we take our breaks together and reinforce each other by doing things like cursing the teacher for giving so much to study, agreeing with each other on the stupidity of the required in-

2. Merton (1957:382) indicates that the empathetic process has an underlying structural base; the "empathy that obtains among members of a society is in part a function of the underlying social structure—for those who are in the role sets of the individuals subjected to conflicting status obligations [i.e., fellow students—especially those taking the same course] are in turn occupants of multiple statuses [and therefore] . . . subject to similar stresses. This structural circumstance at least facilitates the development of empathy."

3. As Merton (1957b) would predict, students sharing similar non-student status sets tend to affiliate with each other (i.e., married students with children associate with others sharing the same role set and the same problems). Thus, he provides a structural base for the sympathetic process and places Schachter's (1959) social psychological predictions (as to why students orient themselves to others who are similar to them) in a larger theoretical context.

formation, and discussing how we have to rearrange our entire lives for study purposes."

Discovering others from the same class who also delay studying provides an occasion for catharsis and the expression of role distance, a technique by which students separate themselves from the role they are playing, or at least from what the role activity implies about them (Goffman, 1961a). Complaints concerning the stupidity of the material among this population are more frequent than among students who begin studying earlier. While it may reflect a greater measure of role strain, the complaining is also designed to express distance between their conception of self as basically "non-keeners" and the role activities in which they are engaged.

Complaints about what they "have to do" create some distance between students "doing" (studying) and "being" (non-keeners), which facilitates study without compromising their sense of identity.[4] The relief in being able to air sentiments and discover that these are shared by others reinforces their sense of identity, generates a sense of social solidarity, and increases self-confidence: "I feel more secure when I know its not just me taking on the professor, but all my new friends as well." Sympathetic interactions "with others in the same boat" are invigorating and enable students to return to their books with renewed energy. Indeed, it may well be that some roles can "be performed without any net energy loss at all (Marks, 1977:926); they may even create energy

4. Nolan (1981:100) suggests that Goffman's (1961) role distancing behaviours and Durkheim's (1954) "monstrous acts of suicide" should be placed on a continuum; "suicide might indeed be envisioned as the most extreme display of role distance". He demonstrates that Goffman and Durkheim use similar underlying modes of analysis, and Goffman actually goes beyond Durkheim in rooting the causes of role distance (i.e., suicide) behaviour in the social structure. Durkheim assumes a tension between the individual's social (i.e., a desire to be at one with their group) and non-social (i.e., unique personality characteristics that wish to rebel against or escape from the group) selves. As long as these forces exist in a proper balance, individuals are protected from suicidal impulses. While Goffman also sees tensions between the individual and societal expectations for behaviour, for him, the self is always socially grounded. Whereas Durkheim is not always certain whether the "unique" self is fully social, in either situational structures which are rooted in the socially generated expectations of the moment or permanent ones like roles or subcultures. Thus, Goffman actually outdoes Durkheim in applying his dictum that "the determining cause of social facts should always be found in preceding social acts and not in states of individual consciousness."

for use in that role or in other role performances."[5] Thus, the desire for affiliation plus the benefits that accrue from exchanges lead students who study on campus in libraries or other study areas frequently to schedule their breaks at the same time. And when they do study at home they frequently exchange phone numbers.[6]

A minority of students use this more open availability of others for purposes such as "averting their own exam preparation." Here they selectively search out others who, even at this late date, a couple of days before the exam, have not begun to prepare. The response to finding someone else in the same predicament "makes you feel better because you're not all alone." These students also frequently engage in a type of game which Erik Berne (1966) calls "Ain't it awful?" and they themselves label "pity parties", where they complain about the unfairness or the irrationality of the work they must do and, consequently, further postpone studying. Bernstein (1976) describes these activities as "commiseration fritters".

Exams can even provide opportunities for romantically inclined Machiavellian types: "Exams serve as a perfect conversational tool to meet attractive women. During these periods, students are a lot more open about things that bother them. Obviously, the troubles associated with exams serve as an easy topic of conversation. If I show I'm genuinely interested in their problems, they seem to show a genuine interest in me. This way I use the exam period as a manipulative tool." While such an attitude characterizes a small minority of students, it nevertheless demonstrates the wide variety of meanings and adaptations present during events like exams.

Students search each other out not only for expressive support, but for instrumental purposes as well. For example, as they go into the exam preparation role, it is not at all unusual for them to discover that they lack complete information for some aspect of the course and must seek out others for assistance. Indeed, the announcement of an upcoming exam leads to "the great

5. This observation is especially significant because traditional theories (Freud, 1930; Goode, 1969) hold that persons have finite amounts of time and energy, and every role consumes a given amount of each commodity. Thus, the only way to increase the energy flow for a given role is to refrain from other roles (i.e., decrease the socializing role and channel the energy into the study role). However, Marks (1977) suggests that taking on particular kinds of additional roles, especially those to which one is committed or those that provide high degrees of socio-emotional support, may actually add to one's energy supply. For example, during study breaks students seek each other out and engage in the process of social comparison. It may add to their energy state when they find they are lagging behind and "provide an incentive to work even harder." However, it appears that this proposition holds only to the degree that lagging students feel they are within reach of their better prepared comparison others. Being too far behind "to ever catch up" frequently results in a decline in energy and motivation. Conversely, non-committed students who find that they are far ahead of others in terms of preparation may use this fact as a justification or fritter to "cool it—at least for awhile." Thus, the choice of comparison others can be strategic for students who wish to continue working to capacity.

6. Around exam time, the meaning associated with the exchange of phone numbers also changes; the security (giving one's phone number to a comparative stranger) and romantic implications of ordinary times largely disappear.

note hunt." Practical benefits may also accrue from this interaction with others. Many students borrow notes not only to copy a missed lecture but also because they want to compare their information with that of others to obtain the most complete and accurate material possible. Wise students act early because, as the exam date approaches, others become increasingly reluctant to loan out their notes: "It's amazing how precious notes become and how uneasy we are about lending them out. This is in contrast to earlier times when I thought nothing of it." Unless the borrower can be "trusted" the request will be met with polite refusal—"Sorry, but I left them at home" or "I'm planning to study tonight." The person who makes the request usually gets the message and tries to borrow from someone else.

Besides the comparison function served by borrowing notes, students also find that in talking about the subject matter "new points are brought up and others get fitted into larger conceptual categories. It's really amazing how much you pick up in these short meetings and how much gets clarified." Students who assist others can also "learn in the process of explaining." However, when it comes to explaining particularly difficult concepts, not all are equally capable or willing to give of their information or time. The few who do meet these conditions are much more frequently sought out.[7] One such focal individual states: "If you are classified as smart it's amazing the number of friends you have come exam time." Interestingly, we now see the emergence of a new status structure among students: "The leader, instead of being attractive, witty, or athletic, is the knowledgeable student who is willing to help classmates. He is worshipped at exam time, though before this he may have been scorned." This is one of the latent consequences of the exam—providing a recurrent set of circumstances in which those who best embody its values are given academic rewards, as well as status and influence among their peers.

Exams also serve to spawn the formation of new study groups. Such groups are especially frequent in classes where professors provide long lists of potential questions beforehand. Since, due to time constraints, one student cannot possibly prepare an ideal answer for each question, there is a division of labour among a number of individuals who will then pool the results. While these small groups of students share answers among themselves, there is no effort to involve the class as a whole and the groups tend to compete with each other: "Anyone suspected of being indiscrete (i.e., giving 'inside' information to other groups) is subjected to strong social pressures, including ostracism." Study group information is encouraged by certain personality characteristics as well as structural factors. For students who are highly gregarious, group study becomes a solution because "it helps combine the necessity for serious studying with the entertainment that comes from socializing." However, group

---

7. Many "top performing" students are members of pre-established study groups who restrict their time allocations and expertise to each other. Hence, students who "know their stuff" and are willing to share it with "outsiders" are especially valued.

study is subject to many strains which may detract from both its studying and entertainment functions. Since grades are awarded on an individual basis a sense of competition is always present: "Even though we share ideas and other resources, we are still competitors. Secretly I know everybody wants to be just a little better than the others—if not the best. So, as we shared information, I couldn't stop asking myself: 'If I give everything I know, will they do better than me? And are they thinking the same thing and keeping some things back?' What I did was share most of my resources and hope that they would do the same." "Feelings of resentment and anger surface if I suspect someone is taking more information than he is giving." Though study group members may cooperate, the individualistic nature of the university reward structure means that much of the interaction occurs within pretense and suspicion awareness contexts (Glaser and Strauss, 1967). Individuals know others are competitors but pretend that this is not the case; at the same time they are continually vigilant to possible signs of concealment by others.

Another disruptive influence comes from "those persons who do not come to study but to get a guy or girl to notice them." These students contribute little to the group and "destroy the development of communal feelings." Unless such "communal feelings" or sense of discipline is present, study groups, especially ones which meet in the evening, are prone to transformation and "can easily get out of hand and even turn into parties." Interactions may then change from ones that have a high instrumental component to ones that are expressive. Empirical research (Jones, et. al., 1980) demonstrates that if sufficient discipline exists, however, group study can be a particularly effective tool for answering exam questions focusing on relationships and interpretations. Group study is less useful if the exam material requires mostly memorization.

In conclusion, as students begin investing more time and effort in their studies, they begin to affiliate more with others who share similar role set positions and experiences. While this selective interaction occurs for social comparison and social support reasons (Schachter, 1959), there is also a strong instrumental component to it. The structural base of these interactions is consistent with Merton's (1957a) theory of role set. Exams also have consequences for other sectors of the student role set; namely classroom role behaviour and interaction with the professor outside the formal lecture situation.

B. Studying and Changes in the Student-Professor Role-Sector

i) Classroom Interaction

Even though attendance in university classes is almost always voluntary, professors do want their students to appear for lectures. While stimulating and informative lectures attract students, most professors find it difficult to make each lecture equally absorbing and after a time even good lectures become routine. When student interest wanes, the professor faces problems of motivation and control. It is at this point that exams can come to the rescue. Although students may not find the subject matter involving in its own right, there is the chance it may be covered on the exam and so they tend to plow on. The professor can also use the fact that material covered may appear on the exam to encourage attendance and attention, for as Jules Henry (1963) aptly notes, exams are the nightmares of student life: "Just the word 'exam' strikes fear in me," it's "the day of reckoning."

Professors face not only the problem of lectures becoming routine but they are also forced to compete with outside attractions for the students' time. Any possibility that class material "may appear on the exam" greatly increases the likelihood that class attendance will receive top priority. The fear of failure is another strong incentive which operates to ensure that the professors will lecture to full classes: "I now attend classes faithfully instead of drinking coffee or going downtown." Comparisons show that class attendance is higher just before the exam time than at any other time during the year, save for attendance at the exam itself. Along with an increase in class attendance just prior to exams there is a general "tightening" of the classroom role. For example, there is a marked decrease in the time required for the class to settle down once the professor arrives and begins to lecture. While whispering and fidgeting decrease, note-taking increases. One can trace note-taking patterns by checking through student note books and counting the number of pages written during any particular period. Discipline in class is more likely to be maintained by the students themselves because "no one wants to lose out on notes because of some loudmouth in the row ahead of you." Students also "always keep an open ear for possible hints as to the content of the exam."

Greater involvement in classroom roles is indicated by changes in the frequency and the nature of questions directed to the professor. Students, especially those in large classes, usually experience a great deal of apprehension about speaking out in front of others, even when the questions concern clarification of important points: "Often we are afraid to put up our hands because we think we are the only ones who do not understand. . . . I fear being embarrassed because my question might sound stupid." Students also fear violating the informal student code of appearing to "try to get on the good side of the professor." As the exam date approaches however, students tend to overcome these fears and "no longer wait for others to question a misunderstanding but attend to it themselves." Persons who do not normally ask questions now do so: "Its almost like we're no longer afraid our questions will be viewed as stupid or irrelevant . . . there is a greater eagerness to get down to business." The nature of questions to the professor also changes to focus more directly on exam-related topics and the entire class pays closer attention to the answer provided. This contrasts somewhat to "regular" lectures where students sometimes raise questions of peripheral interest to the course as such.

The result of this "wandering" is two-fold: it steers the professor away from core ideas and, at the same time, it allows many students to engage in conversation among themselves.[8] With the approaching exam, more questions focus on core course material and there is more efficient use made of class time. The net result is an increase in the amount of information conveyed, recorded, and absorbed in a given class period. This phenomenon recurs in so many spheres of student life that we will formalize it with the term "role concentration"—the packing of more activity than normal into a role performance in a given space of time. Needless to say, professors find it easier to teach under such conditions.

ii) Extra-Classroom Interaction

As the exam date approaches students also extend interaction with professors beyond the time allotted for formal lectures. Once again there is apprehension about approaching the professor and many fear they may be imposing upon the professors or "wasting their valuable time." However, as in the case of asking questions in class, the pressure to avoid interaction with professors can be "broken by the greater pressure to do well on the exam." Therefore, near exam time, more students than usual approach professors at the end of the class period to ask for clarification of various aspects of lectures, readings, or exam-related procedures. The concept "professor" is now extended from "a person who just gives lectures to someone whom we can get answers from in an emergency situation." Under certain "emergency" conditions students will telephone professors at home on evenings, weekends, and even ritual holidays.

iii) Negotiations

The number of visits students make to professors' offices also increases just before exams. While the number of visits increases, the duration of the visits tend to be shorter than non-exam related calls. Although most students come with a few specific questions for clarification and then leave immediately, others have more strategic aims like prolonging the interaction in an attempt to gain hints as to the relative importance of particular course material. One such technique is to ask a long list of specific questions. This list is supposed to serve as an invitation for the professor to state or at least imply that certain topics are less important than others. Another strategy is to establish a "friendly" base for the interaction and then mention that the grades received to date are not commensurate with the amount of effort exerted. Some students also inform the professor that they "have" to achieve a certain grade

---

8. A few students admit the questions are "engineered to avoid having to cover more material" or even "to have a break during classtime." The result is an effective altercast, because every question demands an answer. If the question is directed slightly outside of the focal concern of the course, the answer will not be "exam material." Thus students strategically use questions to "force" professors to behave in ways congruent with student "interests."

in the course in order to graduate or enter a chosen professional school. They then move on to the next step and ask the professor's advice for rectifying the situation. At this point students attempt to create the role for the professor of a friend-counsellor (i.e. an altercast) which would support the goal of obtaining more information about the exam. If the appropriate atmosphere emerges and the style of presentation is good, students indicate that the technique can be quite effective.

A related strategy which occurs with some regularity among students for whom English is a second language is to inform the professor of this fact and stress that, even though they have studied long and hard, their command of the English language puts them at a disadvantage with other students. Occasionally they will appeal for a different mode of evaluation for example, oral versus written. Seeking such a grand concession is seldom the main goal, but rather is related to a more general strategy of making the professor aware of the student as an individual with a particular handicap. The student also hopes to influence the professor to give the benefit of the doubt when grading by not deducting too many marks for shortcomings in punctuation, grammar, and general writing style, or at least increase the tolerance threshold when reading through written assignments. Students also occasionally band together in groups in an effort to "persuade" the professor to alter the type, scope, or date of the exam. For example, students sometimes attempt to dissuade the professor from giving a formally administered final exam by stressing the merits of an in-class or take-home test. They emphasize that the similar classroom situation of learning and testing makes it easier to recall the information: "If I can't answer a question, I'll look around the room and something like a crack in the ceiling that I noticed while the professor was discussing a concept will help me to remember it during the test."[9] There are also frequent attempts to negotiate the amount of material that should be covered in a given exam, the type of questions, and how much weight should be given to assigned readings relative to lectures. Students who feel a sense of injustice on any of these issues

9. This is technically referred to as a "contextual effect." Experimental studies consistently demonstrate that memory is most effective when the conditions at the time of recall are identical to those at the time of learning (Reed, 1931; Smith, et al., 1978). The finding even extends to "inner experiential contexts," where matching drug states (amphetamine and amobarbital) at the time of learning and testing improves memory (Bustamante, et al., 1970). Abernethy (1940), in a more naturalistic study, demonstrates that scores are lower when students write exams in unfamiliar classrooms or with unfamiliar proctors. A combination of changes in classroom and proctor was associated with the lowest exam scores. Superior students (who "internalized the material") were least affected by contextual changes, while inferior students (those least prepared) were most affected. The situation is somewhat akin to that of small children who have not yet internalized language. They must still depend on external referents (e.g., fingers or pictures on the wall) to "count." However, once language is internalized and they can operate at a more symbolic level, they are able to count (e.g., "think") silently to themselves. In the exam situation, less well prepared students depend on external referents (e.g., cracks in the ceiling) to "jog" their memories and help them to recall the imperfectly internalized material. One solution, of course, is overlearning.

can, through collective protest, exert considerable pressure on a professor. Extreme examples of this situation have lead to legal battles in the courts and to professors being assigned different courses to teach the next year. A more usual form of pressure comes from students attempting to persuade professors that the demands of their classes are "excessive" when compared to other sections of the same course. These pressure tactics are particularly effective if the professor is a novice and still uncertain as to the "level" at which to lecture or the volume of material that ought to be processed. Students also take advantage of overt and covert cues to evaluate which professors would be most open to such negotiation: "Professors who continually have a serious attitude, seldomly smile, and are rarely humourous are not good prospects."

In the vast majority of cases, the exams, as set by the professor, are accepted as a matter of routine and most negotiations prior to writing centre around single individuals attempting to negotiate an alternative time to write. Interestingly, there are comparatively few reasons, excuses, and justifications offered by students during these negotiations. The most frequent excuse, in terms of Scott and Lyman's (1968) typology of accounts, can be subsumed under "appeals to accidents" or generally recognized environmental or bodily hazards. The most frequent bodily hazard is some form of illness which prevents students from adequately preparing for the exam on the given date. The style of the student's presentation varies considerably according to the presence or absence of medical documentation of the illness. Students who have documentation make little attempt to emphasize or dramatize their illness. Their interactional posture during their encounter with the professor could be described as "consultative", "objective", and "matter of fact" (Scott and Lyman, 1968). Some students do not even make an effort to provide accounts;[10] professors who do request them are often merely referred to the "authority figure" (i.e., physician or psychiatrist) who wrote the note. However, when students lack medical documentation, they introduce a measure of dramatic realization[11] into the performance—the overall appearance is somewhat "droopy", the posture is hunched over, the hair is "limp" (has not been washed for a few days) the face is unsmiling or, in the case of females, is without

10. When behaviours fall outside the range of the "socially expected", "offenders" are usually expected verbally to "bridge the gap between action and expectation" with an account (Scott and Lyman, 1968:46). The most prevalent strategies for avoiding accounts are: (1) referrals—as in the case here with "sick slips"; and (2) mystification—where "the actor admits to the seriousness of the act, frequently via body language, but verbally attempts to "get away" without an account by simply stating: "It's a long story", "family trouble", or "I had to be out of town—it's part of my job". Generally the latter strategy is less successful than the former.

11. Goffman (1959) uses the term to refer to the tendency to add a bit of drama (i.e., make work) to performances to make aspects of self, that might otherwise remain unapparent, more evident. For example, dramatic realization also occurs when students carefully choose the book with the most impressive title and "face" it outwards, while at the same time they "hide" their favorite magazine on the inside of the stack of books they carry around with them. The purpose, of course, is that others, for example, riding on a bus or in a public area see the most impressive book and so identify students in ways they wish to be viewed.

makeup in order to present a pale, suffering look. The voice is often "weak" and the head tends to be carried somewhat forward of the body, resulting in a closer approach than usual. The overall style of the presentation is more "subjective" and "intimate." Students who give "accounts" on the day of the exam usually phone them in. The vocal presentation is at least equally as dramatic, not only is the voice dull and weak but, when phlegm is blocking the vocal apparatus, it can produce a striking vocal effect and result in vocal "breaks." The conversation may also be interrupted by the occasional hoarse cough. Other, less frequent accident accounts centre on a sudden illness, heart attack of a significant other, or a death in the immediate family.

There is also a conventionalized style of presentation that dramatizes the importance of the relationship and its disabling effects upon the student's performance. The voice takes on a slowness we have come to associate with grief, and occasionally it breaks while the eyes may tear at the same time. A convincing style of presentation does affect the probability of having an account honoured, especially in the absence of socially legitimate forms of documentation. Even though students really are ill or grief-striken, they still "must" engage in some measure of role idealization where presentations are organized to convey how a sick or grief-stricken person should ideally look.

Another category of excuse may be classified, in Scott and Lyman's terms, as an appeal to loyalties and defeasibility (or, "I didn't know"). For example, students report having made bookings on a flight or holiday accommodations "long before the test date was set." This excuse is most common among married students whose working spouse has arranged for a winter holiday. Of course no professor would want to be responsible for the "break up" of a happy marriage! A more frequent appeal to defeasibility comes from students who request a postponement: "I swear I didn't know the exam was today" or "I thought it was this afternoon." They also appeal to various other extenuating circumstances such as role overload (e.g., when two or more exams are scheduled on the same day). The usual argument here is that study time is reduced and, since they have only a limited amount of energy on any given day, performance on the second test will automatically suffer. On rare occasions, students ask for postponements on the grounds that they could not possibly pass the test because they were too lazy to study.

C. The New Emergent Study Atmosphere

As late starters become aware that almost everyone else is studying, they also "begin to feel the effects of the general working attitude . . . in realizing that everyone else has already begun, a kind of panic sets in which causes me to start." This emergent work atmosphere leaves its mark on all facets of campus life. It is first evident from the fact that libraries and other study areas begin to be filled to capacity especially during final exam time which is December for half-year courses and April for both full and half-year courses. Signs suddenly appear outside formal study areas: "EXAMS ARE COM-

ING. PLEASE, NO TALKING IN THE HALLWAYS." Seats in libraries and study areas become scarce so students begin to leave valuable objects behind as "markers" or "seat savers" when they go off to attend classes or take breaks. These "markers" usually indicate a "colonization" of the space and thereby serve to transform a public territory into a home territory (Lyman and Scott, 1967). We measured the extent of the "colonization" in the Coloured Room, one of the most popular study areas on campus. Twice a week, at approximately 7 A.M., a count of colonized spaces in the room was taken. To ensure validity, a space was considered colonized only if there were at least two objects left in it as a marker (e.g., pens, notebooks, posters, and time tables stuck to walls, cut flowers inserted into old liquor bottles, and potted plants). One marker only could mean that a janitor found a pen and put it on a table. Two associated objects in the same area could hardly be by accident. The eight counts for the month were added and the cumulative total recorded as shown in Graph IV.

As may be seen, the number of colonized spaces increases consistently over time and peaks sharply in December when many students are studying for exams. The second term begins slowly but rises quickly to peak in March and April when all students are preparing for final exams in both half and full courses. At this point study space is at a premium and so must be protected.[12] When study space is in short supply students become ingenious at finding and colonizing unused rooms; the colonization is achieved either by marking the area with actual bodily presence or by leaving markers when they must be absent. When rooms are exposed to distracting noises, students often make and post their own signs demanding quiet. A typical example was a $10'' \times 12''$ sheet of white poster paper with the message "Silence is demanded by order of serious students." The atmosphere in libraries and study areas becomes "superquiet" in comparison to earlier times in the year. "The slightest sound is met with stern warning glances, and if the noise persists, clearing of many throats will reinforce the earlier disapproving stares." It is difficult to escape this emerging ethos; commercial posters and the student union sponsored newspaper make mention of the upcoming exams. A recurrent example in the student newspaper is a large-lettered advertisement sponsored by the University of Manitoba Student Association titled "THE UMSU EXAM CRAM SESSION" followed by offers of assistance to students: "The University Centre Building will be open 24 hours a day . . . Study rooms will be available. . . . The Music Listening Room and Nap Room will be open. . . . Free coffee will be available in the late evening on the third floor." Finally, students are wished "Good luck in your exams" (The Manitoban, April 5, 1982). City newspapers carry feature articles on upcoming exams, and the difficulties students face,

12. The greater frequency of markers during the second term as compared to the first also suggests more students are studying regularly thereby overcoming sources of role strain we mentioned earlier.

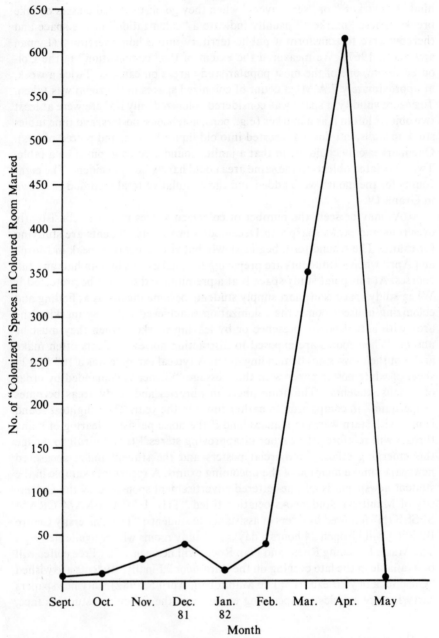

Graph IV: Cumulative Total of Colonized Spaces by Month*

No. of "Colonized" Spaces in Coloured Room Marked

Month

Sept.　Oct.　Nov.　Dec.　Jan.　Feb.　Mar.　Apr.　May
　　　　　　　　　81　　82

*8 Counts/Month for all months except December for which there were 4 counts.

while local television newscasts often feature exam related reports. Reminders even appear in student washrooms where exam related problems become part of the graffiti: "I've got the exam blues." "Fucking's finished, exams are here," and "Exams consume 47x's their weight in excess reality."

By the time procrastinating students finally settle down to concentrated study, they usually realize the limited amount of time remaining will not permit absorption of all the required material. Their conception of time then changes and it becomes "a valuable resource like money"—"Were it possible, I'm convinced that many of us would buy time." As the exam date draws nearer, one often hears: "If only I had another day to study." The high premium placed on time motivates students to intensify their study efforts: "I find it easier to study when I know the deadline is close."[13] While some students give up on the task altogether, others, after experiencing the initial "panic", "give up trying to understand the material and settle down to memorizing what they can in the hope that it will be enough to pass." Students who allot themselves sufficient time to absorb the material find that they are able to take advantage of the increasing motivational pressures which come with the approaching deadline. They use the analogy of a "pressure cooker" to describe the increased efficiency with which they now absorb and understand the material, and, as they act out the role expectations, a new found energy is generated which facilitates the process. The body now "exceeds its capabilities." This role concentration contrasts with earlier behaviour where students would study "off and on"; and it's not at all unusual for students to report that before the exam they "studied all day without stopping for a break." These "marathoning" stints frequently extend well into the wee hours of the morning and, if the exam is scheduled for the morning, some individuals simply continue right through the night: "When preparing for exams I make sacrifices which, under normal conditions, I'd never dream of making." Along with the increased endurance level is an experience of heightened perception "which comes as a natural response to signs of danger." "As exams draw near, the adrenalin in my system works overtime to keep me alert and increases my retentive powers." Thus, both physical and mental energy peak just prior to exams.

13. This statement is true up to a point, but students who delay studying until the deadline is "too close" often experience pressure levels which actually interfere with learning: "I kept putting it (studying) off because I feared I really didn't understand the material. When I finally 'got to it' I was stricken by the task before me. Instead of sitting down and rationally doing what I could, I just got more and more frustrated." This episode, along with most of the other behavioural changes we describe as being associated with upcoming exams, are consistent with the famous Yerkes-Dodson Law. That is, increasing motivational states (i.e., exams and the associated increase in anxiety levels which accompany them) result in increased learning and performance, so long as the task is easily mastered. However, optimum motivation decreases as the task becomes more difficult. Consequently, students, who delay their studying to a point where they cannot possibly learn the material, may easily become overly motivated and thereby frustrated in their attempts at learning particularly if the material is difficult to comprehend.

For many students the real learning for the entire course is concentrated into these pressure packed periods. It is especially noticeable when test requirements go beyond memorization to creative effort and when merely reading through assignments and being able to repeat lectures "chapter and verse is no longer enough." There is now an impetus to "sort out and organize one's thoughts on the course." "The slightest 'fuzziness' about any topic appears as a real gap in knowledge which must be filled if I am to pass the test with the grade I require for professional school." At this point, many students move beyond having to force themselves to study and become increasingly impelled by the very logic of the ideas they are pursuing. They become aware that they do not fully understand a concept and are motivated to fill the gap. Incompatibilities among various items of "knowledge" result in what Festinger (1962:3) terms cognitive dissonance: "just as hunger impels a person to eat, so does dissonance impel a person . . . to change his cognitive state." A new interest in the subject develops simply because it was neglected before. One biology student reports: "I went through most of my labs with a vague, disinterested conception of the theory behind the experiments. Now that exams are forcing me to study, I find myself understanding things I did months ago. . . . 'Oh, so that's why we did this experiment and this is its meaning in the larger scheme of things.' " Students find their past being reinterpreted in terms of knowledge they are obtaining in the present, while activities carried out in the past sensitize them to ideas they are now absorbing. These prospective-retrospective shifts in perspective can add interest and even excitement to learning. As the student goes on to explain: "It's amazing how interested you can become when you really have to."

In this chapter we examined the nature of the study role itself and how students negotiate their way in and out of relations with other students and instructors. At this point students are completing their studying activities and are ready to enter into the transitional "pre-exam phase" which carries them into the examination proper.

Phase II—Immediate Pre-Exam

1. Transitions: From the Study Role to the Pre-Exam Phase

The pre-exam phase of the examination situation is a time of anxiety for students and calls for coping strategies which may be instrumental (e.g., as in the study phase) as well as expressive (e.g., controlling feeling states through psychological and social means). The transition period from the study role to the exam phase lasts from the point when students complete most of their studying, usually the night before the exam, to the point when they enter the exam room. The psychological ploys and social supports used by students during this period are described in detail in this chapter and analyzed for sociological sense within the framework of Malinowski and Gmelch (for those words and acts of anxious persons in isolation from others) and also of Goffman, Schachter, and Wrightsman (for behaviours of anxious persons that propel them either toward affiliations or away from them). Indeed, as we will see this study in a natural setting sheds light on an apparent contradiction in Wrightsman's laboratory experiment.

Coping with anxiety through expressive means becomes especially important in the transition period—between the point when studying is defined as "finished" and yet there is time to fill before arriving at the exam site—where students can get together with others who share their plight. However, when students are alone and cannot rely on others for social support or comparison, they are forced to use self-oriented word and action strategies. As the works of Malinowski (1954) and Gmelch (1971) suggest, many students turn to rituals, taboos, and fetishes in the belief that these will aid performance by reducing uncertainty.

A. Word Oriented Self-Management Coping Strategies

Many students go beyond engaging in self-reassuring conversations such as "I've done my best and that's all I can do" to enter into conversation with God: "As exam time nears, a feeling of humbleness comes over me and I turn to God for some extra strength and wisdom." "After saying my act of contrition and before going to sleep, I usually pray to God that He help me do my best. . . . I also pray to the Virgin Mary that She might intercede for me." "Since I left home I only pray now and then. One thing I can say about exams, particularly about difficult ones, is that they get me reacquainted with God." Some students even attempt to bargain with the Almighty: "If you let me pass this exam, I promise I'll mend my studying ways." In a similar "religious" vein, there is also a concern with taboos: "It's dangerous to write an exam without God on your side . . . so all sins should be confessed to God and man before writing." Taboos may also arise against taking an optimistic view of performances: "I don't dare think I'm going to 'ace' an exam for fear it will bring bad luck." Indeed, some students ritually entertain the thought of failure in hopes it will "bring about the opposite."

B. Act Oriented Self-Management Coping Strategies

The religious orientation is also evident in act oriented self-management strategies: "Since I want to get whatever divine help I can, I make a special effort to keep myself pure while exams are in progress."

Other "act oriented strategies" diversely and widely distributed throughout the student population involve rituals and taboos concerning food: "You may think what I do is weird, but I know it works. In India we know that eating almonds before studying allows us to absorb much more material. Almonds are a sort of brain food which helps us cope with the pressures that come from studying and writing exams (fetish). But you have to be cautious— too many almonds will "heat up" your mind and have the opposite effect (taboo)." Many students also attribute magical powers to coffee which is believed to increase "retentive capacities."

Another popular strategy to control exam-related anxiety is to stress the role-enabling aspects of appearance which come from either "dressing up" or "dressing down" "I'm very particular about the way I dress and comb my hair. It's as if I'm putting on a special uniform reserved for exams. If I feel good about the way I'm dressed, it makes me more confident." Others stress the continuity of clothes and general appearance in exam preparation: "If I'm dressed the same way I was when studying, it somehow helps me recall the material better." While there may be a contextual effect at work, most students cannot explain why they choose to wear selected items of clothing to the exam: "I like to wear the same clothes I studied in the night before. I don't know why, but it makes me feel better," or more directly, another student states, "it's a superstition with me." Similarly, students often "wait until after exams are finished before getting a haircut." The familiar length and shape of the hair is comforting and provides an additional element of continuity between their everyday lives and the world of exams: "It gives me a feeling of security, especially when I twist it—I swear that sometimes it even helps me remember facts." Once again, the contextual effect may be at work; where there are more continuities between the times of learning and the exam, powers of retention are enhanced.

Miner (1956) suggests that science exists on a continuum with magic. Both magic and science attempt to manipulate the world for practical gain but science, unlike magic, is backed by a rational understanding of the cause and effect relation between events. The dividing line between magic and science is a fine one. Miner suggests that ritualized behaviour performed for goal attainment be classified as magic when practitioners are only vaguely aware of any cause and effect relationship, "I wear articles of clothing that brought me luck in the past." This can quickly take on the character of a taboo where students become reluctant to change their ways and dress for fear their "luck" may make a turn for the worse. Other objects, like coins, pens, and books may also be viewed as possessing quasi-magical properties. One student brought a bent, almost distorted, dime to the exam and placed it on the top right hand corner of his desk. He reports: "I found it just before my last in-class test and just happened to keep it in my pocket. I did much better on the test than I thought I would. . . . I've been carrying it around with me ever since. It's for good luck." "I always take the same pen I used for study to the exam. Since it was always with me when I studied and even wrote down much of what I'm supposed to know, I feel it knows all the information—which is a comforting thought." Yet another adds: "Like many of my friends, I bring every book we've used in the course to the test only to place them all on the floor at the front of the room. This is one phenomenon I must admit I've never figured out." Another typical response, in accord with Malinowski's (1954) proposition, is "Although my books and notes are no longer necessary, I feel more secure if I have them to hold onto." One second-year student who was enrolled in two introductory level courses never carried her textbooks for the classes with her: "I've got a phobia about being identified as only a first year student, but somehow for final examinations, I make an exception." At the point where feelings of anxiety begin to peak, students may attribute magical meanings to events: "On exam mornings I sometimes interpret ordinary events as omens of things to come—a simple thing like the failure of the automatic garage door opener distressed me because I felt it foreshadowed my failure on the exam. Other things like victory of a favorite team or even good weather lead me to be optimistic about how I will perform."

A source of considerable anxiety for some students is the possibility of having their honesty questioned. They attempt to forestall such possibilities by engaging in behaviours best designated as "accentuated acts of honesty." For example, they check all objects to be taken to the exam to insure that nothing might be interpreted by the invigilators as "tools for cheating": "After hearing that people sometimes cheat by putting notes inside their calculator cases. I left mine at home." "I cleaned my purse of all extra pieces of paper that might possibly be misinterpreted because I've got enough to worry about as it is." "For open book exams, I always double check to make certain that my book is clean of any extra pieces of paper that might be stuck between the pages—even though I've never cheated, I still find it comforting to enter the room with the feeling that I'm above suspicion." "Once I forgot to remove study notes from one of my shirt pockets. I suddenly became aware of them about mid-way through the exam. I almost had a 'shit fit' . . . now as a precautionary device, I always check through my pockets before I go into the exam room."

Other students control their feelings of uncertainty through more instrumentally oriented strategies. That is, they make sure they have an abundant supply of exam-related equipment: pens, pencils, erasers, cough candies, extra batteries for calculators, and Kleenex. In one instance, an individual thought he had the beginnings of a cold but neglected to bring along an adequate supply of Kleenex and as the exam progressed so did the cold: "Here I was completely embarrassed and distracted from answering the questions because I imagined everyone was listening to me sniffle."[1]

Another strategy which contains both instrumental and expressive components involves maximizing control over the environment and thereby reducing feelings of uncertainty. Students attempt to extend their range of choices over matters they see as affecting the outcome of the exam and feel that by so doing they gain control of their fate.[2] For many students one of the most important "moves" tends to center around the choice of the seat they will occupy during the exam: "A good way of building my confidence is to get to the exam site early; this way I'm one of the first to enter and get a choice seat. It puts me in a confident mood, and I'm ready to tackle the exam the minute the signal is given." Choice seats are normally those furthest from where invigilators spend most of their time because, even though one of their major functions is to enforce rules of quietness, they tend to be associated with most of the distractions: "Due to a last minute call of nature, I entered the exam room late and was forced to sit near the professors. All through the exam, they spoke to each other in hushed tones and frequently interrupted my train of thought. Because of my position as a mere student I was hesitant to ask them to be quiet. I also found my writing time was cut short because the early finishers stopped by to say their good-byes to the professors. One individual

1. Gross and Stone (1970:175) highlight the importance of embarrassment for understanding the nature of social interaction: "Embarrassment always incapacitates persons for role performance . . . and . . . occurs whenever some central assumption in a transaction has been unexpectedly and unqualifiedly discredited for at least one of the participants." They classify over one thousand specimens of embarrassment into three general categories: (1) disturbance in the assumptions of confidence individuals make about one another; (2) loss of poise; (3) inappropriate identity. The above example of embarrassment is largely associated with a loss of poise as a result of lack of control over self and situation. Working from the outside in, Gross and Stone sub-classify five elements of "self and situation" wherein a loss of control over (1) spaces (domains), (2) props, (3) equipment, (4) clothing, and (5) body gives rise to embarrassment. The "cold episode" above involves a loss of control over the body which must be in a situationally appropriate state of presentation. In this case, a lack of physical equipment (Kleenex) was a large part of the problem.

2. Seligman (1975) emphasized the importance of a sense of control over the environment for a feeling of well-being. Schulz and Hanson (1975) support Seligman's findings by demonstrating that students who feel in control of their academic worlds achieve higher grades.

even went so far as to discuss his plans for an upcoming trip during the summer."

To understand why some students come to the exam site early in hope of securing "choice" seats we must introduce a number of interactions that take place in the exam phase. Many students who regularly sit near the front of the classroom to see or hear better would like to sit further back during in-class exams precisely to avoid the disruptions that come with sitting so close to the invigilator. However, they are reluctant to move for fear others might think they are moving because they want to cheat. On the other hand, students who normally finish their exams early do not mind an upfront seat and occasionally they even choose their regular classroom seat with exams in mind: "I always try to get to the first class very early so I can choose a seat near the front and at the very edge of a row because, when exams are passed out, you receive yours first. This is an especially important factor when time is limited." Most students prefer to write in-class tests in their regular classroom seats and frequently cite reasons which contain an element of magic: "Knowing you have a place to sit before the exam starts makes for one less thing to worry about, so I must have my regular seat in class—these things help to give me confidence—and I always come to exams early to ensure I get my seat."

Frequently aisle seats are also considered to be non-door-choice locations because professors cause distractions by moving up and down aisleways to answer questions or hand out extra exam materials: "As supervisors come closer, I become aware of their presence and they temporarily destroy my flow of thought."[3] A more extreme form of distraction comes from invigilators who happen to pause to glance at a student's paper. "It completely blows my concentration." "It's like I'm being graded on the spot."[4] On the other hand, students who ask clarification-type questions benefit from greater accessibility to invigilators; it takes less time and effort for the invigilators to arrive because they do not have to "crawl in" between rows of students. Consequently, these students don't "feel as guilty for asking many questions." Other students suffer from claustrophobia: "Since aisle seats only have a cheat partition on one side, this location makes me feel less hemmed in." "While the supervisors moving around do cause a few distractions, I find that being a little less confined makes me more relaxed—especially if the exam is one I'm really nervous

3. Zajonc's (1965) principle can be used to explain these breaks in concentration; physical proximity increases arousal which in turn hinders the performance of "underlearned" tasks. Students who do not yet have the appropriate dominant response are especially susceptible to adverse audience effects while invigilators may stimulate greater performance in students who have mastered the material.

4. The effect is accentuated for students who are not well prepared: "The worst type of feeling I've had was when the professor walked up and started to look down at the 'snow-job' answer I was trying to compose. I got the distinct feeling that he was actually snickering at me and that everybody was looking on—it gave me a terrible sense of inferiority." Beyond producing embarrassment, others indicated that such episodes accentuate their feelings of guilt: "It lets the Prof. know I don't know my stuff and that I didn't work hard enough."

about." Some students prefer aisle locations for more social reasons: "When my boyfriend and I happened to be taking the same class, we always tried to sit across the aisle from each other during exams so we could at least see each other. Even though we seldomly availed ourselves of the opportunity just knowing I could, if I wanted to, made me more relaxed."

By far the most frequent reason for arriving at the exam site early is a desire to affiliate with others who will be undergoing the same ordeal. In terms of the typology of coping strategies we outlined in chapter III, priority shifts to the verbal mode of interaction, and the most proximate audience also shifts from self to other. In the study phases of the exam act we noted how students change their relationships with family, friends, and others in the work place to facilitate more study time. The withdrawals in these relationships are associated with an increased interest in other members of the student role set, namely other students and professors. Affiliation reaches a peak in the half-hour or so before the exam, just when most students have finished studying and are waiting to enter the exam room. To the uninitiated the interaction may resemble the "milling" scenes associated with crowd behaviour. In contrast, however, the participants in the present situation self-consciously fit their lines of action together within a context of shared understandings and expectations.

2. The Pre-Exam Phase and the Anxiety-Affiliation Hypothesis

The immediate pre-exam phase begins approximately one half hour before the exam, the moment the first two students arrive at the exam site and become aware of each other's presence thereby creating a social situation, and ends with the beginning of the exam proper. Interactions within these situational and temporal parameters have a sufficiently bounded and coherent character to provide an experiment-like setting which allows for an examination of how people cope with anxiety socially. In particular, we can clarify, even test, hypotheses developed from the anxiety-affiliation literature: (1) In anxiety-producing natural situations do people express greater desire to interact with others and do they translate these anxieties into behaviour by increasing their rates of interaction? As we noted earlier, Schachter (1959) merely asked his subjects if they would like to interact and with whom. He did not take the next step to see whether or not they actually did. This point is important because many persons who express the desire to affiliate (e.g., the lonely) do not actually do so. Also, Deutcher's (1973) review of the literature shows a pervasive discrepancy between what people say (words) and what they do (deeds). (2) If people do increase their rates of affiliation, what reasons do they give—is it for purposes of social support, social comparison, or for other reasons? Schachter (1959) believed he had successfully discounted all other possible alternatives (e.g., interaction as a means of diverting attention away from the "shocking" ordeal his subjects were about to experience), but did he really? (3) In searching out comparison others, are people motivated principally by accuracy (Schachter-Festinger hypothesis) or by the desire to enhance or at least protect their role-identities (Goffman hypothesis). Beyond providing a test of these questions, we will attempt to extend Schachter's work by using a symbolic-interactional perspective to describe how people go about managing their interactions to handle anxiety.

As students approach the exam site, their anxiety levels tend to rise and, as Schachter would predict, "Others from my class suddenly become more attractive to me. I now talk to individuals I normally try to avoid." Beyond a pervasive search for social support, many students also want a better idea of their relative state of preparedness (social comparison) so they can "locate themselves in the hierarchy of probable student performance." Thus, since students from one's class provide a source of comparison, they ought to be the focal concern. And, students do in fact tend to restrict their affiliations to others writing the same exam—even to the extent of interacting with a comparative stranger in preference to a friend who, though physically near, is writing another exam. However, contrary to Schachter's contention, students do offer additional reasons for affiliating. Indeed, many students state that interacting with others provides a mental diversion and "takes my mind off the exam."

Since students do seem to affiliate, the next step is to focus on the relative importance of accuracy versus self-enhancement in the social comparison process. Support for an affiliational orientation based on accuracy would be found in students seeking out others who represent a wide range of ability levels, particularly those on the higher end of the preparation continuum. Using these criteria, we found that only the 'big-leaguers', the most confident and top-performing students were strongly motivated by accuracy of comparison since they do tend to search out other well-prepared classmates: "I generally like to interact with others I consider to be a direct threat to my relative performance. This way I'm able to test their knowledge and state of preparedness relative to my own.[5] It gives me some idea of my position in the class and provides me with a final mental preparation before I actually write the exam." Many such students take on a very instrumental orientation and attempt to interact with others whom they judge to be even better prepared than they are to gain additional insights: "The first final exam I had was in Political Studies. After mingling for awhile, I joined three other students who were discussing the content of the course and possible exam questions. By joining them, I was able to expand my store of facts and examples. On the exam, I

5. Students pick up cues for this classification as they circulate from one encounter to another and supplement them with information from previous interactions (either directly face-to-face, or indirectly from the types of questions asked in class or rumours as to who scored the highest grades on the last test).

was actually able to use two of these facts. As a result, I now arrive at the exam early and search out the best students who happen to be discussing the course material."

Being motivated principally by accuracy is not without its dangers when students find themselves to be less well prepared. The following "big leaguer" states: "I was not properly prepared for my Sociology exam. I had only read through the assigned readings once. In an effort to discover my relative state of preparedness, I 'tested' some individuals I considered to be in 'my league'. If their position had been similar to mine, I would have entered the exam feeling quite secure. Instead, I found them very well prepared and a great deal more secure in their knowledge than I was. As a result, I was 'shaken up'." Wheeler (1966:30) also found that highly motivated students expressed a desire to compare themselves with others who were superior to them. This creates a paradox where the "individual with the greatest motivation to achieve subjective feelings of success has the greatest tendency to make social comparisons which result in subjective feelings of failure or inferiority." Wheeler (1966) attempts to explain the paradox by suggesting that highly motivated individuals tend to assume greater similarity between themselves and others of superior ability; when greater than expected differences occur the result "is a feeling of failure" or, in the case of the student mentioned earlier, a break in self-confidence.

Most students are less than fully confident in themselves or in their mastery of the required material and are concerned mostly with receiving social support: "Just before the exam, my feelings of tension are at their highest point. By talking with others I get a measure of relief." These students are more concerned with self-enhancement of their role-identities and, as Goffman would predict, they actively avoid others who are better prepared: "It makes you feel more confident if you only talk to classmates you think have studied about the same as or even less than you have." Given the limited amount of time before the exam begins and the importance of maintaining a sense of confidence, the search for others with whom to interact can result in considerable risk. One of the most demoralizing of all experiences is "talking to someone you know has studied a whole lot more than you have, and hearing that person state that she still doesn't know her stuff well enough for the exam. . . . It makes you feel sick, and thoughts like 'Oh no, I should have studied more,' and 'I'm probably going to fail,' run through your mind." The safest and most usual interactional choice for students is to interact with those persons they have sat beside throughout the year. They know each other's performance levels and the feelings of friendship that normally develop are especially comforting at times like this.

Other students attempt to maintain their poise by "totally" refusing to discuss course material or even the upcoming exam. They keep interaction strictly within the bounds of sociability and hope to obtain social support as well. At almost the opposite end of the continuum is a small number of highly instrumentally oriented students (sometimes labeled 'parasites' or 'wingers') who affiliate with others solely for the purpose of learning enough from the talk going on around them to "wing it" on the exam. Typically, they have done little or no studying and have virtually no interest in either social support or social comparison motives. Their sole aim is to gather whatever information they can: "It can only help—it may even be enough to pass the exam."

Generally, an orientation to accuracy is a luxury limited largely to top performing students because they are the only ones who can afford to be motivated by such elite desires; they have much to gain and little to lose. First, top students may gain additional insights which directly benefit them on the exam. Second, they now have a better idea of how well they must do to remain competitive with or to outperform others in their 'league'. And since they tend to be better prepared than most, many of their comparisons turn out to be self-enhancing as well. Thus, top performing students demonstrate both Festinger's (1954) accuracy and Goffman's (1959) self-enhancement motives at the same time. Most other students who feel less confident in their abilities are motivated more by the self-enhancement motive. They feel threatened by others better prepared than themselves and avoid them whenever possible (the opposite of what we would expect if accuracy was the principle motivator). Hakmiller (1966) also questions the general applicability of Festinger's accuracy motive hypothesis, especially when comparisons threaten an individual's positive sense of self. He found that subjects who experienced a threat to their self-esteem responded by searching out others they considered inferior (in the hopes of regaining a more positive sense of self). Likewise, students who found themselves in encounters with better-prepared others tended to "anxiously look for the first opportunity to retreat to a group that was on their level, or even lower, so, as one of them states: "I can regain some of my lost confidence."

While some might argue that since students, by and large, search out others within their own 'league', they are acting in accordance with Festinger's predictions. Festinger feels that the major motivation here is accuracy of comparison. Students in our study clearly indicate, however, that their concern is more with self-enhancement than accuracy. Schachter and others have also not explored how students, in their search for social support and comparison, actually go about affiliating with each other. We will now look at this dimension, and examine whether or not the affiliation actually does result in a reduction of anxiety.

3. Pre-Exam Encounters: Managing Anxiety

The earliest arrivals at exams usually come alone and stop just outside the closed doors, much as they would when routinely waiting for their classroom to become accessible. However, this is where the similarity ends. The arrival of subsequent students transforms the physical setting into a sociologically significant entity—the situation. The usual norms—which dictate a state of nonfocused interaction between unacquainted students—are suspended. Civil inattention,[6] maintenance of an appropriate public distance, and impersonal angling (180 degrees) of the body are replaced by focused interaction. Students search out each other's eyes and, when contact is accomplished, the usual accompanying eyebrow lifts signals that the participants recognize each other (although it is sometimes a purely categorical recognition based on the fact that each is carrying the appropriate textbooks for the course) and are eager to converse.[7]

Interaction is facilitated by the fact that the upcoming event provides readily available opening lines which are of immediate interest to all and offend none:[8] "What do you think the exam will be like? What do you think the questions will be? Have you studied much?" These statements tend to occur at the end of the greeting (while the participants have a smile on their faces) and serve as a metasignal which brings to the fore the bond that presently unites them. These questions are not only effective means to get interaction underway, they have the further advantage of immediately allowing students to begin reducing uncertainty via the social comparison process.

The topics of probable exam questions, their level of difficulty, and generally how wary the students think they ought to be provide a guaranteed store of conversational resources to maintain the discussion once it begins. As a consequence, the most usual problem faced in interaction (i.e., a lack of "safe supplies" to talk about) is solved. For example, when one engages a relative stranger in conversation it is easy to run out of impersonal things to say even while the body is still posturally positioned for talk (frontally oriented and in close proximity, with much eye contact). In such a case, each looks to the other in the hopes that the other will provide a signal for talk, but, since they have such limited knowledge of each other, topics of mutual interest are difficult to come by. The situation is aggravated by the fact that it is considered rude to "hold" a relative stranger's eyes without speaking. The situation is usually

6. Civil inattention (Goffman, 1963) is the most frequent interpersonal ritual used to convey that persons are indeed objects of ultimate value. When "actors" come into the presence of strangers, the ritual begins: actors glance and thereby acknowledge the presence of the strangers (civil), but then remove their eyes so as to respect the stranger's privacy (inattention). We frequently make use of this ritual when we encounter strangers on sidewalks, elevators, etc., at a distance, we may "look them over," but as we approach our eyes tend to move away.

7. The situation is comparable to one which occurs when two unacquainted persons from the same country meet on foreign soil. There is mutual recognition, even though the persons are really strangers, and an expansive greeting followed by talk.

8. Every encounter must meet what Goffman (1963) calls the problem of "safe supplies", that is, there must be a store of topics for discussion which are of immediate interest to all and yet offend none.

solved by angling the body away from the other and taking a step backwards. Understandably, then, people are reluctant to start conversations with strangers, especially if there are few potential topics or "safe supplies."[9]

A. Managing Anxiety by Expressive Means: Words and Acts Directed to Others

As other students arrive for the exam, there is a definite tendency for them to engage in behaviour similar to that of the first arrivals. Soon the entire physical space that contains the gathering is socially transformed into an "open region", since all have rights of access to each other for purposes of talk, even if "they barely recognize one another." Interaction is facilitated as never before because there is a common bridge to cross; a joint ordeal which generates an interactional atmosphere somewhat comparable to that found at the scene of disasters: "It serves to make one feel less tension in just going up and talking to others." "During the regular year, I would like to meet more people but I usually feel too awkward and I'm afraid of being embarrassed. However, it's much easier when I'm waiting for an exam to start."

Another factor promoting the social comparison process is that students exist in a closed (or at best a suspicion awareness) context as to how well prepared others are for the exam. This is a topic of great concern and interest because performances are always, to some extent, relative and dependent on how well prepared others are. Although such information is vital, participants work at disguising and containing the fact, since open reference to competition undermines the generation of solidarity and build up of poise which are, of course, the major aims of the pre-exam frame (i.e., "self-confidence is built via group confidence"). Solidarity is facilitated by maintaining the interaction within a pretense awareness context (Glaser and Strauss), where each student knows that the other is a competitor, but acts as if this were not the case. Indeed, individuals display concern for the welfare of others (social support) and actually help to build their self-confidence (poise), which in turn probably aids performance during the exam.

Another rule which serves to generate social support discourages the expression of purely subjective states that might run contrary to the goals of

---

9. Schachter neglected this feature when he dealt with various alternative explanations for the relationship between anxiety and affiliation. He dismissed the hypothesis—that people may affiliate as a means of diverting attention from their "miserable" situation—on the basis that students who expected to receive electrical shocks preferred to wait alone rather than with others who were in a completely different condition. Schachter's logic was that interaction with others could divert attention from the ordeal they were about to undergo. Since students did not choose to wait with others, he inferred that diversion was not important. However, this interpretation might be considered problematic because several other variables are not controlled. Schachter's subjects would be reticent to talk to strangers because we have cultural rules against such a practice (Goffman, 1963), especially in the absence of a shared compelling situation to provide an opening line and a store of safe supplies to keep the talk going. Since these conditions were not present, it may well be that Schachter's subjects considered that the potential costs in attempting to meet strangers (i.e., embarrassment) would outweigh any benefits which might occur.

the encounter. Individuals are not allowed to show their true emotions: "It's the calm person who commands respect." "I avoid nervous looking people; just talking to them makes me feel nervous too." Individuals act more calmly than they feel and the interactional effect generates some measure of composure. Several students freely commented on their use of ["impression management"] in this situation. "We all put on our masks of calmness over the stormy sea." "I pretend to have a worry-free nature, though sometimes my insides feel as tight as the stretched cat guts over a violin." While individuals probably know that the others are concealing fear, they co-operate by not making pointed reference to their attempts at expression control. For example, no reference is made to the presence of torn fingernails, the number of cigarettes smoked, or the large number of individuals who come to the exam with pale faces.[10]

Yet another rule concerns being modest in terms of describing one's state of preparedness for the exam and the proscription of an attitude of open confidence. As one student, in her graduating year, noted: "Personally, I have yet to enter an exam room with another student who freely announced, 'I sure worked for this exam;'[11] the emphasis is inevitably on how little prepared one is." Students tend to accompany statements of how little they studied with accounts which draw on the various sources of role strain, especially role overload: "I had two other exams to study for." "I had a major essay due the same day." Concealing the amount of studying helps to keep the underlying competitive element in check and facilitates the generation of social support.[12]

These rules are consistent with the more general, informal student norms which hold that "it's not cool to study one's brains out for an exam"; nevertheless, a reasonable amount of studying is expected. While students may say how quickly they covered the material, when someone else happened to mention that area X is important, they are likely to reply that they "didn't study that much overall, but I did concentrate more on that part." Behaviour is still within the normative boundaries and students do not lose face by appearing to be unable to differentiate between what is more or less important. Concealing the amount of studying also serves as a mechanism to protect one's self. If students do not perform as well as they hoped to they have a ready

10. A survey of the physical context after the students have moved into the examination room will reveal a vast number of pieces of styrofoam, which were once parts of coffee cups, littering the floor. A closer look will often reveal pieces of torn fingernails. Argyle (1975) points out that fear is associated with an increased flow of adrenalin which increases bodily functions (i.e., rate of breathing and probably general body movement, especially finger work). It also causes a restricted flow of blood to the skin, hence the white faces.

11. While this type of statement is comparatively infrequent, it does serve as a "test" of the postulated norms. We would expect such "deviant" behaviours to be accompanied by sanctions. Indeed, these persons are resented and generally soon find themselves without an audience. Occasionally, they may even be yelled at by others who are especially uncertain and irate.

12. Although students are frequently aware that others understate their level of preparedness, the information "still makes me feel good because, at a time like this, it's just what I want to hear." Thus, even though the comparisons take place largely within a pretense awareness context, they nevertheless do generate some measure of social support.

made excuse, whereas "if you said you really studied and then failed, you'd simply be thought of as 'dumb'."[13] If the exam results are positive "there is more prestige in hearing 'What a brain, she never studies and always does well' than 'Sure she gets good marks, but anyone who studies as hard as she does could get straight A's'." Thus both personal and social functions are served by students "understating" the amount of studying they do.

Indeed the typical routine involves individuals dramatizing their weak points while at the same time stressing the strengths of the other. For example, when talking of tests the professor had previously set, students went through the following interaction:

A: "You know . . . I don't think I'm going to do very well." [Self denial which has the effect of encouraging others].

B: "Oh, don't say that . . . "Of course you will, you know your stuff." [Positive encouragement]

A: "I wish I was as confident in myself as you are in me." [Reciprocal encouragements].

C: "You're sure to do well." [Emphathetic encouragement].

A: "There was so much material to study and he didn't even cover all of it in class" [Same boat attitude].

B: "There's nothing we can do" [Fatalism].

C: "He's a hard bastard" [Joint enemy].

This last remark brings a round of "yeh's" and supporting nonverbals from almost everyone in the group. These "after you Alphonse" routines are particularly effective in obtaining social support. Individuals are allowed to disparage themselves knowing the right is not likely to be abused and, in so doing, they create an obligation on the part of others to deny the negative traits and actually emphasize their strengths. This is exactly the message people are looking for at this point in time because, in comforting, supporting, and reassuring each other, there is a collective bolstering of courage for the upcoming event. In these more intense dialogues, the postures tend to mirror each other and generate further cohesion (Scheflen, 1964). Vilifying professors and identifying them as the cause of present woes is a particularly effective mechanism to deflect students from their identities as competitors, thereby

---

13. Hewitt and Stokes (1975:2) introduce the concept of disclaimers—a verbal device actors use to "ward off and defeat in advance doubts and negative typifications" which may result from future actions. They contrast disclaimers with Scott and Lyman's (1968) concept of accounts which have a retrospective orientation. Accounts attempt to smooth over problems that have already made themselves apparent. Disclaimers seek to define forthcoming conduct as not relevant to the kind of identity-challenge or re-typification for which it might ordinarily serve as the basis. For example, when students say they haven't studied, they are protecting themselves from being labelled 'dumb' (although they might be regarded as lazy).

facilitating social support among them: "To the extent we make the teacher our enemy, each person we speak to becomes our ally."[14]

As interaction proceeds, a mood or ethos emerges which is quite at odds with what would be expected at an exam situation. As assurances are traded, details are swapped and the more memorable classroom incidents are retold and dramatized, especially if one of the persons now present figures in the incident. The interaction becomes enveloped in a mood characterized by banter and laughter which tends to increase in tempo and intensity as time goes on. This mood is due to the special conditions associated with exams and to the fact that a very large number of people are crowded into a small area, with each encounter located within the sphere of intimate distance[15] (Hall, 1966) and each person trying to talk loudly enough to be heard. The effect is perceived by an outsider as a "high level of chatter." At this point, participants also report a greater feeling of emotional preparedness for the exam. This talk, then, has a powerful influence on emotional attitude because it convinces the participants that nothing more can be done. "We co-operate to make this tense and unknown situation a little easier to handle or cope with." Many students who have been remote and standoffish for most of the year are now congenial, gregarious, and supportive. This is quite an achievement, considering the underlying competitive element: "Basically students do not deeply care how others fare so long as it is worse than themselves."[16]

In describing how students manage anxiety, we go beyond Schachter who largely limited himself to identifying social support and social comparison processes to locate the processes in context and demonstrate how they are used by the students. In essence, we found that a common ordeal gives rise to feelings of solidarity and provides a store of safe supplies which facilitate affiliation. Once interaction begins students manage their feelings of anxiety either indirectly by making social comparisons or directly by exchanging acts of social support. To reduce uncertainty through social comparisons, while at the same time obtaining social support, requires considerable interactional skill since blunt comparison can undermine the atmosphere of social support. The process is facilitated by a set of pre-existing norms, like being modest about

14. Sometimes the opposite happens and students reassure each other that the professor is a nice person who gives fair exams.

15. Hall describes intimate space as 0–6 inches. The potential for contact is considerable and this is the distance at which "lovemaking and wrestling, comforting and protecting" could easily occur.

16. One can look at the above situation in a more philosophical vein and see that perhaps it is not really that unusual to develop solidarity in the face of competition. The classic reference here is Simmel (1969), who pointed out that any social bond involves dialectic interplays between various forces—helping and harming, harmony and conflict, and open disclosures and closedness. Simmel felt that without such an interplay a social relationship could not be viable. He believed there was no pure form of cohesion—that it was always mixed with some form of competition and conflict. Lyman and Scott (1970) indicate that Simmel went so far as to suggest that even two lovers in an erotic relationship may be in competition as each attempts to outdo the other in demonstrating affection.

one's probable achievements. Even in encounters enacted by persons with the best of intentions, however, surprises can occur. Typical incidents center around students who, in an attempt to prevent having their "confidence jarred," avoid discussions of course-related material. In fluid interaction where one topic naturally leads to another, an assigned reading may be mentioned. Unfortunately, such remarks about assigned readings sometimes cause a dark look to come over a face (eyebrows rise and are brought together with some intensity) as someone mutters, "What article?" This display brings to the fore the tension which is supposed to be contained and all the participants feel the consequences of it. Most often there is some elaboration about "what article" is referred to, the person's memory is jogged, and tension is relieved with "Oh [hand pointed to head], I remember now," or "Ya, I see now." It sometimes happens that the person really did not read the assigned article. Under these conditions, the focal person usually does the interactional work required to suppress the incident and get the interaction rolling again. This is usually accomplished by a rationalization such as (with a swipe of a lowering hand away from body), "It doesn't matter, it's not important." And all tend to agree, verbally or nonverbally, or state, with the beginnings of a smile, "It's too late now." The focal person may also take a humorous posture, and say "I don't know anything". Most participants tend to respond to the cue with laughter and the expressive order is re-established. Sometimes though such focal persons take a more instrumental approach which challenges the socially supportive atmosphere. The fact that interaction can instigate anxiety was never considered by Schachter. Indeed, some students, who have experienced such threats, adapt by refraining from pre-exam affiliations altogether.

B. Managing Anxiety by Instrumental Means: Word and Act Self-Management Strategies

Another tactic used by students who have missed an article is to ask others if they feel the reading contains anything that might be on the exam. As other students reluctantly attempt to summarize the main points, it is not at all unusual for someone from another encounter (who also missed the assigned reading) to enter the group without going through the "proper" rituals and ask, in a panicky voice, for a restatement of the major points. As one such intruder explains, "In other times and at other places I would be hesitant to just go up to a stranger and ask for an explanation of things. But at a crucial time like this, most students understand and are willing to help."

Meanwhile, the expressive focus of the interaction with its emphasis on social support changes to a more instrumental one. This switch in focus is frequently associated with a changeover in personnel, especially in the case of students who fear the instrumental form of interaction might "mess up" their minds and "shoot" their self-confidence "to hell." Students who participate in the instrumental form of interaction search each other out and, as the interchanges become more intense, may disturb those who hold more strictly expressive orientations. Increasing signs of annoyance are reflected in statements like, "I wish they'd shut up, they're making me nervous." Occasionally, someone may even request such a group to "pipe down" or, in one extreme case, an individual yelled "shut up." Some students openly admit to attempting to "psych out the competition." A victim of this process states: "They're obnoxious people who quiz each other—in as loud a voice as possible—on the most insignificant details they can find—they know there is no possible way this information could be asked on the exam. The extra knowledge they flaunt may give them a feeling of superiority, but it only confuses the rest of us."

Given the measure of risk that always accompanies pre-exam interaction we would expect students who have had prior negative experiences to avoid such gatherings (Goffman, 1959). As a student illustrates: "I've gone to exams early and had bad experiences like being approached by a nervous-looking woman who asked me for an answer to a question and then argued with my answer. Not only did she make me feel unsure about my answer, she shook my self-confidence as well." Students who do not want to be reminded of the exam (i.e, they wish mental diversion) may also avoid pre-exam gatherings and replace them with a variety of self-oriented acts which often have an element of magic about them: "I religiously stop studying one hour before the exam, even if I'm in the middle of a sentence. After this point, I don't want to think about course material of any kind—worrying about what might or might not be asked just makes me forget other things I need to remember. Before, when I used to stand around with others, I found it all but impossible to avoid discussing questions without being rude. Now instead of talking to others, I let the material circulate nicely in my brain . . . when I take the fatal plunge, my thinking processes focus totally on the exam questions."

Students who rely heavily on mnemonic devices fear that involvement with others might interfere with their organization and recall schemes: "I don't dare come early and take the chance of disturbing the information I've so neatly packaged away in my brain." Occasionally, students will actually go so far as to lock themselves inside cubicles in washrooms just so they can avoid interacting with others. On the other hand, students who want social support from others, yet fear they might "get flapped" often sit out the last hour or so with trusted friends: "We review possible answers and work on each other's sense of self-confidence. It's amazing how it actually works."

While there are a variety of reasons why students make a point of avoiding pre-exam gatherings, there are also a number of alternative adaptation styles available to the individuals who are present. We can actually categorize some of the students who interact in pre-exam gatherings into three distinct classes: the "crammers", the "just-in-casers," and the "first placers." The "crammers" (an epithet devised by fellow students) are a relatively small number of individuals who arrive at the exam site on schedule, but refrain from engaging in face-to-face interaction. Their faces, posture, and locations set them apart from the larger group. Instead of smiling or laughing they effectively communicate their desire for privacy by clutching their books, reading feverishly, and wearing "pained expressions of deep concentration." The intensity of their message is reinforced by angling their bodies to make them less accessible to others (front part of body is at a 180 degree angle to others or sometimes facing the wall), and by locating themselves on the periphery of the gathering. Other students, the "just-in-casers", engage in intense last-minute review just in case they might now catch something they missed previously. They gain reassurance by combining the solitary last-minute review with the presence of others: "I feel most secure when I've done everything I possibly can for an exam." Finally, some students come to the pre-exam gathering early simply because they want to be among the first to enter the exam room and secure "good" seats. These "first placers" do not want to interact with others in case the interaction might upset their recall ability; they just want to acquire favoured places quickly. Not surprisingly, others who are socializing usually attempt to ignore the "crammers", "just-in-casers", and "first placers." Unfortunately for them, however, this isn't always easy to do since these groups challenge the dominant mode of adaptation and may evoke feelings of guilt. As one student notes: "I feel that last minute cramming just doesn't work and yet, watching all the others in action, I fear they might pick up something I missed."

In overall terms, most pre-exam interactions work to control and moderate feelings of anxiety through acts of social comparison (especially when participants feel they are as well or better prepared than others) and social support. Social comparison and social support are facilitated when interaction is contained within a pretense awareness context (Glaser & Strauss, 1967). Individuals suppress competitive aspects of the situation and use whatever materials are available to build and fortify feelings of solidarity. A successful outcome depends on cooperation, skill, and a measure of luck; a lack of any ingredient results in problematic interaction and an increase in anxiety. These observations in a natural setting are not only consistent with those of Wrightsman's (1961) laboratory study but enable us to offer a more detailed interpretation of his somewhat surprising results. Wrightsman attempted to extend Schachter's (1959) research to determine whether acts of affiliation did indeed result in anxiety reduction. Like Schachter, he frightened his subjects and then had them wait for five minutes in experimental conditions where they (1) were in the company of others and could converse with them (i.e., focused interaction); (2) were prohibited from talking to others around them (i.e., nonfocused interaction); or (3) were all alone (i.e., isolation). Subjects who were first born or only children experienced greater anxiety reduction when in the presence of others. However, subjects in the non-focused situation experienced the greatest overall reduction in anxiety levels. On the surface this finding seems surprising because joining in the conversation would seem to offer greater opportunity for uncertainty reduction through acts of social comparison and social support, but a closer inspection of the range of scores revealed that the focused interaction situation was associated with more extreme changes in anxiety scores. While most subjects in the focused interaction situation experienced anxiety reduction, a minority of others actually experienced an increase. The positive and negative scores cancel each other out and result in a lower overall score compared to the non-focused situation where students experienced moderate but consistent decreases in anxiety. This finding left Wrightsman somewhat perplexed. By using a participant observational approach we were in a position to observe how, where, and with whom participants interacted as compared to Wrightman's experimental design where only the effects of interaction were recorded. Our observations suggest that interaction is a formative (causal) process in its own right, beyond the personalities of individuals and the structural features of situations. In other words, when interaction is free to develop on its own, later phases of interaction cannot necessarily be entirely predicted from a knowledge of earlier conditions (Blumer, 1969). Thus, individuals who refrain from talking to others may nevertheless experience a reduction in anxiety because they have the comfort of knowing that everyone is in the same situation as they are. Further, there is no risk of having self-confidence shaken by discovering some sort of deficiency in knowledge as would potentially be the case with focused interaction. The convergence of our results with those of Wrightsman supports the notion of underlying commonalities in both situations and provides a theoretical base to explain why students resort to such a variety of coping strategies (i.e., from making a point of staying away from pre-exam encounters to actively participating in them).

Chapter VIII

Phase III—The Exam Act Proper

1. Setting

We begin the discussion of the exam phase with a description of the context within which the examination occurs because many behaviours can be made sense of only in terms of the setting that provides the background for them.[1] One such context which serves to structure the behaviour of the participants (students and professors) is that of a series of interactional rules regarding territoriality. Territories have socially-constructed boundaries that encompass interactions and, when violated, they evoke defensive behaviour. The outer boundaries of the territory extend beyond the walls of the examination room and include sound spaces which, if violated, have an effect upon the exam situation. For example, a group of noisy workmen creating a disturbance outside the building merely has to be informed that an examination is in progress and the territorial boundaries will normally be re-established. Signs outside the examination room serve as another device to mark off this territory from its surrounding context. When individuals perceive the sign, one usually can detect a drop in the volume of the conversation.

Final examinations at universities are usually administered in large gymnasia. The expanse of these areas allows for division into well-spaced columns or aisles consisting of approximately twenty desks to a row. Each desk is numbered. Administrative officials know the number of students per class, so desks are pre-assigned to specific classes. Separate classes are often marked off from each other by a row or two of empty seats. The pre-assignment of the numbered desks allows professors and their assistants to distribute the answer booklets, exam papers, and any other items which might be necessary before the students arrive. This permits more efficient use of the allotted examination time, and also helps to keep interaction within an examination- like context. Students are informed of the location of the exam and their "area" within the gymnasium by announcements which appear on official bulletin boards approximately two weeks before the end of regular classes. On the day

---

1. Like Birdwhistle (1970), we hold that bodily signals have little or no meaning in themselves, but acquire their meanings in particular contexts.

of the exam professors tend to mark, with their presence, the particular "area" their class is to occupy and so aid the students in locating their desks.

It is usual that places in which institutional transactions are held are outfitted with characteristic furnishings, and architectural features that come to symbolize the activities that occur there (Stone and Farberman, 1970). Since exams are written in close proximity to other members of the same class, the physical and architectural features of the setting are strategically arranged or staged to communicate the type of desired behaviour and facilitate its control. To this end, then, furnishings and accessories such as desks, tables, chairs, plywood dividers, and writing material are assembled and arranged in particular patterns. The aim is to integrate architectural and social elements so as to create, for each student, institutionalized islands of privacy. Our understanding of privacy comes from Simmel (1969:334) who describes it as "the control of stimulus input from others and a degree of mutual knowledge and separateness of people from one another." However, we are adapting the concept for the benefit of the educational institution which may not always correspond to the desires of the individual (as Simmel intended it). Thus, even though two or more students may wish to continue interacting and sharing their knowledge, the furniture and accessories are arranged to create a sociofugal space[2] which is designed to keep people from interacting and so maintain the institutionalized definition of the situation.

In particular, the examination room is organized to conceal students' papers from each other while making an efficient use of space. To this end, tables are arranged in rows (so writers sit side by side and not face to face and hence are less accessible to each other). In addition there are plywood partitions between students. The divider itself runs the width of the table, stands approximately two feet high,[3] and is attached to the table by clamps. It serves the function of allowing students privacy as well as preventing them from having eye contact with their neighbours or their examination papers. The use of such walls is somewhat unique to exam situations. They were adopted in response to problems which arose with the booming enrollments of the 1960's. Prior to this time, students in the same class were insulated from each other by alternating them with members of other classes. Students were preassigned seat numbers so that a student writing a biology exam might well sit next to someone else who was writing a sociology exam. The huge influx of students created many difficulties for invigilators—in large classes it was frequently not possible to recognize all the students and, also, lack of space meant that classes often had to be split up at examination time and assigned to two or

2. Sociofugal space is in contrast to sociopetal space which is arranged to bring people together (Sommer, 1969).

3. Lyman and Scott (1967) would designate this as a mode of insulation; that is, the placement of some sort of barrier between the occupants of a territory and potential invaders. Insulating barriers can take many forms, from the wearing of an expression that tells others one is not accessible, to the construction of physical barriers that keep people out.

more writing areas. The introduction of "walls" between students solved many of these problems because examination papers were "shut off" from persons who were actually sitting right beside each other. Thus, invigilating was facilitated and most classes could be fitted into one examination room.[4]

In all exam situations, except possibly the take-home variety,[5] there is concern with sequestering writers of the same exam from each other. From earliest records of examination settings, we find that barriers between writers were consciously erected to facilitate the institutional definition of the situation. A participant in an Oxford Locals Examination (1864) writes that "boys who undergo the examination sit at desks about a yard apart from one another, so that they cannot look over each other's papers or take any unfair advantage" (Roach, 1971:181). In institutions that have sufficient space this is still the most frequent mode of social control; students typically are seated in gymnasiums at single desks located some distance from each other. In classroom situations professors frequently ask students to leave an empty seat between them and their neighbours. An historical form of extreme insulation occurred at the Imperial University in Peking where, instead of desks, there were rows of "examination cells"—fully enclosed hut-like structures which gave the impression of rows of outhouses—each containing a single writer (Monroe, 1918).

The opening of the doors into the exam room and appearance of the "chief invigilators" may be viewed as triggering the transformation of phases. That is, interactions previously marked by their informality, egalitarianism, and expressiveness (i.e., "loose" roles) evolve into a set of relations marked by formal hierarchy and high observability (i.e., "tight" roles). Participants now indicate to themselves "It's time," and a new definition of the situation emerges. This new situation is reflected by a gradual decline in talk and movement, as the participants disband their focused clusters, turn to the door, and take on parallel postures[6] that have the organizational features of the queue.[7] These actions result in the appearance of a "people pipeline" as individuals

---

4. Despite such innovations, disciplines which have large enrolments and a single exam for all sections of the same course (particularly introductory chemistry and biology) tend to be split up into different examination areas, although not as many as before.

5. In this work we limit ourselves largely to the investigation of closed book exams written in the presence of other class members at examination sites and, to some extent, in classrooms (i.e., in-class tests).

6. Scheflen (1964), more than any other social scientist, has emphasized the relational significance of posture. He indicates that a change in the definition of the situation is usually marked by an alteration in the postural behaviours of group members. In the present case the group members (students) are moving from one "presentation" (the larger, enduring definition of the situation which is characteristic of the pre-exam interaction) to another where a certain number of "positions" (topics of conversation, types of relationship) are developed and sustained by a vast number of "micro points" (glances, gestures, turn-taking signals, etc.) (Goffman, 1971).

7. The queue is conceptualized as another territory of the self where claim is made to a turn. The claim establishes the right of individuals to come just after the persons arriving before them and just ahead of the persons arriving after them.

proceed through the doors on the basis of accessibility, which corresponds to order of arrival. Since a turn in a queue, however, is a right, not a duty, those early arrivals who linger to talk to friends must forfeit their position of priority. The priority of arrival determines claim of a scarce good; that is, the choice of a more desirable seat.

Students who enter the exam room in the company of a friend ritually tend to acknowledge the suspension of their open accessibility to each other with a faltering smile and the exchange of "Good luck." Any materials, such as study notes or books that might have an effect on the outcome of the exam are deposited just inside the doorway. The next step is for students to find the territory reserved for their particular class and especially their own seat. Once seated, students proceed to colonize or personalize their "stalls"[8] by setting out pens, pencils, and erasers. At this point, females usually place their purses under the desk: "Although I'm not sure whether purses are allowed in the exam room, I usually bring mine. My insecurity is bad enough already because my books are not in close proximity." These acts serve symbolically to transform a desk into a place that will be home for the duration of the exam.

The usual response to finding an unoccupied niche is one of relief. However, those who always carry their notes or books with them and who feel these are, like clothing or jewelry, part of their identity, report feelings of "nakedness," "defenselessness," or "waiting for the massacre armed only with pen in hand." To lose control over objects with which one identifies, to have to sit further apart than usual, and to be separated from fellow students by a physical barrier creates a "further feeling of being unarmed" and a distinct sense of vulnerability.

By the time the exam begins students have experienced several sub-role changes, each of which has its own relevant bundle of norms that serve as guidelines for behaviour. Students move from the back regions of the sociable, pre-exam phase—a relatively open, fluid situation that allows for considerable leeway in role-enactment—to a more structured role when they enter the front region (exam room) and are greeted by the solemn-faced examiners. We now witness a collapse of the sociable expressions that were, until a moment ago, so much in evidence. The demeanor and facial expressions take on a more serious tone, and the talking, joking, and smiling virtually disappear. The participants now display a new decorum that excudes a sense of respect for the occasion.

The atmosphere of the exam room has many parallels to that of a solemn church service. This similarity might even be extended to the sociable pre-

---

8. The stall is conceptualized by Goffman (1971) as a space to which an individual temporarily lays claim (i.e., chairs, tables, booths, desks). It has clearly marked boundaries in a definite setting. This contrasts with personal space, which is the area surrounding individuals to any point where an advancing other causes them to feel uncomfortable. While personal space and the stall are both territories of the self, they differ in that the stall is fixed in a setting and has visible boundaries.

service interaction and accompanying transformation as individuals enter the church. The beginning of the exam proper signals the final move from relatively unstructured interaction to structured interaction where norms and roles are predetermined by the educational institution and ultimately by society. The roles are institutionalized in the social positions of student and professor and, while they may lie dormant for most of the participants' social lives, they become activated during the social occasion of the exam.

2. The Exam as a Semi-Focused Gathering: Conceptualizations

The various contexts which envelop, penetrate, and help to organize exams were previously mentioned, and their consequences for the larger society, the school, and the participants were discussed.

Exams, however, have another side; they are not direct, unmediated replications of the larger institutional structure of society or the school. Indeed, exams as social occasions may be viewed as systems in their own right. They possess natural boundaries, or a type of "metaphorical membrane" (Goffman, 1961a), which selectively cuts them off from both the larger society and the classroom. Aspects of these systems which are allowed to penetrate the exam membrane now perform somewhat transformed functions and are given unique interpretations. Thus, these aspects gain a new status in the reality of this particular interactional world. Since Goffman (1961a) suggests that situations which possess these attributes can be considered as social encounters, it might be useful to look at the exam as an encounter.

At first glance, this may seem surprising because the common sense view of exams is that they are composed of isolated acts with little or no social interaction between any of the participants. However, a closer inspection reveals both focused and unfocused social interaction. Thus, while the students are faced with tight normative proscriptions regarding mutual accessibility, they do engage in considerable diffuse nonverbal interaction with others in their immediate vicinity as well as with the invigilators. This nonverbal interaction, of course, is the central defining feature of non-focused interaction. The exam also possesses characteristics which might lead one to describe or conceptualize it as a semi-focused gathering. While unfocused interaction is characterized by the absence of "an official center of attention" (Goffman, 1963:64), the reading and answering of the exam questions serve as both visual and cognitive foci. The participants in the exam situation are primarily engaged in individual tasks so the setting cannot really be described as an encounter. However, the exam is organized in such a way that the professor can, at any moment, summon the attention of the writers and transform the assembly into a focused gathering. This is clearly a step beyond the realm of the unfocused gathering where, as Goffman (1963:19) states, "no one participant can be officially 'given the floor.' " Exams also share other features with encounters in that they include ceremonies which "bracket the initiation and termination of the activity." There is an emergence of a "we rationale or shared sense of the single thing that we are doing together at the time," and the provision of a base for a "circular flow of feeling among the participants as well as corrective compensation for deviant acts" (Goffman, 1963:18).

We will first survey the state of the examinees as they wait for the opening ceremonies and follow up with a description of the ethos or group atmosphere which emerges as the participants, following the rules of the occasion, focus on the central theme, namely the examination questions.[9] As participants focus on the same question, labour under the same conditions, and cooperate one with the other in order to get through the occasion, a circular flow of feeling, which is characterized by a sense of "we-ness," emerges. From here, the discussion moves to consideration of the elements which are allowed to penetrate the "membrane" of the event and their transformation as they are worked into the interactional processes of the occasion. The terminal behaviours involved in winding down the exam provide the final focus of discussion.

3. Opening Ceremonies

Once students are seated at their desks, they begin to fill in information on the front of the examination booklet. Their identity is then concealed by a sticker glued over it which may only be removed by the professor after the paper has been read. Once this is accomplished, students await the ceremonialized opening ritual.[10] As noted earlier, because of the value orientations of the participants, the brief period of waiting is charged with considerable emotion: "Since the beginnings of our life, we have been told by our parents that our destiny is in our own hands and here it is literally at the tips of one's fingers." Since the outcome of the task cannot be known in advance, the writers get the feeling "It's all up to God and one's pen." The "no talking" rule is now in effect and so the students must deal with their emotions without the verbal support of others. At this point, tension is evidenced by increased blinking behaviour and reports of "sweaty palms," "dry mouth," and "butterflies in the stomach."

The chief invigilator begins the acts which are associated with the opening role by walking towards the front of the room, stopping at approximately the centre, and turning to face the students. Eye contact is directed towards

---

9. The question-answer format of exams serves as the equivalent of the topic of conversation in the encounter. Exam writers, like conversants, soon become involved and carried off into another world. While exam dialogue may be silent, it is nevertheless focused by the questions and has the advantage of leaving traces of the symbolic interchange.

10. Exams, like other social occasions, have ceremonialized opening and closing brackets. These brackets act as boundary markers and provide a sense of stepping, not only into a new role, but beyond into a new world.

them and the voice is loud enough to embrace the entire gathering.[11] The chief invigilator offers a greeting, makes whatever relevant announcements are necessary, and finally ends with some form of the ritual statement: "You may now begin."

4. Ethos of the Exam Phase

The opening signal might be compared metaphorically to a detonator that sets off a charge of explosives; a sea of heads and eyes are lowered simultaneously, and the sound of turning pages fills the air as students open their examination papers to read the questions. The once closed, perhaps suspicious, awareness context is now transformed into an open one. This point marks the climax of the exam act, because the dominant definition of the situation now takes hold. The examination paper itself becomes both the normatively specified dominant involvement and the occasioned main involvement. Any discrepancy between the two is psychologically taxing and potentially costly in terms of career.

The exam questions tend to be involving, not only because most distractions are temporarily controlled,[12] but also because of a basic rule of interaction which dictates that a question requires an answer (Sacks, 1968). As a consequence of this internalized rule, the writers enter into symbolic interaction with the professor. That is, writers assign meaning to the question by attempting to view it through the professor's eyes and by composing an answer they think the professor will consider the "most mark-worthy": "you don't just answer the question [with] what you think is the right answer, but rather think of what the professors had in mind when they wrote the question." In this process many top-performing students get caught up and carried away in the evolving logic of their answers: "When I look at the questions and realize I've

11. It is interesting to note that the announcer role involves an invariant sequence of acts; announcements are not made from the back or sides of the room or from a wide angle at the middle of the room. All of these actions would probably violate rules of etiquette and procedure because they would detract from the clarity of the communication. Merely proceeding to the ecological centre of the area and facing the audience frontally communicates that the message is meant for everyone. This pattern of opening behaviours is much less time consuming and explicit than in the past. For example, according to a participant in an Oxford Local Examination (1864) the invigilator took centre stage and "read out the rules of the Examination and cautioned against copying, etc. . . . he specified the time allowed for the paper and said he would speak for five minutes before the exam could begin" (Roach, 1971:181). Today, most instructions are written on the cover of each examination booklet (e.g. "Candidates must not have in their possession at the time of examination any unauthorized books, tables, notes, or other extraneous material").

12. Exams, in addition to the various levels of control that serve to screen out potential distraction, also have special rules of irrelevance which dictate that the writer should disengage self from concerns which cut across the time limits of the exam frame. All of one's other identities (as well as the invigilators') are to be ignored, and other individuals are treated as non-persons. This is a role much like that played by ushers in a movie theatre; they are to be inconspicuous unless their services are required. Thus, exams are designed to eliminate all competing roles and so produce one-dimensional persons.

got the answers, a feeling of well-being comes over me. In the process of composing the answers, I get so involved in the thinking and writing that I'm completely unaware of others around me. Barring a severe disturbance, I'll remain in this state up to a full hour. It's only then I realize where I am and become interested in others around me." Evidence of their involvement can be seen in the bodily cues given off; for example, people "huddled" over the papers, with "think faces" characterized by a look of concentration, and eyebrows knitted to such an extent that trace lines may remain after the expression is relaxed. Even though every student is writing a separate paper, their fates are linked so they tend to remain somewhat "alive" to each other. Thus, the jointly exuded cues come to take on a normative quality which, in turn, gives rise to a jointly sustained atmosphere or ethos of "silent industriousness."[13] Writers have described this state as a "covering blanket of silence" or, emphasizing the cognitive process, as a "silent, thinking atmosphere." This jointly sustained character or ethos carries with it a sense of moral responsibility: "I feel self-conscious about disturbing the silence, so even when I feel the need to clear my throat, I frequently restrain it until someone else does." "I even feel guilty about having to cough." "I don't dare blow my nose. It's too quiet."

Questions do vary, however, according to their relative capacity to involve the students. As a consequence, if the questions are very easy the atmosphere which evolves may be much "lighter," the possibilities and probabilities for distraction are much greater, and students may exchange "knowing" side glances or gestures which indicate "it's a piece of cake." On the other hand, if the questions are too demanding, students also find it difficult to get involved, and one may hear weakly audible groans (acts oriented to others) which are actually comforting because they indicate others are having difficulty as well: "exchanging sighs helps us regain some of our lost togetherness."[14] Such information exchange and expressive support reduce anxiety levels and help to lessen the "mental blocks" some students experience (Schachter, 1959). The importance of such sharing is made apparent by its absence: "It's particularly demoralizing when others around you are frantically writing and you can't even think of a word." The experience of seemingly being "the only one" is the source of many exam "blank-outs." Many of those students who, for whatever reasons, are unable to get caught up in the questions (normatively specified dominant involvement) report feelings of self-consciousness and pressures to "fit in." Some adapt by engaging in acts of impression management like "putting on a perplexed facial expression to give the impression that I'm deep in thought" while others remain quite immobile.

13. This ethos contrasts with that of the pre- and post-exam phases where participants draw themselves out into jointly sustained states of sociability.

14. However, when these groans are widely distributed through out the class, they can cause deep embarrassment for the professor involved. While these nonverbal indicators of displeasure eventually die out, the professor feels the "coldness" when the examination papers are handed in.

One student who read and re-read the questions and who, each time, drew a complete blank, reported: "I remained stone-faced for several embarrassing minutes . . . [finally] I wiped my forehead to remove the perspiration that had accumulated from worrying." Such situations tend to have many instrumentally oriented strategies attached to them; one of the most frequent is to answer the easiest questions first and leave the most difficult ones until later. This technique is suggested in one of the earliest works on exams (Scott, 1908:209) which advises that "by answering an easy question first you will regain any 'nerve' you may have lost, and will be able to proceed with other questions with greater assurance." Scott also advises writers to forget questions about which they "know nothing . . . spending time on others and answering them better." Our students suggest a variety of additional strategies: "When all else fails, I put my head down on the desk and wrap my arms around it. These actions relieve the extreme stimulation of the moment, and clear my head so the answer comes to the surface." "I very slowly and meticulously recopy the 'problem' question in my exam booklet." Such ritual acts directed toward self can, as Gmelch and Malinowski suggest, moderate feelings of panic to the point where "a relevant fragment of an idea crops up" and, when it is jotted down, may "ignite further insight into the question."[15]

Exams are one of the few social occasions in our society where one is given license to engage in extreme forms of self- concentrated withdrawal and allowed, temporarily, to forget personal appearance and the impression that facial expressions give off. Thus, behaviours such as hair twisting and facial contortions, which in other everyday settings (e.g., elevators) would lead others to question one's sanity, are considered "normal." However, even though there is license for a range of acceptable behaviours, there are also normative limits beyond which behaviours may not stray. As in all gatherings, the writer must maintain at least some margin of self-command. If the margin is transgressed, such behaviour would be a violation of the norms of over-involvement (Goffman, 1963, 1974). One example which is frequently mentioned is when writers become so engrossed in the task that they lose control over the noises they make. Often students unconsciously move the tongue when coping with a difficult question and create a clicking sound which disturbs others in the vicinity. Other such emissions come in the form of over-zealous erasing where the desk and its walls actually rattle, leg jiggling, pencil drumming, and gum

15. McKeachie, et al., (1955:98) offer some empirical evidence for the anxiety reducing effects of expressive acts on exam performance. Some students writing a multiple choice exam were encouraged to write comments about their questions as a means of releasing anxiety while the control group were given no such encouragement. Students who felt free to comment performed at significantly higher levels than did the others. Furthermore, since the test scores of students who wrote comments only differed significantly from the control group on the second half of the test, it eliminates a purely cognitive explanation of the differences; that is, the comments did not improve scores on the specific questions about which they were written. As a result, the authors conclude "When a person is frustrated or anxious, the discharge of tension through almost any available response will help decrease the effect of the anxiety on later problems."

chewing. One student, in a reflexive frame break, reported, "I just saw the guy in front of me shaking his legs nervously and I then realized that I was chewing my gum quickly and making crackling sounds."

Other frame breaks come from coughing, sneezing, and sniffling. Sniffling is one of the most frequent and grave offenses, especially when the offender is drawing on a "full nose." The sound stands out not only because of its regularity but also because it is psychologically experienced as revolting. Students even report the feeling that the immediate space is contaminated. Such actions extend the writers' powers of selective inattention to the limit and hamper their cognitive engrossment in the dominant involvement.[16] Only rarely however, do students ask to be transferred from one area to another.[17] Invigilators also find it difficult to deal with this matter; about the most they can do is offer the offender a tissue which, on occasion, has been politely refused with the statement, "I have some, thanks." Frequently it is only at this point that the offender becomes aware of his transgression. Needless to say, these types of situations generate embarrassment for all concerned. Other forms of distraction come from students who, despite the fact they know that smoking is prohibited, light up cigarettes; in this situation students feel much freer to inform invigilators of the violation.

Some students also indicate that invigilators cause distractions. One irate writer noted: "those incessant clicking shoes of the white-haired professor in the green jacket are rattling me no end."[18] A more routine form of disturbance comes when students raise their hands and request vocal communication with the professor in order to clarify the interpretation of a question.[19] The interaction which emerges is adapted to fit the particular occasion; that is, students initiate the act by adopting a non-congruent posture (sitting up straight versus others who are huddled over their papers, raising an arm, and focusing their

16. Although students regularly report these violations, they rarely sanction the violator directly and openly, probably because the sanctioning of such behaviour is itself a violation of societal rules. The normatively appropriate reaction, at least among adults, appears to be "studied non-observance." Occasionally students will indicate to the invigilators via nonverbal means (usually facial expressions) that they are aware of the violation; presumably this occurs because they also heard "the draw."

17. The offender is almost invariably male. Females seem to experience this practice as more contaminating since the only two persons throughout the study who requested transfers were female, and they moved as far away from the offender as possible. Most students can recall incidents of being "grossed out" but did not request that the invigilator move them because "it would have caused too much commotion and been embarrassing for everyone." In classroom exams where they are not separated by partitions, students can exercise greater measure of control over "snifflers" by giving them "that socially acceptable wilting look."

18. Students, especially those who are least prepared, are easily distracted by competing stimuli: "I only find it irritating when an invigilator walks by if I don't know my material very well. Otherwise, I'm either not aware of them or may even use them as 'safe' objects to look at when I want a rest."

19. Answering questions is about the only time professors act in their role; most of the time they are mere supervisors.

gaze on the professor).[20] As soon as the professor perceives the situation the writer's signal is acknowledged by a sequence of behaviours which very much resemble a long-distance greeting.[21] The professor acknowledges the student with an exchange of glances (eyes are slightly rounded, eyebrows are lifted, and a head toss may be initiated) and thus signifies availability for verbal encounter. Almost simultaneously, the student will drop the lifted hand and reorient his/her eyes to the "safe" region of the desk. The body may remain erect or may be angled toward the desk. Such exaggerated acts of honesty directed to invigilators serve to moderate feelings of anxiety: "In no way does one lean back or look around while the professors make their way over; there is too much fear; one might somehow be thought of as cheating."

Meanwhile, the professor starts off in the direction of the student.[22] The walk is now faster than usual and conveys a sense of purpose. The greatest disturbance occurs at the point when the professor reaches the row of desks where the student is seated because now other students must pull their chairs forward so that the professor can pass behind them to reach the particular desk. The usual response from students is that they do pull their chairs forward and occupy the least amount of space possible.

Professors must still angle their bodies sideways and move horizontally between the rows if they are to minimize touching others—hardly a dignified professorial posture. The professor comes very close to the student. Their shoulders are usually parallel and the head and trunk are bent at an angle which maximizes hearing. The actual distance between heads is negotiated so that both parties feel fairly comfortable. However, even at this distance, each is very sensorily aware of the other, since, as Hall (1966) points out, it is possible to smell the other (breath, lotions, perfumes) and detect body heat and

20. This gazing process seems to add something to the situation. People are particularly sensitive, it seems, to sets of eyes which follow them.

21. Greetings serve to single out people and acknowledge them as separate from others around them. In the usual atmosphere of the exam frame, writers and invigilators take on the status of non-persons who are treated somewhat like background features of the setting. When students raise a hand, the situation is transformed and the interaction is now between two distinct individuals. However, the status difference between professors and students is maintained by the fact that professors acknowledge the particular student's request but the students simply maintain their position and do not respond to the professor as one friend might respond to the other.

22. In the past, students caused louder interruptions of the silence than they do now because nonverbal indicators were supplemented by verbal ones. Participants in the Oxford Locals Examination in 1864 indicated that students who wished assistance would hold up their hand and would call their number, whereupon the person who conducted the examination would immediately attend them (Roach, 1971:181).

breathing rates.[23] Given the tension associated with the exam situation, it is not unusual for students to have bad breath. However, in accordance with Goffman's (1967) "protective practices," every attempt is made by the professor to control facial expression so as not to seem to notice it.

In order to create as little disturbance as possible, the students wait until the professors have positioned themselves before engaging in conversation. The usual ritual is that the student places an index finger on the troublesome question and both sets of eyes orient to it. Both are expected to be as quiet as possible. Further, the professor must also face another bind: there is a normative obligation to be helpful but, as one student noted, "not violate professional ethics" by divulging information that "would give the student unfair advantage over others present."[24] These requirements can be most easily achieved by keeping the encounter short and keeping the verbal information communicated to a minimum. Thus, head nods, head shakes, and shrugs of the shoulders are often used as means of communication. This tactic sometimes results in the professor being seen as "closed and cagey . . . careful not to divulge any information that would give away the question."[25] The extensive use of nonverbal communication helps to maintain the expressive order and atmosphere of the exam. Despite all attempts not to disrupt the situation, nearby students invariably listen to the conversation in hopes of gaining valuable "clues". Students who sit nearby and who are also members of the same

23. The closeness involved in answering questions creates some difficulty for Hall's (1966) conceptual system. He indicates that physical closeness with its attendant disclosure (e.g., seeing the veins in the other's eyes, cosmetic work on the face, etc.) tends to be associated with psychological closeness (e.g., scenes of intimacy). Yet, in exam situations, the social and psychological distances between professors and students are at their greatest: "Professors become eagle-eyed disciplinarians and, for this period of time, nobody's friend . . . they don't even look like nice people." The conceptual difficulty is resolved by introducing Argyle and Dean's (1965) equilibrium hypothesis; that is, even though people are physically close, they create distance through acts such as placing their shoulders at 180 degree angles, much like strangers sharing a seat on the bus, rather than in a face-to-face orientation. Eye-contact and talk are kept to a minimum and faces are unexpressive.

24. A professor, who recently emigrated from an eastern European country and was still learning our language and exam customs, looked over a student's shoulder and began to read his answer. The professor read only enough to realize that the student either didn't know or had misinterpreted the question. He began to offer assistance in the form of concrete ideas for a more worthy answer. The embarrassed and almost incredulous student jotted down some of the suggestions and finally informed the professor: "I think it's unfair of you to continue helping me." Here is a situation where a subordinate who has the requisite knowledge is socializing an authority figure as to the norms of his position.

25. Students may exert some form of control over professors. When the information given by professors is clear, students respond with head nods, glances, and finally a terminal nod. When students accompany the head nods with questioning looks, the result is a rerun of the sequence and an increased possibility that "more information can be pried out of them." That is, opening rituals (e.g., greetings) are tightly paired with rituals of departure—the first demands the second. If the ritual of departure is not forthcoming, something is felt to be missing and participants are left in a ritually exposed state. In order to gain closure, professors feel pressured to provide "better explanations," thereby increasing the likelihood of their being "properly" released (i.e., given the terminal nod).

study group as the questioner may get "very riled up" and think that "they must have missed something" because, "if we studied the same material and yet we don't have a question, maybe he's got one up on us."[26] Once the conversation is ended the professor must leave and again cause disturbance for the writers in that particular row. Given these circumstances, it is little wonder that questions come more frequently from individuals who sit near the aisles than from those who sit in the middle of the row.

A. The Exam as a Time-Bound Event

Since exams are also time-bound events, any in-depth discussion of them must involve some aspects of the temporal dimension. Indeed, time becomes something against which the students must compete and they frequently check the large clocks in the gymnasium. An interesting occurrence that appears with some regularity is the removal of the watch from the wrist and the laying of it on top of the desk. If there are no clocks present, it is not at all unusual for students (in panicky voices) to ask the invigilators for the correct time. The request frequently takes a non-verbal form; students raise an arm as if to ask a question and when they catch the examiner's eye, point to the top part of their left wrist (where they would ordinarily wear a watch). The request is readily understood and the examiner usually writes the time on the blackboard for everyone to see or at least to inform the individual concerned. The importance of time is shown in the following illustrations: "I frequently glance at the time, worrying if I have enough left to complete the questions to the best of my ability." This type of thought intensifies the atmosphere and helps to make it a "pressure period."

The importance of the time factor is further emphasized by the fact that a formal announcement of the time is made by the chief invigilator at the end of the second hour in a three-hour exam, and at the end of the first hour in a two-hour exam. This process involves actions similar to the opening ritual (i.e., the invigilator goes to the front of the room, stops in the centre, turns towards the students, and with the least possible disruption states the time in a loud voice). This last point is important because many students are lost in concentration and a loud announcement with no fore-warning can create chaos. For example, one chief invigilator, who was playing the role for the first time, did not excuse himself and boomed out: "Just one hour of writing time left." Heads jerked up, eyebrows flashed, many students literally jumped from their seats, and one student was heard to whisper, in a very irritated tone, "I'm going to shoot that guy." The professor realized the faux pas and responded by lowering

---

26. Occasionally other members of the study group may also raise their hands and ask the professor to repeat the question and the response to it. While such acts are rare, they do show how competitive small study groups can become: "Even if you make 90% and someone else makes 92%, that person still has one up on you . . . besides, in the end, it could be the difference that gets you into medical school."

his eyes and shaking his partially bowed head to indicate "I'm sorry." The effectiveness of the message was evidenced by the ensuing laughter which, in turn, helped to restore the appropriate expressive order.

B. The Atmosphere of Solidarity

Many writers in the exam situation experience a sense of "we-ness" with each other. At first glance, this seems paradoxical because, by their nature, exams are competitive and constraining events. Feelings of solidarity appear to be facilitated by the fact that all examinees are answering the same questions under the same conditions. As one student noted, "Knowing that I am one of many students in the same situation makes me feel a little better." Another person added, "We all write the exam together and I therefore don't feel all alone." Furthermore, each writer contributes to the construction and sustenance of the emergent ethos, which is tied to the capacity of all to concentrate on the task. However, since concentration itself is such a delicate psychological process, each student depends on all the others to control the expression of self-acts like coughing, excessive erasing, and asking frequent questions. Also, students are dependent on each other for the more subtle definitions of reality which concern the nature of the exam. Thus, "If you are not quite sure about how the exam is going or if it is not going as well as it should, you glance at others to find cues as to how you should act or feel." Also, "If you feel that you're whipping through the exam and then, after looking around it appears that other students are having a tough time, you think again about the exam, look it over, and may go more slowly."

Another factor which adds to the solidarity of the situation is that students actually depend on each other for their grades, since grading is usually carried out on a ranked scale: "Every once in a while as I'm writing, I want to know how others are doing—not only for reasons of empathy but because I also want to pick up clues as to how I'm doing relative to them." Thus, the institutional rules of "information preserve" which are found in exams create a situation where each student knows how he/she interpreted and answered the question, but does not know how others have responded. Since all students are graded on the same questions there is a desire to find out how others handled the situation. As Simmel (1969:334) points out, "While secrecy sets barriers between men, it at the same time offers the seductive temptation to break through the barriers." In some ways, then, the exam serves to pull the participants together. Interaction is easier once the exam is over because people are eager to see how others found it.

A feeling of solidarity is also created by the fact that many students have been classmates for at least four and sometimes eight months. Their identity as a group is further enhanced because now they are collectively in the presence of many other strangers (and so the notion of an outgroup categorization becomes salient). The definition of the other classes as the outgroup naturally serves to intensify the ingroup consciousness. Another factor which serves to create a sense of solidarity is that classes occupy specific areas in the gymnasium which are bounded off from the other groups. Therefore, physical boundaries are created which announce to all their membership in a certain social group.

This situation occurs at a time when the reality of the group is about to be dissolved, since final exams are final acts. Indeed, the exam performs ceremonial functions, intensifying the reality of the group as it is about to be dissolved.[27]

C. Accentuation of Hierarchical Differences: Rituals of Subordination and Superordination

Exams accentuate the authority differences between professors and students. Professors have the authority to decide when exams will be written and they design the exams without consultation with students. Students frequently view exams as something professors impose on them (witness the moans and groans when the announcement of a test is made). They view professors as being capable of "forcing" them to spend time studying and "destroying perfectly good weekends." Indeed professors can come to be viewed as despots, "mean persons who put us through all of this hell." During in-class exams the accentuated authority differences are apparent when professors, without giving an account, ask students to leave "their" desks (i.e., an area they have colonized all year) and move to the next one over in order to leave some distance between them and their neighbours. Compliance is virtually absolute whereas, at any other point during the year, students might resist moving. Furthermore, students are subjected to detailed control. In fact, we might compare their situation to that of a total institution, where, in this case, professors and their assistants become enforcing agents for larger institutional structures. This creates a sharp, caste-like division between students and supervisors. The supervisors, of course, are at the top. Goffman (1961b) refers to such positions in total institutions as "inmates" and "staff." Any member of the staff (from the lowliest teaching assistant to the professor) can exercise control over the inmate (student) for such seemingly trivial occurrences as "letting one's eyes wander." The power of sanction is great: "If you are suspected, they will select you out for attention and may even ask you to leave, making you feel about one inch tall." "If asked to leave, it could mean the end of the course and potentially even the end of one's career as a student." While these perceptions are exaggerations of the "objective" state of affairs, they nevertheless demonstrate the felt differences in power between positions: "I

27. Exams not only serve as the basis for class rites of intensification, but classes, like other groups when they are about to die, make an all out last ditch effort at survival by gathering their energies and spontaneously resurging just at the moment of dissolution. Several other factors help to intensify this meaning. First, exams are held in a much larger setting than usual, and size is frequently associated with importance. Second, there are many more authority figures and students present than usual. Third, exams involve the whole class, with virtually no persons missing.

feel further removed from my professors than ever before— it's like exams exaggerate whatever status differences exist between us." "However friendly you may otherwise be, you can no longer joke with professors or even consult them." Thus the "looser" role relationships which characterize everyday student-professor interactions are now so "tightened" that they leave little room for the "selves" of the participants to peek through and display their individuality.

These hard divisions of power and authority are further accentuated by the nonverbal symbolism of the occasion. First, the availability of and control over space symbolizes status. In the exam situation, each student is given equal space, the boundaries of which are marked by the high walls of their "stalls", to indicate uniformity of status. Students must remain quiet and relatively fixed within their "containers" while the staff can move anywhere in the room, engage in quiet conversation, and observe students or their papers. The only persons the student can acknowledge are professors, and even then they must be discrete, since frequent glances not only distract from the task at hand but also arouse suspicion. One student expressed the contrast in perspectives this way: "The professor walks around with roaming eyes, while the student remains in one place, tense, eyes glued to the paper, and gets writer's cramp." These features are further reinforced by the fact that supervisors stand and tower over the students who usually labour at their tasks with bowed heads. The fact that professors are silent during this occasion is also noteworthy, because students have no idea what they are thinking about. These, then, are some of the rituals that tend to increase feelings of subordination.

The extreme self-consciousness of students regarding suspicious readings they think invigilators might give their acts is explained by Lofland (1976:54–5) who indicates, "Acute strategic consciousness seems to be the consciousness of underdogs . . . they become highly sensitive to the impression their actions are making on the overdog." Argyle and Williams (1969) experimentally verified that subordinates in role relationships (i.e., interviewee versus interviewer, adolescent versus older person, young female versus young male) feel more self-conscious and demonstrate a greater concern with self-presentation. The extreme forms of consciousness verging on paranoia that we described earlier can now be viewed as a normal reflection of extreme differences in power that come with exams. Consistently, students who are least well prepared (i.e., most subordinate on the hierarchy) are the most self-conscious. They have the greatest difficulty losing themselves in the dominant involvement and consequently put more effort into giving off the impression that they are hard at work. They are also the ones most easily distracted by invigilators walking up and down the aisles and most concerned about concealing answers from them. A related finding by Argyle and Williams (1969) also helps to make sense of why students are so self-conscious even though invigilators tend not to do much deliberate searching for acts of deviance (in fact invigilators are much more concerned with answering questions and bringing extra exam booklets to students as quickly as possible). They demonstrate that actual observation by others has little effect on how highly subjects feel they are observed. The key variable resides in the relationship of subordination. Thus, even though invigilators do little direct looking for acts of deviance, we would expect students who occupy positions of subordination to feel closely observed.

D. Transformations

The exam, as mentioned earlier, is marked by a special boundary which excludes many factors that would normally be permitted in other closely related frames like the classroom. Books and note pads are deposited at the front or excluded from the exam room altogether; this serves to remove a potential source of framework tension. Food or snacks are prohibited in the examination setting, although it is not unusual to see students eating their lunches during a regular lecture (especially if the classroom is very large). Also, friends or interested persons who are usually welcome in classrooms are barred from the examination room.

Aspects of the larger world which are allowed to penetrate the situation become transformed in their meaning. Hence, the exam becomes a world with a moral alchemy all its own, transforming whatever passes through it. For example, the room in which the exam is written is somehow changed from a place of sociable pleasures (basketball or other sports, socials, films, etc.) to "the place that is approached with fear and dread." One of the basic characteristics that pervades the examination room is the presence of a context of suspicion which leaves its tinge on everything. As students enter the examination room they become aware of the fact that not only are they transformed into non-persons but also that they are now non-persons who cannot be trusted. This message is implicitly conveyed by the arrangement of the writing areas as well as by the presence of extra staff whose only real function is to "keep an eye" on the writers and ensure that actions fall within the rules of the occasion. Persons who enter as professors are also transformed into supervisors, invigilators, or proctors and students frequently see them in even less sympathetic ways as "patrolmen on the look-out for cheaters" or "watchdogs". Although students are permitted to write their exams in close proximity to each other, the introduction of plywood dividers (though appreciated by most for the privacy they afford)[28] prevents students from having eye contact with

28. Students, when questioned, reported that they did not necessarily find these walls to be aversive. They noted that when one must think "hard and fast," it is preferable to have a setting that reduces the number of potential distractions and provides more space within which to write and think. This notion is supported by observations of examinations held in the classroom setting. In this situation, many students will, if space permits, spread out and away from their neighbours. Hall (1966:95) quotes a passage from Thoreau's Walden which is perhaps also applicable to exam writers: "One inconvenience I sometimes experienced in so small a house was the difficulty of getting to a sufficient distance from my guest when we began to utter the big thoughts in big words." Note that when we are discussing difficult thoughts we prefer to do so at some distance. Touch, at these times, is difficult to tolerate because it is just not part of the frame.

their neighbours or from seeing their papers. The implication is that students cannot all be fully trusted. Students aptly call these dividers "cheat partitions." The dividers visually remind the writers of the ever present moral precepts against cheating. Thus the vast number of rules and physical supports come together to "contain" and "insulate" students from each other in a "normative cocoon." One implicit norm is that the plywood dividers are to remain in position and may not be rearranged to suit the tastes of individuals. Not only are writers physically contained in a box-like area but their movements within it are also tightly circumscribed. Hands are expected to be "on desk". Placing hands under the desk or in pockets can arouse suspicion. Movement of the trunk of the body is also limited. The permissible arc a body may describe ranges from an angle of about 90 degrees to an angle of 20 degrees, which allows a reading and writing position for even the most short-sighted of students. Leaning back involves a stretching of the norms as well as the body: "With these professors continually walking around, you sometimes feel you can't even tilt your head." Even the conduct of the eyes is regulated: "roaming eyes are not permitted . . . and if you must look around, make it obvious to everyone you're not looking at someone else's exam." Writers are continually reminded of the boundaries of their world by the implicit normative message contained in the spatial arrangements, "Don't look over or beyond." "Even though I'm writing the exam and would like to get an overall view of the setting I find I cannot make myself turn my head for fear of being sanctioned for violating the non-gazing rule." "The solemn faces of the professors, as they authoritatively walk up and down, say 'Don't you dare'."[29]

The context of suspicion is further enhanced by the fact that approximately one-half hour after the exam begins the invigilators pass or bring around

29. We observed quite contrasting behaviours in a group of United States undergraduates who were taking an in-class test. Essentially, they exhibited much looser styles of demeanor— they looked about much more frequently, leaned back in their desks, and, where space permitted, propped their legs on the desk ahead of them. Some students who were sitting next to walls angled their bodies and used the radiators as props for their legs. Such postural displays are relatively infrequent among Canadian students, and yet they were observed in as many as one-third of the American students. There are several possible explanations for these differences. On the whole, American society tends to be more informal than Canadian society. As Friedenberg (1980) expresses it: "American society itself is less like a school and feels less like a school than Canadian society." Differences in posture can be linked to differential levels of anxiety; one Canadian student who had attended and taken exams at both American and Canadian universities indicates: "While I felt nervous and tense the week before and during exams in the California system, it was never as intense as here . . . in the other system, if you don't do well, you can always write a supplemental. Furthermore, everything is so much more formal here . . . it's even evident in the names we give to the event (test versus exam) and the staff (teacher versus professor or invigilator)." Further insight into the differences between the two countries comes from the instrumental and expressive meaning Canadian students attribute to their postures: "Leaning intently towards my desk helps me to concentrate better." "In an exam setting, a lax posture conveys laziness." "Slouching shows disrespect for the professors and the setting." The latter observations are particularly consistent with Lipset's (1964) perception that Canadians are more elitist than Americans, and Friedenberg's (1980:261) observation that Canadians are "more than normally prone to respect their betters, and demand a corresponding respect from their own subordinates."

a sheet of paper on which students must sign their names and enter their seat number. This practice actually serves as a safeguard for both student and professor. For example, if a student did not sign the sheet, the professor would be protected from any charge that an examination paper had been misplaced or lost. By the same token, students are protected because their signature indicates that they did indeed write the exam and turned in a paper.[30] The exam situation even transforms the manner in which one responds to biological needs. During a regular class the student will slip quietly out the back door and reenter in the same way while in the exam situation one must raise one's hand[31] and ask permission to leave. When this permission is granted, one is expected to be accompanied by a same-sex invigilator. The identity of professor now temporarily becomes that of "washroom warden."

One might pose the question, "why go to such elaborate lengths?" Students tend to perceive these actions as a normal part of the world of exams and, as one noted, "it imposes a sense of honesty on you." Indeed, some students freely admit they would experience a greater urge to cheat if the controls were not present. Here are some of their remarks: "When I see an uncovered paper, I'm always tempted to look at the answer;" "If a person was guaranteed he wouldn't get caught cheating, he probably would." While the impulse to cheat may always be present for some, there are several levels of control, ranging from internalization and self-sanction to the realization that when we look around we are encroaching upon another's personal space. Encroachment functions to make both the one encroached upon and the invader feel uncomfortable (Barefoot, Hoople, & McClay, 1972), and if it does occur it is not unusual to see students "crouch over their papers and locate a strategic arm" in an attempt to re-establish the boundaries of their territory: "If someone on your right or left drops something and they go to pick it up, you automatically cover up your exam." Presumably this is done not only to suit the demands of immediate normative behaviour but also for protection: "If tests are marked, and answers are found to be the same, you could be accused of cheating. The question in this case would be, who cheated off whom?" Since isolating one's paper effectively eliminates this problem, those who are not sufficiently vigilant are seen as accomplices conspiring in the act. Although the rate of cheating here is probably less than in normal classroom exams, it does still occur. Many students who witness these acts tend to be angered, especially at professors for "not doing their job." Students seem to attribute much greater

30. At the end of the exam, the papers are counted and the number is matched with the exam roll. If the numbers are equal, the professor presents the exam roll to the chief invigilator who signs it and then carries all of these rolls over to the administration building for safekeeping.

31. During a regular class, the raising of a hand would be acknowledged by professors but would not likely result in a change of their physical location. In an exam professors come to the student's desk. Also, the process of requesting permission to go to the bathroom would likely be seen as an actual disruption in a normal classroom setting (out of frame) while in the exam situation it is a normative act.

powers of perception to the invigilators than is actually possible; indeed, invigilators infrequently catch students in the act, and if they do, they tend to be reluctant to push the point. In fact, when professors do happen on such acts, they tend to be taken by surprise (e.g., eyes rounded, eyebrows raised and mouth dropped) and embarrassed (e.g., show signs of disorientation and reddening of the face). These reactions can be explained by the fact that most don't expect or especially look for such acts. Also, the identities of both professor and student are built up and maintained by adhering to the legitimate rules of the occasion; when jarring acts on the part of one individual "break the harmony", the foundation upon which the identities of both depend is suddenly gone. Consequently, the identities of both individuals are no longer tenable and the result is reciprocal embarrassment. Signs of embarrassment on the part of students are taken as evidence that an offence has indeed occurred. When signs of embarrassment are not present, professors are less likely to take action because they fear they might "discover that the other's show of innocence was not merely a show, and that the exposer [may be] exposed at wrongly exposing" (Goffman, 1974:343). Furthermore, invigilators are often reluctant to pursue the issue because of the drastic consequences for the student. Thus, the usual response is an attempt to inconspicuously sanction and control the cheating before it goes too far.

Students are aware of the dire consequences of these situations, and by far the majority of them wish to be viewed as persons who are above reproach. This brings about a heightened concern over the meaning their acts may have for invigilators and, as a result, some of their actions become exaggerated (i.e., they engage in acts of dramatic realization). For example, to reach in one's pocket or purse for a tissue, a cough candy, or a pen is no longer a completely neutral act; in an attempt to give off the appropriate impression that no cheating is intended, students move slowly and, when the desired object is located, it is often openly displayed.[32] Such exaggerated acts of honesty moderate feelings of anxiety by insuring that they are "properly interpreted." Perhaps the most vivid example is provided by females who must "root around" in their purses for the desired object. Failure to locate the object immediately results in a high degree of embarrassment and students have even been observed to raise their hands and provide a verbal explanation of their behaviour to the invigilator; some even feel they "are being dishonest in some way."

Also, if students wish to borrow something from a neighbour, they raise their hands and request permission to do so.[33] When permission is granted the

---

32. Goffman (1971) would refer to these as "body glosses." These actions clearly suggest that the writers are aware of how their behaviour appears to others (invigilators) and that they monitor it to show it has an acceptable purpose. This is a central assumption of symbolic interactional theory.

33. In the lecture frame such actions would be viewed as disturbing. Indeed, students show respect for the dominant involvement (lecture or class discussion) by quietly asking their neighbours if they can borrow the instrument.

students work to keep their eyes fixed on each other's faces as the request is made and then focus on "safe" objects as the transfer is made. These transactions are characterized by their brevity. Another interesting aspect of this situation is manifested in the manner in which the writers deal with writing-related concerns like a cramped neck. Students often report that they experience constraints in terms of how they can relieve such symptoms—"I feel loath to twist my head around or even lean back for fear of being accused of taking a look at someone else's paper." One solution which is widely used is to tilt the head back as far as it will go, while keeping the eyes closed. Students who wear glasses tend to remove them before engaging in any such activities and so, as one reported, "couldn't cheat if I tried."

In the classroom setting the professor provides the main focus of interaction but this is not the case in the examination situation. Indeed, students who spend a great deal of time watching the invigilators usually end up provoking their suspicions. Also, a conversation between students in the classroom is often interpreted by the professor as an attempt to clarify information. If the student does speak out directly in class, it is in a voice which can be heard by all. Such behaviours in the exam situation are interpreted as cheating or an indication of mental illness.

Other phenomena also undergo transformations in the exam setting. For example, time in both its material and non-material forms takes on a new meaning. If no clocks are present, blackboards are transformed from a learning-tool into something of a time piece.[34] Furthermore, clock watching in the exam has a different meaning from clock watching in the everyday work world. In the everyday world, bored and alienated workers count the minutes until their day is finished, a process which also occurs in most routine lecture situations. Workers and students depart from their respective situations at the first available opportunity. During the exam, though, time becomes an enemy against which one struggles. Students frequently hang on to the very last moment before their examination papers are taken from them and "try to 'steal' whatever time" they can by continuing to write after the official time limit is past.

Other material objects[35] which undergo a transformation in the exam situation are the chairs and desks. One student noted, "At home or in empty classrooms, a chair is seen as a means of relaxation; now it is a place of work." Even the relaxed posture in an exam has slightly negative connotations of not concentrating, while in the larger world a relaxed posture may indicate some measure of composure or sophistication. The pen which is usually a tool for recording someone else's thoughts now becomes a device for transmission of the student's own creation.

---

34. In a sense, then, chief invigilators also become transformed into momentary time pieces.
35. Study notes, which have a positive connotation (hard worker) outside of the exam room, become transformed into objects of infamy—"cheat notes"—in the exam room.

While the exam is written on paper, a real substance, it also undergoes a transformation that might best be thought of in terms of a transmutation (Durkheim, 1954). The exam can be viewed as a social representation of the class. It is set by the most basic representative of the class, the professor. Furthermore, the questions are usually designed to tap the intellectual experiences which the class, as a collectivity, has shared. Exam questions also stimulate the student to recall the accumulated stock of social knowledge, making it immediately relevant. Re-searching the group's collective past serves not only to place experiences in a somewhat new perspective, but also to revitalize them. Hence the exam is social in its content, as well as in the fact that it is written in the presence of others. Note, though, that the exam is also a representation of the writer's self, a means of displaying an attribute which in this setting is at the core of ego, that is, intelligence. Thus, the shared intellectual past is individually recalled, evaluated, and presented.

Since the exam comes to be viewed as an objective embodiment or representation of the professor, the students, and their relationship to each other, one would indeed expect—following Durkheim—that the paper upon which the exam is written will undergo a transmutation and emerge as an object which carries with it a sense of the sacred. Some possible evidence for this notion can be noted by examining the elaborate rituals involved in its preparation and presentation; looking at another student's exam can virtually constitute an act of intrusion into a sacred realm. Further, final exams are treated with much more reverence than are ordinary assignments by the professor and the administration alike. To illustrate, exams are matched with student signatures and counted to be sure this number tallies with the total number on the exam roll. Finally, after the exams are graded, they are returned to the administrative offices and retained for a period of two years; only then are they destroyed.

E. Departure Rituals and Conclusions

Interestingly enough, even though exams are unpleasant events for almost all students, "no one wants to be first" to hand in his/her paper and leave! One frequently mentioned reason for this is the perceived impression such acts might create, especially in cases where an individual completes the exam in much less time than others: "Questions arise as to whether that person is actually finished or simply giving up." In an even more negative light: "If persons leave [too] early, there is usually general concensus that they did not know their material and probably bombed out." Others feel guilty about disturbing the silent working atmosphere of the exam. Also, the first person to leave breaks the existing pattern of action and feels "somehow awkward and embarrassed because most everyone looks at you."[36]

Students also fear that the professor will begin to read the exam and give off cues, usually via facial expressions, as to how they will eventually fare. Students expect such information to be strictly confidential and not to be broadcast to their classmates.[37] When several papers have been handed in the situation is no longer so problematic because now others do not know whose paper is being scrutinized. Indeed, students sometimes slip their exams into the middle of the pile so this situation cannot occur. Finally, and consistent with theories of anxiety and affiliation, a significant reason that students provide for not wanting to be the first to leave the exam is: "I couldn't stand the tension of waiting outside for someone else to finish so we can talk over the questions and all." Consequently, students who complete the exam early tend to remain. Given the working atmosphere which pervades exams they feel the need to "look busy" and ritually "check over" their paper, while at the same time remaining alive to cues from others that they are also finished. Thus, there is now selective attention to others' actions which a short time ago would have been ignored (selective inattention). One student noted she used the professor's face as a rear view mirror to see what was going on behind her. Another tactic frequently used is tentatively to begin gathering up papers and pens; if such action is repeated by others, the frame is set for at least a couple of people to stand up and leave. Occasionally this sets the stage for a mass exodus.[38] On the other hand, some students are reluctant to leave at the same time as the person beside them for fear the professor might think they've been cheating. During the leave-taking process every attempt is made not to disturb others or to mar the seriousness of the occasion. Leave-taking itself can be a problematic process since students may feel "dizzy" after concentrating so hard in such cramped conditions. It is not all that unusual for students accidently to bump one of the plywood partitions. The ensuing noise makes the offender the centre of attention. This loss of control over props (Gross and

36. Students who "know their stuff cold" feel fewer such constraints. Indeed, occasionally they even see it as an opportunity to demonstrate their "smarts": "If you finish before anyone else it just means you're mentally 'quicker' than they are."

37. Students expect this relationship to be kept on a one-to-one basis. Any deviation, as for example reading the exam while the examination is still in progress, constitutes a frame break.

38. During exams where many students finish before the deadline, those left behind are affected: "It breaks my concentration and makes me feel dumb for being so slow." Others who feel guilty about their lack of studying see it as a "sign that I must not have prepared well enough. It leads me to hurry through the rest of the exam so I can be like the others who are talking in the hallway."

Stone, 1970) leads to a feeling of embarrassment[39] and is usually followed by a non-verbal apology which might take the form of lowering the head and shaking it in disgust.[40]

At the end of the examination period, the chief invigilator makes the ritual announcement, "Time is up". The response is much muttering and a flurry of last-minute activity as a few students try to "steal" a few more minutes to note those all-important last points. This is only the case if students are fortunate enough to have an answer in mind because increased motivation enhances the emission of dominant responses (Zajonc, 1965). On the other hand, for less well-prepared students who don't have an answer, the urgency of the situation along with the complexity of the task calling for original thought will, consistent with Zajonc and the more general Yerkes-Dodson law, produce disorganizing results: "I suddenly ignore the question and begin to write everything I know about the subject." The second request to cease writing brings a "feeling of relief" to most students, but for those who have rational answers in mind, it can become a real problem to separate them from their exam papers, which are symbolic representations of themselves.

When all exams have been handed in, professors count the number of examination booklets and compare them to the number of signatures on the examination roll. If the numbers correspond, the chief invigilator signs an official statement to this effect and then files it with the student records office. Finally, when invigilators are satisfied that all examination papers are accounted for, they tend to take a final "tour of inspection" and check for anything students might have left behind them (e.g., books, purses, sweaters, etc.). The exam phase normally ends with the ritual of invigilators switching off the lights as they leave. Meanwhile, students move out into other areas and begin to engage in post-exam interactions.

39. Embarrassment is based in part on the fact that the body must continually give the appearance of being in a state of readiness to interact, and any evidence to the contrary (as in the case of clumsiness) may produce it. In any social transaction, certain activities are called for—they are in the foreground of attention and termed dominant activities. On the other hand, others—to be disattended or at least relegated to a background role—are termed side activities. This distinction is similar to Goffman's notion of main and side involvements. Behaviours like getting up and walking out of the exam room ought to be side activities. However, knocking over a divider during a final exam or dropping an armful of books after an in-class test are cases where side activities accidentally become dominant ones. In the process adjunct identities (e.g., students walking out) become dominant identities (i.e., the centre of attention and exposing selves as "real Klutzs").

40. Once the paper is handed in, an implicit rule dictates that one does not remain in the exam room but must wait for friends outside the door.

Phase IV—The Post Exam

The post-exam phase serves as a transition between the discipline and strains (i.e., "tightness") of the exam phase and the more diffuse (i.e., "looser") role expectations associated with everyday life. Essentially, it provides students with an opportunity for permissive release. As Schwartz (1970:485) points out, "every social organization exhibits structural features which both guarantee the regular performance of duties and ensure release from such performances." The more elaborate role-release behaviour takes place in back regions which are areas that are "bounded by barriers to perception" (Goffman, 1959:106). In the case of students, post-exam interactions make exams more bearable and so serve as important modes of social control.

Post-exam interactions provide another opportunity to examine how people cope with uncertainty, stress, and anxiety. As we noted earlier in Chapters II and III, both Malinowski (1954) and Schachter (1959) assert that people cope through acts of hyperaffiliation. Schachter draws on Festinger's (1954) assumption that there exists in people a drive to evaluate their opinions and abilities. Comparing oneself to others reduces uncertainty and anxiety. The assumed basic motive behind the comparison process is accuracy. However, Goffman (1959) questions Festinger's assumption that people are motivated solely by accuracy since too accurate a comparison might prove threatening. He suggests that there are pervasive, unspoken, institutionalized rules to protect individuals from such contingencies; for "without such mercies . . . unsatisfactory persons would be left to bleed to death from the conversational savageries performed on them" (Goffman, 1971:68–9). Goffman also assumes a vast store of individualized strategies designed to protect and enhance one's sense of self.

One objective of science is generalization obtained from demonstrating that concepts and propositions apply consistently from one situation to another and over time. While we found considerable support for Schachter's theory of affiliation across all phases of the exam act, there is some need for modification. In the pre-exam phase we demonstrated the need to balance the accuracy motive behind the social comparison process with the desire for self-enhancement. Furthermore, although Schachter explicitly eliminates mental diversion from a miserable situation as one reason for affiliation, we found convincing evidence of its presence and suggest his rejection may have been a bit hasty. In addition, monitoring the developing interactions allows us to go beyond

Schachter to suggest not only why anxious people are propelled toward affiliation but also why some are propelled away from it. Post-exam interactions also provide another situation where we can examine the affiliation hypothesis since students have now completed their ordeal (as compared to the pre-exam phase and Schachter's original hypothesis testing situation where subjects were observed prior to the time when they were supposedly to be shocked). In the post-exam phase the theoretical conditions for affiliation are still present since students are anxious and uncertain as to how they fared so this phase provides us with yet another opportunity to see how well Schachter's hypotheses about behaviour and our modifications of them become translated into actual affiliative behaviour.

As students leave the exam room and close the doors behind them, they are finally freed from the tight regulations and seemingly ever-watchful eyes of the invigilators. This move from front region where the main performance is given in full view of authority figures, to back region is marked by varying types of role-release behaviour. For example, students sometimes stop just outside the doors of the exam room and heave audible sighs. One such "heaver" explained the sigh was meant to convey that "It's so good to get out of there." "Finished!" "The End." Smokers almost invariably light up cigarettes and inhale deeply. On rare occasions, individuals (usually females) turn around to face the door and stick out their tongues. Males more frequently flash an upraised middle finger and, for added emphasis, may hit the elbow of the raised arm with the palm of the other hand. A more elaborate, typically male, form of emotional release associated with the last exam of the year consists of a few wild yelps accompanied by a leap or two towards the ceiling.

As the theories of stress would predict, students also demonstrate a heightened orientation to others who have already gathered following the exam. This heightened awareness extends even to starting conversations with strangers: "Something extraordinary occurs . . . you will just approach others and start up a conversation with them even though you don't know them by name or even by face." Female students point out that exams are one occasion which gives them license to "initiate interactions with male strangers and yet not convey sexual connotations." This sudden sense of comaraderie is in some measure brought about because the participants have shared a "joint ordeal." In turn, this joint ordeal provides a readily available opening line: "What did you think of it?" Indeed, most students report and demonstrate an eagerness to engage in the social comparison process: "Even though it's too late to do anything about it, I like to find out as much as I can about how I did on the exam and about where I fit relative to others." Since there are as yet no objective criteria with which to compare oneself, students, in accordance with Festinger's (1954) notions, rely on a social reality produced by searching each other out. Furthermore, as Festinger predicts, when representatives from several different classes are available for interaction, students for the most part orient themselves to others in their own class.

1. Accuracy and Self-Enhancement Motives in the Management of Anxiety in the Post-Exam Phase

Contrary to Festinger's predictions, however, only a few students are interested solely in accuracy of feedback. Once again the ones who are so interested tend to be those who feel most confident about their performance. Since their exam-related role identities are secure, they can afford to be motivated by such elite and objective concerns. Most other students harbour varying degrees of doubt as to their performance and are concerned not only with accuracy but also with the implications for achieving and maintaining a positive sense of self even at the expense of accuracy: "When comparing answers, I find that it's me that's on the line and so I'm on edge. My defense mechanisms are on the alert and ready to work at the slightest threat." Indeed, students usually elect to interact with others who appear most compatible (i.e., the least threatening) and in so doing, adopt a variety of masking strategies (e.g., acts of guarded or contrived disclosure) where any claims regarding self are hedged with qualifications supplemented by rituals of apology and accounts. One student who felt most inadequate about her performance noted that after leaving the examination "I looked for others from our class who looked as miserable as I felt; I wanted to be comforted with the impression that I wasn't alone." Such students make initial selections based largely on nonverbal cues: "I look for those who look like they've done about the same or even worse than me . . . those who look depressed, tired and deflated . . . their bodies droop and their faces just seem to hang from their hair." As these statements indicate, when accuracy of information threatens to discredit selves, individuals will give highest priority to maintaining the integrity of their role identities. Given the competitive nature of exam writing, even students who feel relatively confident may experience some measure of anxiety as they leave the exam. One male student who felt that he had done well still feared that his friends, who were also consistently top performers, may have done even better. He reports: "When comparing yourself with your friends, you are putting yourself out for public view. Should you turn out to be subordinate, it's not only embarrassing but it might set a permanent lower status relation with them in the future." This can lead, in the words of another student, "to always hoping that others didn't do any better, or, even better, that they didn't do as well."

If post-exam interactions are to be characterized by an air of sociability, one central rule must be the suppression or masking of any element of open competition. Thus, although each student knows the other as a competitor, each pretends that this is not the case. One top performer elaborates upon the situation this way: "During discussions [of the exam questions] with peers, all that goes through my mind is the phrase, 'I hope I did better than they did.' But you can't let this be noticed because it would create grudges and maybe even ruin friendships." This "working agreement" (Goffman, 1959) which characterizes post-exam occasions can be seen to inhibit further the exchange of accurate information. Once in an encounter, students employ acts of guarded disclosure to "size up" their exam-related identities: "I always like to know how others fared before I volunteer any information." The reasons given for such guarded disclosure centre around loss of control over the interactional situation or, more generally, the fear of being discredited: "I'm afraid of immediately telling others how I found the exam for fear they don't share my plight." On the other hand, those who feel they have done well fear negative reactions from others who found the test difficult: "Because of the competitive nature of exams, I'm hesitant to reveal how I found it. Not only would I arouse antagonism on the part of many, but I'd also be considered a gloater, a braggart, and an outcast to most." Often persons who feel they have done well seem to enjoy moving from encounter to encounter and, when the situation calls for it, they are quick to console others. This freedom of action would be curtailed were they to provide an accurate assessment of their position.

Because of these difficulties, initial interactions tend to have a hesitant quality about them; they are likely to begin with such global generalizations as, "Isn't it nice to get that over with?" or, on a somewhat more focused level, "How did you find it?" Answers, in turn, tend to be vague and non-commital: "I don't know for sure," or "It's the type of exam where you don't know how well you did until you get your mark back." Such a response is "not only the safest reply, but also the most polite." Also, it "could be pleasing to the listener because it suggests uncertainty" on the part of the speaker. In such a situation, students are protecting "selves" against compromise by exposing information in small doses and waiting for responses from others before proceeding. If they sense others' performances are along lines similar to their own the topic soon is narrowed down to what they call the "real point" (e.g., "What did you put down for question 10? You know, the one . . ."). The impact of the request is frequently softened by divulging one's answer and "hoping and praying your answer is the same as his." This strategy almost always works because the other now knows where you stand and you seem less threatening. At the same time, the rules of tact learned during socialization obligate support for the extended self (Goffman, 1959). Disclosing the answer first perhaps signals that one trusts the other sufficiently to believe that the exposure will be received in some acceptable fashion. The other, following Gouldner's (1961) norm of reciprocity, feels obligated to reciprocate since "If he trusts me, I can trust him." Frequently, persons who feel quite uncertain about their performance and yet wish to engage in the exchange of answers start with a question they are certain they answered correctly. Likewise some receivers attempt to save face by engaging in acts of controlled disclosure such as stating that they provided the same answer when, in fact, they did not. On occasion, however, even this strategy fails because some students simply refuse to discuss exam questions as a matter of policy. Even though they may indicate "Gee, I'm sorry but I never exchange answers after an exam" and offer accounts as to why they will not, the interaction tends to end abruptly. Each then looks for more compatible company.

As more students finish the exam, interaction tends to take on a highly fluid character, with conversational circles forming, quickly dissolving, and reforming as individuals "browse and search" rather than conform to the opinions or moods of a particular group: "It's hard to participate in a discussion when your thoughts and feelings are in opposition to those of the majority." Students who feel more secure in their performance may search for encounters where the discussion centres around questions they're unsure about (i.e., social comparison based on accuracy). On the other hand, students who feel less secure may only join and remain in an encounter as long as the discussion focuses on questions they feel confident about: "When others begin to talk about questions I don't feel I've answered well, I try to deflect them to the ones I feel confident about. If I can't, I'll leave. I don't like feeling inferior." At times the circulation of individuals is so fluid that the "group" may maintain its approximate size, yet change its entire composition in the space of a few minutes. Through this sifting and sorting process compatible others are eventually found, and friends who finished the exam at varying times are reunited. At this point encounters become more stable.

As the area outside the exam room begins to fill, individuals stand much closer to each other than they ordinarily would; talk speeds up, gestures become more animated, and voices rise to compete with the increasing level of background noise. Occasionally there is a cheer when a number of students discover they have provided the same answer and assume, because of the agreement, that it must be correct. This intensification of interaction can give the setting a carnival-like atmosphere which, in turn, may disturb others who are still writing. Even though invigilators may come out of the exam room and ask the assembled horde to "move on" or "tone-down," the result is not usually permanent, for within a few minutes the noise level begins to increase again.

When most students in an encounter agree on the "correct" answers there is a "comfortable, assured, and occasionally jubilant" atmosphere. There are, however, always those who have selected other, presumably wrong, answers. They feel the need to engage in "face-work" to "make-up" for their compromised position: "I thought that was the right answer, but my choice looked right, too." There is almost always agreement from someone else in the group; individuals support one another so that no one is "judged as stupid." At the same time other students are thinking to themselves: "I had that answer. Why did I go and change it, especially when I swore after the last test that I'd never go back and change answers again." If several people chose an alternative answer, the discussion may become lively as they argue over the merits of "their" choice. Before the interaction "gets out of hand," intermediaries usually move in to smooth over the differences. If the minority group is not satisfied with the exchange, they may well move on to look for others who agree with them.

Selves can easily be compromised in post-exam encounters and, as Goffman predicts, we find numerous tactful acts of social support, especially from students who feel secure in their performance. In the case of multiple choice tests, for example, students often say "I chose 'B' but I could be wrong," even though they know they were correct. Others remark, "There could be two right answers for that question," or, in the case of an essay question, "The Prof. will probably read between the lines and understand you know it, even though you didn't say it outright." While this polite fiction can be a source of social support, it also works against the accuracy of social comparisons. More overt acts of social support may be observed when someone hears general consensus for other responses and blurts out, "Oh no, I'm going to fail." One top-ranking student states: "When this occurs, my automatic response is to lean towards them and suggest they'll probably do just fine." A related tactic is negative bargaining, where one person whose performance is uncertain may mime a knifing slash across his throat. Someone else then asserts, "No, it's I who am going to fail," followed by others who say the same thing. The first person usually then responds, "No, I'm sure you're all going to pass—it's just I who am going to fail." While "deep down" students may doubt the accuracy of these statements, they are nevertheless effective: "It's just what you want to hear." Furthermore, "some who say they haven't done well are just plain telling the truth in hopes that someone will offer sympathy to bolster their sagging ego." "Such people give great comfort and support just by virtue of the fact they may have done even worse than you. Even if this isn't exactly the case, it's still reinforcing to hear others say they didn't do well either. Let's admit it, misery loves company and no one likes to suffer alone."

One of the strongest unspoken rules governing post-exam interaction is that students who know they have done well do not mention the fact before "beleagured others." However, as with all norms there are deviations, and an occasional transgressor may announce with a smile: "Boy, did I ace that one. I'll bet I got at least 95% on it." Such "gloaters" are "easy to dislike. They are the type who kick people when they're down." "At this point, even the most peace-loving person gets the urge to kick the nearest object" or "grab the bastard's throat and squeeze it." While students may have these inclinations, we have never actually seen them carried out.

The general result is that most students understate their probable level of achievement and, by so doing, add to the solidarity of the encounter. The feeling of commonality also works to conceal their potential identity as competitors for grades: "Even though I knew I had done better than most, I didn't let on . . . it increases our feelings of togetherness, because it's easier to identify with people who say they've done poorly." Others understate their potential levels of achievement because of social pressure: "Since the majority say they found the test difficult, I feel I must fit in if I'm to be accepted." Still other students see underestimating probable performance as a means of avoiding discrediting themselves in the future if they don't happen to do as well as they thought they had: "I actually say I've done worse than I think I have to protect myself from possible future embarrassment. It would be foolish to give myself more credit than I actually deserve." Occasionally students suggest that it is a way of adapting to the worst of all possible outcomes: "It prepares me for failure, especially since it's a distinct possibility."

While the various concealment practices do make for a more supportive atmosphere, they reduce the accuracy of information required for social comparison. As we noted, most students place greater priority on self-enhancement than on accuracy, especially as we move down the performance ladder. Students who feel they performed least well tend to lose interest in accuracy and devote themselves entirely to seeking support via account-making from others who share their "plight", thereby adding some credence to Schachter's notion that "misery loves only miserable company."

2. Protective Self-Management Strategies

A. Sharing Accounts

There are always a number of students who find that not only are their answers different but they are also probably wrong. Instead of apologizing, they may finally release their frustrations with a string of profanities. Discussing the exam "only succeeds in making you feel worse." Besides, "you can't just stand there and accept the possibility of failure because it's like admitting to being a dummy—it's too humiliating." A student who feels this way is forced to adjust "to an impossible situation—a situation arising from having defined himself in a way which the social facts come to contradict" (Goffman, 1952:456). In effect, the person who enrolls in a class makes claim to competence sufficient to pass the course and this competence is now being questioned. The person "must therefore be supplied with a new set of apologies for himself, a new framework in which to see himself and judge himself" (Goffman, 1952:456). These persons frequently attempt to protect their student role identities by seeking out others who are no longer comparing answers to questions, but rather engaging in account-making.

Given the fact that exams are designed to differentiate performance levels, conditions ensure a recurrent and somewhat standardized "vocabulary of motives" (Mills, 1940) which can be catalogued along lines suggested by Scott and Lyman (1968). Accounts[1] can be classified as excuses or justifications.

---

1. Scott and Lyman (1968) define an account as "a linguistic device employed whenever an action is subjected to valuative inquiry," whether by persons themselves or by others. Accounts are likely to be invoked when people do something they, or their audiences consider "bad", "inept", "wrong", or "unwelcome." A key feature of accounts is moral management which is to be distinguished from questioning that involves cognitive management (i.e., explanations versus accounts). Motives are not to be seen as the "real" spurs to action: rather, they are transacted words which attempt to legitimate or provide "adequate grounds for . . . conduct" (Mills, 1940:900).

Excuses "are accounts in which one admits that the act in question [i.e., failing] is bad, wrong, or inappropriate but denies full responsibility." The responsibility lies in factors that are not under one's control. Justifications "are accounts in which one accepts responsibility for the act in question but denies the pejorative quality associated with it" (Scott and Lyman, 1968:47). In terms of a vocabulary of motives, excuses are by far the most frequent type of account provided. Excuses can be subclassified as scapegoating, defeasibility, and appeal to biological drives. After a difficult exam the most frequent excuse takes the form of scapegoating, where behaviour is viewed as "a response to the behaviour or attitudes of another", on whom they "sluff off" the burden of responsibility for their actions (Scott and Lyman, 1968:50): "When I do poorly, I usually hold it against the Prof for being so rough." "That exam was totally unfair, you'd think he thought we had a Ph.D. or something." "The questions were too vague" or "too specific—she was nit-picking." The professor's style of delivery also comes under attack: "He didn't prepare us properly." "She speaks too fast . . . and uses too many big words. . . . You can't follow her, forget taking proper notes." "If the Prof gave half decent lectures we'd all have better marks." "Yea, he's just plainly a lousy teacher." Occasionally the professor's personality characteristics are also blamed: "He's a nasty person. He enjoys seeing people suffer." While professors may deserve much of the criticism directed at them, there are perhaps other reasons why they are so frequently singled out as a source of the problem. One insightful student noted: "If there was no professor, there would be no exam. And if there was no exam, there would be no grades and so no one could fail." Students also seem to need time to work through the reasons for their poor performance: "He knows why he failed, but he finds the truth too painful to bear. Therefore, he blames his poor mark on the difficulty of the test. It isn't a complete lie because any test will be difficult for someone who hasn't studied." Making the professor the cause of present woes also helps to unite students into more cohesive units which, in turn, work to reduce anxiety. Most importantly, scapegoating moderates feelings of guilt because the reality is one in which the professor must bear at least part of the responsibility.

Another method of mitigating responsibility for exam performance is through "appeals to defeasibility,"[2] especially the "had I only known" types of excuses: "I studied the wrong notes . . . had I known there was going to be so much emphasis on the information in the textbooks, I would have studied them more." "I misinterpreted that question. If I'd only known that's what he wanted. . . ." "Why can't he ever ask the questions I know?" After the first test of the year, one frequently hears: "The lectures seemed so straight-forward and easy I thought I could 'wing it'. . . . As a matter of fact, I didn't start studying until the night before . . . had I known we were going to have

---

2. Scott and Lyman's (1968) "appeals to defeasibility" contain two rather distinct kinds of excuses, a lack of information and a lack of free will.

a test like that I would have been better prepared." Many accounts begin with appeals to defeasibility and end with something approaching scapegoating: "I misinterpreted that question. If I'd only known that's what he wanted, I could have easily done it . . . if only he would word his questions more clearly." If a sufficient number of students express the same problems in each other's presence and no one contradicts the developing theme, they will occasionally talk each other into going to the professor and making a case for their interpretation. Hence the construction of accounts carries along with it the possibility of collective action.[3]

Yet another popular account, "appeal to biological condition," reflects the experiences of individuals. Social acts require bodies, so state of health or tonicity can always be called upon to excuse an unsatisfactory performance: "I wasn't feeling well." "While I was writing, I developed such a bad headache I couldn't think. I considered handing in my paper early and explaining my problem, but that seemed as if it would only cause more problems so I just went on trying to write." "I had a hard time thinking because I couldn't sleep well the last few nights." Since extremes in environmental conditions affect the body which in turn can affect acts during the exam, they can also be classified under appeals to biological conditions: "The room was so cold I could hardly write, let alone concentrate." "The place was so hot, stuffy, and smelly that it almost made me sick to my stomach . . . besides, I had to listen to a disgusting sniffler." Students also may appeal to their mental state on the day of the exam: "I was too nervous." "I experienced a 'blank out'." Another appeal which extends the "biological condition" concerns an absence of "fit" between a student's basic character type and the task at hand: "I'm just not mathematically (sociologically, etc.) inclined . . . some people are and others are not." The absence of "meshing" behaviours may even be applied to the format of the exams: "I'm not good at multiple guess questions because they trick me rather than test my knowledge." "I'm better at objective (multiple choice) tests where you either know the answer or you don't." An interesting point here is the connotational differences in the words chosen to refer to the same exam, depending on the student's attitude towards the type of evaluation and perspective of the moment.

Appeals to accidents are a fourth type of excuse used to disclaim the results of one's performance and mitigate responsibility for it. Students often point to "the generally recognized hazzards in the environment, the under-

---

3. However, vocabularies of motive are specific to situations, so when actors switch roles they also switch the type of account used. For example, after an exam a student, who was participating with others in derogating the professor's abilities (i.e., scapegoating), turned around to leave the group, only to be greeted by the professor who had just opened the door of the exam room and was about to leave. The professor asked the student how he found the exam. He responded: "I don't think I'll do as well as I hoped to because I concentrated on studying the wrong stuff." Note, as the student switched role-sectors, the specific type of accounts he appealed to also switched from scapegoat to "appeals to defeasibility."

standable inefficiency of the body, and the human incapacity to control all motor responses (Scott & Lyman, 1968:47): "My dad just had a massive coronary and I didn't get much of a chance to study." "Its just my luck; I had a fight with my girlfriend (boyfriend) and so I had trouble concentrating."[4]

Over time individuals talk themselves out of excuses and begin to accommodate themselves to their performance. At about this point someone may make a tentative suggestion to the effect that individuals are at least partly to blame for their own performance. As the conversation picks up momentum and more students join in there is a movement from the realm of excuses to justifications. They not only acknowledge greater measures of responsibility for their acts but may even come to see something positive in the experience; that is, while they recognize the general unacceptability of an inadequate performance, they may claim that this particular occasion permits or even requires a compromised performance. Scott and Lyman draw on motives used by juvenile delinquents to neutralize their behaviour (Sykes & Matza, 1957) and classify justification as "denial of injury," "denial of victim," "condemnation of the condemners," and "appeal to loyalties," as well as adding "sad-tales" and "self-fulfillment."

In "denial of injury" actors acknowledge responsibility for an act but assert that it was permissible because no one was harmed or the consequences were trifling. Scott and Lyman originally meant the term to apply to injuries ego perpetrates against others. If we make ego the object of the injuries then a number of post-exam accounts can be classified as 'denial of injury': "So what, it wasn't worth that much. I can still make it up on the final." During final exams one frequently hears: "No problem, my term marks are high enough to balance this grade—even if I fail, it won't hurt me." The results of the exam can also be seen as "trifling" either because of special credentials or because the person may make no claim to full mastery of the area: "It's not my discipline." "It's not my area." "It's not my major." "It's just an option." "It has no relevance to my job." "It doesn't matter, it's a course I had to take to get my degree. I really wasn't interested in the subject anyway."

In "denial of the victim" actors take the position that the action was permissible since the victim deserved the injury (Lyman and Scott, 1968:151). Once again, if we make ego the victim, we hear students say: "I really deserve to fail, I didn't even open a book," "I deserve it, I've been sluffing off all year."

In "condemnation of the condemners" students attempt to discredit or challenge those professors who they believe are unfairly challenging them. To the degree students believe professors are condemning them, condemnation of professors is related to scapegoating. There is a difference in attitude, however, in condemning professors for being unfair, students implicitly justify,

---

4. We are modifying Scott and Lyman's "appeals to biological drives," which they subsume under the larger category of fatalistic forces (i.e., uncontrollable sexual appetites). Such forces are assumed to drive people unwittingly into certain socially proscribed acts.

rather than merely excuse, their own performance: "If he wouldn't give such difficult exams, he'd get better results." "With an exam like that what can you expect?" Students occasionally also dismiss their parents' challenges with: "I'm only grades to my parents."

Scott and Lyman's appeals to loyalties and sad tales can actually be treated as instances of the more generic concept of "role overload" at times when demands placed on students are so heavy they exceed the students' abilities to cope: "I hardly had any time to study for this exam. I had to finish off two final term papers, write up a group project, and study for three other exams this week." "I've just had so much to do—besides all of the school work that's piling up, I have two children, a husband, and a house to take care of. Just how am I supposed to fit in enough time to study properly for a test like 'that'." Such a problem of role overload usually demands that some roles must be sacrificed. In the selection process, both role identity hierarchies (e.g., "Since my other exams were more directly related to my field of work, I felt they required more attention") and appeals to loyalties (i.e., where actors feel their actions are appropriate because they serve the interests of others to whom they owe unbreakable allegiance or affection) are important determining factors (Scott and Lyman, 1968:151). The mother quoted earlier viewed her parental role as personally more important than her student role and she justified her choice by appealing to societal values: "Society says good parents put the needs and desires of their children above their own." Hence, neglect of the study role is justified by the fact that certain identities are expected to take precedence over others (Merton, 1957a). A more direct appeal to loyalties comes from another mother: "I was studying for an exam and one of my children asked for help on a project. I said I was busy right then with my own studying. After a few interchanges, my child said, 'All the other kids in my class get help from their parents. Why won't you help me? Don't you love me?' This appeal to loyalties was particularly effective. 'Believe me, that last one is the best. It works everytime. Of what importance is my exam on the tribes of New Guinea when my own little tribe thinks I don't care?' " Other students also use appeals to loyalties to justify their lack of studying: "My friend just happened to come to town on business. He was leaving the next day so I had to go out with him." "My dad just suffered a heart attack so I had to console my mother and take charge of things." Finally, there are a number of students who accept responsibility for their performance and justify it on the basis of appeals to self-fulfillment: "I get a lot of fulfillment out of seeing how well I can do without studying at all. I know then how well I can do just relying on my natural abilities . . . I feel especially good about myself when I'm still able to pass." On the other hand, another student who experienced considerable difficulty in achieving his "full potential" states: "A 'shocker' [tough exam] like this is probably just what I need to make me buckle down and do some serious work." More philosophical types justify their performances with the notion that "experience broadens": "It's just part of the learning process. . . . I don't feel good about it, it's just life. . . . I've got to get my study habits down pat."[5]

Most students cope with the various sources of uncertainty associated with exams by seeking out others who have undergone the same experience and then engaging in acts of social comparison and social support. Others, however, instead of working through their anxieties directly in the give and take of social interaction, prefer to remain physically close enough to others so they can hear their conversations, yet not have to take part in them. They tend to stand with their backs to the wall; selectively attending to conversations most relevant to them. At most they may contribute a smile or nod in agreement with a point being made. By adopting such a posture they can "soak up" the information, without any of the costs that come with being a participant.[6] There are also a significant number of students who leave the exam site at the first available opportunity and refuse to have contact with anyone present. Keeping such behaviour in mind, it is necessary to qualify Schachter's (1959:103) basic proposition that "anxious subjects want to be only with those in a similar plight."

B. Switching Audiences

On close inspection these "deviant" cases turn out to be alternative strategies for coping with anxiety. One reason for avoiding other students after the exam is the fear that interaction might actually increase anxiety levels through possible discreditation of self rather than reduce them. Since interaction is structured in the process of its occurence, it may take unanticipated turns which place insecure students in compromised positions: "When I don't know my material well enough to back up the choice of one answer over another, I worry about getting cornered and exposing my ignorance to all." "I don't like feeling inferior or intimidated, so I conceal my lack of knowledge by simply leaving as fast as I can and avoiding others who want to talk about the exam." These students feel that withdrawal is the safest preventive strategy for coping with their inability to exercise full control over discrediting information which may surface during interaction.

Other students avoid discussions about the exam because they know that now they cannot do anything to change the situation and to find out that their answers are less than ideal only increases anxiety: "Not talking about the exam allows me to retain confidence in my performance." "I usually try to stay away from others who want to talk about the exam because, now that's out of my control, I want to forget about it." "If I happen to put down the wrong answer,

5. Quite a different scenario occurs if the exam turns out to be easier than expected. Post-exam discussions take on a jubilant tone, with students making comments like: "We deserved it", "We sure studied hard for it", and "The Prof is not such a bad person after all," followed by a listing of more admirable traits, especially teaching quality.
6. These students are somewhat like Wrightsman's (1960) subjects in the "no-talk" condition which was associated with more consistent, though less intense, reduction in anxiety.

talking about it won't change anything. It only succeeds in making me worry, which is the last thing I want to do." Essentially many of these students find comfort not by interacting with others but from the knowledge: "I did my best and that's all I can do for now."

Another reason, besides concealment and inability to change the situation, for not interacting with other students after the exam concerns exam-related phobias. Some students indicate that "particularly trying exams that seriously question my right to be here as a student" arouse so much anxiety that the most effective way to relieve it is immediately to put as much physical and mental distance as possible between themselves and the event: "Exams like that make me want to get away as fast as I can, then I'm not as likely to think those awful thoughts." "I almost literally throw in my exam and run." "I take special precautions to leave the room alone. . . . I leave fast and don't let my eyes get caught. . . . If I am questioned by someone I just nod, shake my head, or at most give a monosyllabic response and keep going." Superstition is yet another reason why some students avoid participation in post-exam gatherings: "I'm reluctant to discuss an exam for fear it will bring bad luck." One girl wriggled her way out of an encounter with another student by stating: "I'm not saying anything about the exam because, whenever I do, I don't do too well. . . . It never fails."[7] As Malinowski noted, superstitions tend to emerge when there are risks of failure associated with something of consequence.

It takes effort to interact with others, especially when one must recall answers and be ready to defend them. Most students are already mentally and physically exhausted, particularly if they stayed awake most of the night before studying or simply faced difficulties sleeping: "The whole re-hash of the exam is sort of like beating a dead horse, and its something I'm not up to after having had my brain systematically picked for the last three hours." Other students indicate that after checking over the exam for a final time "a feeling of relief comes over me and the information starts to drift from my mind. I'm tired and don't want to have to discuss the exam." It may also be the case that some students lack energy to help others "get over the exam"; "I keep my distance because I'm afraid others might dump their anxieties on me, and I just don't have the energy to handle them." Students who have to write other exams especially later the same day, also tend to avoid post-exam interaction: "I have to relax and save up my energies for the next one . . . besides I can't afford to take the chance of discovering my answers were wrong. If I get upset about the exam, it affects my performance on the next one." Although Schach-

7. The first person one chooses to interact with after the exam is crucial. If students don't find a sympathetic response, they tend to withdraw entirely from the scene: "Here I geared myself to her looking for reassurance, and all she said was that, 'for anyone who studies, it was pretty easy.' Of course, she was the absolute authority—it was in her voice and in her words too. I felt like an idiot. . . . My next thought was to get out of the building, away from campus, and go home where I could find comfort."

ter (1959) did not take into account energy level or fatigue, they do appear to be salient factors to explain why people might withdraw from interaction.

Now that the exam is ended, non-student identities become more salient and many students leave to fulfill workday roles or to search out significant others (i.e., friends or mates) for social support. For example, one student in an evening class found the exam very difficult. Initially she looked around for someone who might share her state but instead met up with one of "those" people who indicated "it was a snap." "That response prompted me to flee and seek comfort from my husband in the security of our home. However, when I got home, my husband had already gone to bed and was, in fact, asleep. I was disappointed to the point of being depressed. Here I was with all these feelings I wanted to share with him so he could tell me I was wrong in thinking so negatively of myself. I was too worked up to go to sleep, so I turned on the T.V., but couldn't get involved in any of the programs." She then did what many married, female students do—she engaged in frantic housecleaning. Many of them report an accumulation of guilt over neglecting household chores while studying for exams and they see this frenzied activity not only as a way to "get caught up," but also as a means to "wind down" and return to the routinized world of everyday life. "My next thought was to go downstairs and clean the basement. I cleaned every item I could get my hands on and worked vigorously until I stopped, exhausted, at 12:30 A.M." She then engaged in another routinized act that further facilitated her "return to reality." "I took a long, hot shower, after which, I bitterly crawled into bed and fell asleep."[8] When she awoke the next morning, she was still resentful that her husband had not waited for her. However, "as soon as he said I was intelligent and he was sure I'd do well, my fears just melted away." Although this interchange may on the surface seem shallow and trite, these little supportive rites from significant others carry considerable weight in removing anxieties and restoring a positive sense of self. These alternate modes of coping with anxiety force us, once again, to qualify Schachter's (1959:103) proposition that "anxious subjects want to be only with those in a similar plight."

On the other hand, students who feel they've done well on the exam are more confident and sociable: "When I know I've done well, I'm more willing to listen to others. I also have more discussions with my husband. I don't have this pressing need to discuss my feelings and anxieties." The exam-related dispositions of students who are also parents have implications for their offspring: "When mom comes home after the exam, the children hope she's in a mood to celebrate because, if she is, they know they'll be included."

---

8. As Schwartz (1970:489) indicates, whenever anything significant disrupts everyday routines (especially evening ones), sleep will be difficult because, "the sleep role, like all roles that require substantial physical and/or mental preparation, cannot be abruptly taken on . . . its assumption must be preceded by an institutionalized 'transition phase' wherein the individual may gradually adapt himself to it." In our illustration, then, routinized acts such as housecleaning and bathing facilitated the shift from the world of the exam to the world of sleep.

C. Switching Settings

A good number of students can be found heading towards restaurants and pubs to "indulge ourselves as a reward for all the hard work we've done." Even if students feel they haven't done as well as they hoped, "The marks don't come out for awhile, so celebration is still O.K." These post-mortem discussions usually begin with an overall evaluation of the professor and the course. Interaction here is frequently more humorous than that which occurs just outside the exam room. For example, a frequent theme after a particularly difficult exam is exactly how they're going "to murder the prof," whether it should be by rope (with considerable imagination as to how and which parts of the anatomy will be involved), gun, or dull knife. Another more frequent topic concerns the relevance of the course for the students' lives. A particularly vivid illustration comes from a night class largely composed of policemen and prison guards who were discussing an anthropology class. The students were wondering aloud about the relevance of learning about Malinowski's Trobriand Islanders; as one of them stated amid gales of laughter "It's sure been a long time since I've had a chance to arrest a Trobriand Islander on the Strip". Finally, talk tends to turn to more everyday concerns such as plans for summer vacation. As people finally run out of things to talk about there is a general move to disband with perhaps a few of the participants moving on to a more serious form of celebration at someone's house. In this manner, post-exam interactions function to ease students back into the routines of everyday life.

This function becomes especially apparent when we examine what happens to students who don't take part in post-exam activities. The end of the exam can be anti-climatic: "After working so hard before and during the exam, I'm left with nothing to show for it. So, instead of emotional release, I experience an emotional void—I usually just go back to residence and hide in my room. If I'm really uncertain as to how I performed, the weeks that follow the exam can be filled with agony until I finally get my results." Since most students face uncertainty as to their level of performance, interaction with others allows them to learn something of their probable overall placement and probably leads to a measure of social support from others "in the same boat." A lack of this interaction, as we just noted, tends to result in students negatively exaggerating their performance. However, when they do eventually meet and converse with someone from the same class, much of the anxiety can be relieved: "The day after an in-class test, I met a very bright girl in the tunnel connecting two buildings. She asked me how I found the test. I just said 'Well. . . . ' She 'opened up' and said it was the most difficult test she had experienced in her two years of university. She was sure she had done poorly. Here was a person of substance, a good friend, and an all round good trouper. Using her as a comparison, I no longer felt like such a moron. I immediately stopped my hysterics. . . . I could begin to accept my performance with more dignity." It seems then that students who delay their post-exam interactions have more difficulty switching back to everyday roles in their "real" worlds.

3. Conclusion

The theoretical implications of the post-exam phase are very interesting indeed. Once again we find self-enhancement motives are perhaps even more basic than accuracy motives to the social comparison process. While the most confident students tend to be motivated by accuracy motives, students who feel vulnerable are more likely to abandon the quest for accurate comparisons with others and instead search for self-enhancement via the account-making process.

We do find considerable support for Schachter's proposition that "misery loves miserable company." Indeed, students who feel they fared poorly prefer to interact with others like themselves. However, we find only qualified support for his notion that "misery loves company" since the most miserable students tend to not to be among the highest affiliators. Proportionally more of those students who are disappointed with their performances (as compared to those who are not) withdraw from the situation altogether and divert their attention from their plight by engaging in other activities. Students who are disappointed in their performance may attempt interactions with others but since the result is frequently too anxiety arousing (i.e., they confirm their fears of poor performance by comparison) they leave. On the other hand, students who feel secure in their performance (and are therefore more confident) tend to have more intensive and extensive interaction both with others similar to themselves as well as with those who are "miserable." Indeed, the most intense and extensive post-exam interaction tends to occur when most members of the class feel they have fared well. This suggests that joy may be an even more potent source of affiliation than is misery.

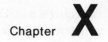

Conclusions and Implications

To understand the nature of student life one must realize just how much of it revolves directly or indirectly around the exam. In order to understand the exam we must look at the reciprocal interpenetration of the micro (face-to-face interaction) and macro (vast behind-the-scenes structures) worlds which results in experiences that make sense to the interactants. Exams are directly linked to our central values of competition and achievement and especially to opportunities for obtaining status, privilege, and power. The importance of these factors when combined with the uncertainties inherent in exams gives rise to intense feelings of anxiety. The major conceptual frameworks used to examine the underlying causes of anxiety and how students cope are structural and symbolic interactional. Instead of seeing them as two theoretical solitudes we attempted to use them in tandem to balance the weaknesses of one with the strengths of the other. In particular, interactional theory, to the extent that it assumes that situations exist in a continual state of construction and never exactly repeat themselves, is weak for demonstrating how students are linked via norms, roles and positions to larger societal structures. It is also weak in explaining how, despite a complete changeover in personnel, students go through more or less stable and recurrent patterns of interaction year after year. On the other hand, structural theory is inadequate for capturing the interactional experiences of actors, especially with respect to how they employ creative acts to cope with role-making demands. Conceptual articulation between these two theoretical approaches was achieved by viewing roles as varying on a loose-tight continuum. At the "loose" end, traditionally focused on by symbolic interactionists, there is greater room for improvisation, while structuralists have largely confined themselves to the investigation of "tight" roles. The study of exam-related experiences allowed for empirical integration of the two perspectives because study roles go through loose-tight cycles. As long as roles are loose there tends to be pervasive deviance, which we attempted to explain through structural concepts such as inadequate socialization to the role, role-personality conflict, subcultural pressures, and role competition.

Even as the study role "tightens" and "forces" students to honour it, a rich underlife of adjustive and creative acts including motive talk and other aligning actions such as role withdrawal, delegation, compression, contraction, and concentration are employed to juggle the multitudinous demands of various role and status sets. In the process of manipulating role systems their structural descriptions can at least be modified and sometimes permanently adjusted as when whole family routines are renegotiated.

Instrumentally oriented strategies designed to reduce uncertainty by setting up conditions that facilitate concentrated study are supplemented by expressive ones designed to increase actors' feelings of control by altering their frames of reference. For example, as Schachter's (1959) work would lead us to predict, students begin directing more words and acts toward others about to share the same ordeal and, consistent with Malinowski (1954) and Gmelch (1971), students begin to direct acts to themselves by using magic to gain greater feelings of control over eventual outcomes of uncertain situations. Furthermore, students who experience difficulties studying rely on fritters (words directed to self) to appease feelings of anxiety and pangs of conscience.

By organizing our research around such theoretical notions we are able to contribute to the understanding of a growing core of social scientific concerns. By investigating the conditions that increase people's desire to affiliate we are focusing on the question that is at the very heart of sociology: why do people want to interact with each other, thereby forming groups and ultimately societies? In grappling with this question we are in essence attempting to provide an answer to "How is society possible?" Although Schachter (1959) laid much of the groundwork he did not follow through to see whether or not "high anxiety" subjects would actually interact with each other; he only asked them if they would desire to do so. And as we know, Deutscher (1973) demonstrates a pervasive gap between what people say they would like to do and what they actually do. By testing Schachter's hypotheses under natural conditions we add credence to his theory and at the same time extend it by demonstrating that participants are not only concerned with an accurate comparison of themselves relative to others but are equally concerned with receiving role identity support. It appears that self-enhancement motives for comparison are stronger than motives of accuracy because whenever self-enhancement is threatened it clearly becomes the dominant motive. Another important point is that although Schachter dismissed the notion that people might affiliate as a means of attempting to divert attention from their "miserable situation," we found considerable evidence that they do. Furthermore, although Schachter found that more of his high anxiety subjects expressed a desire to affiliate with "fellow sufferers," a significant proportion chose not to. His only suggestion in this regard was that those who had siblings and were second born or later were less likely to affiliate. By focusing on deviant cases who specifically chose not to affiliate we found that they were mainly those who had suffered negative examination experiences. Also, and most importantly, people cope with anxiety by directing words and acts to themselves through motive talk and magic as well as through affiliation. Thus, we also found support for Malinowski's proposition that whenever people are committed to a given set of uncertain outcomes magic provides them with a feeling of control. This empirical support is crucial because it demonstrates that Malinowski's proposition holds not only in magic-ridden preliterate societies, but also in supposedly the most literate sector of our society.

In addition to suggesting theoretically oriented contributions, we also attempted to fill an empirical gap on a significant facet of student life. Exams are so much a part of our world-taken-for-granted that social scientists have neglected to investigate them as activity systems in their own right. By studying exams per se, we attempted to go beyond the commonly held assumption that studying and exam writing are highly solitary acts where "students pour out their brains on to paper." Exams are actually imbued with social life as participants orient themselves to each other and are influenced in the process. Indeed, social factors influence everything from deciding when to and how much to study to how rapidly an exam should be written and handed in. The ramifications of exams are everywhere: they influence interactions within the school, work settings, religious groupings, and ultimately in society as a whole. We also demonstrated how, in turn, societal conditions have their impact on exams. As we noted earlier, exams in Britain arose alongside industrialization and the ascending middle class. Industry required reliably trained personnel, and the middle class wanted to compete with the upper classes for more highly rewarded positions. Backed by the rising demands of industry, the middle classes stressed the value of achievement over ascription and sought to institutionalize standardized exams as a major vehicle for attaining positions. By the early 1900's, they had achieved their goal. However, during the middle and late 1960's, students and some faculty members began to question the value of exams in principle: they offered a number of "academic" justifications for the abolishment of exams and suggested benefits which would accrue from their demise. These claims that exams are dysfunctional were rarely subjected to empirical testing, so it might be useful to compare them with findings from the present study.

1. General Criticisms of Exams and Some Empirical Findings

A. Grades Keep "Students From Teacher and Teacher from Students."

We found support for the notion that exams accentuate the social distance between professors and students. Our students frequently use militaristic imagery to describe exam related student-professor interactions. However, we found little support for the idea that the grading system keeps students and teachers from each other. As a matter of fact, student-professor interaction increased as exam dates drew closer; more students attended lectures and the intensity and quality of interaction within the classroom also increased. Students became more actively involved in their role by listening more intently, writing more notes, and asking more questions to clarify potential incompatibilities in information. More students remained after class to ask questions and more availed themselves of help during office hours: "When exams approach, there is something that makes me want to get closer to the professor . . . usually I want to clarify class notes and readings, and if possible, pick up some hints on potential questions." This pattern continues and reaches its climax at the height of the evaluation procedure when the graded tests are returned. Many students want to find out specifically where they lost grades, while others are more concerned with how to increase their standing for the next test. Some students want to negotiate their grades by introducing alternative interpretations of a question or simply pointing out that someone else wrote much the same answer and received more points.

Interactions centering around the alteration of grades may become highly emotional and even conflictual in nature because they focus so directly on the latent conflict built into the student-professor role. It is in the student's interest to obtain the highest grade possible and yet professors are normatively constrained to give grades that "justly" reflect performance. The results of such interactions can be explosive and lead to emotional outbursts on the part of both parties.

While on the surface such conflicts may seem dysfunctional, they do serve the latent function of increasing involvement between the parties, a more productive alternative than apathy, which would more likely occur in the absence of grades. There are also positive consequences of interaction beyond the classroom setting—professors have the opportunity to treat students as individuals and to see whether they are grasping the essentials and underlying orientation of the course. While extensive contact with students necessarily takes away from time available for research and lecture preparation, it does offer the professor the opportunity of being able to validate his/her role-identity as "approachable" and "ready to help."

Overall, we found little support for the assumption that grading via exams keeps professors and students away from each other. On the contrary, exams increase interaction between professors and students symbolically, as students attempt to guess which questions the professor might ask, and in face-to-face encounters.

B. "Exams Create a Negative Atmosphere"

Another argument is that abolishing exams would "promote an atmosphere of partnership, rather than one of jealous competition" (Goldhaber 1973:103). While exams do indeed bring out the competitive aspects of student identities, it is not always at the cost of co-operation. Exams actually make students more dependent on each other and serve to stimulate considerable co-operation between them. Part of this dependency is task-based; for example, students borrow notes from each other so they can supplement their own information or catch up on classes they missed. Once students begin to engage in serious study there are more discussions revolving around clarification and understanding of notes and texts. This interaction might well not occur if there were no exams to "encourage" it. Now "status can be obtained by giving competent help to classmates." The need for information stimulates students to exchange phone numbers and even to form study groups. When an atmosphere of trust among members emerges, group study can be a particularly effective means of preparing, especially for analytic-type questions. There is an intensification of feelings of partnership not only in study groups but also among many class members just prior to and after exams. The joint ordeal of exams seems to have the power to transform strangers into acquaintances and even friends. As Berscheid and Walster (1978:92–3) suggest: "Try an experiment: come to class a few minutes early on a regular school day. You will probably find that few of your classmates approach you. Then, sometime when a tough and important exam is scheduled in one of your classes, arrive a few minutes early. You may be surprised to see how many classmates approach you with friendly remarks or joking comments." Thus, rather than isolating students from each other, exams can actually (with the exception of some isolates) bring them closer together.

C. "Exams Reward the Wrong People"

Another criticism of exams is that "Grades over-reward the wrong people. . . . There is something basically immoral about a system which passes out its highest institutional appreciation to a meritocracy based on memorization," (Simon, 1971:117). The possession of a good memory is certainly a good asset in studying for exams; however, memory is in great measure linked with interest in the subject matter (Robinson, 1970). There is little problem if the persons who perform best on exams are those most interested in the subject matter. The real criticism is that education ought to go beyond "regurgitation" to nurturing students' analytical abilities; students ought to be able to grasp the essence of ideas, relate them to each other, and integrate them into novel patterns of thought. This means professors must construct exam questions which tap this "higher level" of capability. More serious students frequently see this as a major criticism and become angry with professors who give "too easy" exams which can be more than adequately answered with a week or so of "cramming." This sort of arrangement doesn't give an opportunity for them to convey the full range of their knowledge: "Easy exams anger me because they offer no opportunity to push the class variation in terms of quality of answers. They rob me of the chance to prove to myself, and others, just how much I've learned." Another reason for disliking easy exams is that "some students who only crammed for a few days end up with good marks. Since they spend less time studying than you did, they're also regarded as having more 'smarts' than you." Once students learn they can prepare for particular professors' exams in a few days, even ones who normally study a great deal will direct more time to other courses or simply not spend as much time studying. Thus some professors who complain that students don't study enough may actually be responsible for the conditions they observe.

If people object to exams because "they over-reward the wrong people," then as Becker (1968:95) suggests: "the poorer student probably studies longest." Once again we found but marginal empirical support for this notion. In our study only a small minority of students studied for a long time and still received low grades; most of them suffered, not so much from having been blessed with fewer academic talents, but from less efficient study habits. They had problems concentrating on the material and were slow to seek help from others when problems did arise. Most of our students who studied more received better grades overall and those who studied very little were consistently at the lower end of the grade continuum. This association between work invested and rewards is quite in accordance with Homans' (1974) concept of "distributive justice."

D. "Learning Should be Based on Curiosity and Self-Motivation"

Another suggestion is that the elimination of exams would "help develop the habit of continuing education based on curiosity" and "increase self motivation" in students, (Goldhaber, 1973:1027). These hopes seem to be based on the underlying assumption that the pleasure derived from learning is strong enough to keep students at their desks, even in the face of other competing attractions. As we noted earlier, this assumption is highly questionable. Most students experience the austere life of a scholar as aversive, and "anything that is experienced as negative is put off until it has to be done." Even engrossing subject matter cannot guarantee spontaneous study behaviour: "No matter how interesting I may find a subject, it's still hard to really have to learn it." Furthermore, these idealized assertions do not take into account the social nature of studying. Students tend to be immersed in a subculture where the "live-it-up" attitude which prevails is incompatible with regular studying. Also, group norms evolve which help individuals justify not studying, such as appeals to loyalties, and appeals to self-fulfillment. All social relationships, whether with family, friends, work, or school, involve obligations and, except for studying, there is a high degree of role observability. Thus when students are faced with the normal state of role-competition, studying is the easiest activity to neglect because it does not involve immediate relational others. Exams serve to make the study role more observable. The fear of failure coupled with the danger of having to expose a less than adequate grade encourages students to bear some responsibility for their learning, since "nobody gets anything for nothing." In some measure, then, exam results show how well students have borne that responsibility.

In sum, we found little evidence to support the assumption that the removal of grades would generate a more spontaneous and continuous orientation toward studying. As Barzun (1969:87) notes, ". . . a good many plans

140

for independent study have floundered after trial; the cost in will power was too high. For example, in a large mid-western university where a class of 300 in the philosophy of education was asked, after complaints on their part, whether they did in fact want to take responsibility for their own work—reading, research, and preparation for a final 'exit' examination. Ten hands went up." Exams stimulate more studying and, in the process, behavioural conformity tends to be increasingly replaced by attitudinal conformity: "Gaps in knowledge become apparent and implications emerge that would not otherwise have been noticed." The "etc. assumption",[1] which characterizes much of everyday interaction, is also brought to account: "In class when I don't quite understand what the professor is saying I usually play along and hope for more information or an example later that will make the meaning clear. Often it doesn't happen and I forget all about it until I start studying for a test. Then I make a point of asking for clarification." As a result of more accurate information "the subject matter of a course can suddenly become interesting and I'm able to sit and concentrate on it for much longer periods of time." Students are also more likely to turn to each other for answers to questions which appear during study. This "searching for answers" is most apparent just after exams are written when students want to know what others "put down", how others' answers compare to theirs, and what is probably the "more correct answer." Considerable learning occurs during these exchanges and there is no cost to professors' time[2].

Finally, exams are about the only periods of time that the formal organization gets the spontaneous support of informal groups who negatively sanction "too much" studying. Students who study beyond the formal, gradable requirements are subjected to less than subtle pressures: "What's wrong with you?". . . "You must be crazy or something.". . . "Now that's a worm for you." Eliminating grades may well increase the influence of these non-studying groups because pressures against studying subside, and even reverse

1. Ethnomethodologists (Garkinkel, 1967) state that the Etc. Assumption describes the ambiguous nature of many of our everyday communications. Interactants rely on a larger, unspoken context to actually "fill in" much of the meaning of conversations so they can proceed without continual interruption (i.e., "what do you mean by that?"). When meaning cannot be "filled in", we tend to "let it pass" and hope that, as the conversation proceeds, the meaning will eventually become clear.

2. Such exchanges figured prominently in the "breaking" of one of the more infamous cheating routines. A couple of engineering students obtained a master key to their professors' offices. During the exam they would request additional examination booklets and then conceal them when they left the exam room. When the exam was completed, they would engage in the "traditional" exchange of questions and answers with other class members; with the benefit of such "knowledge" they would re-write the exam in the "official" booklets they had smuggled out of the exam room beforehand. After professors had returned the exams to their offices and left for the evening, one student would enter and "pluck out" the "old" booklets and substitute the ones containing the "new" information. Meanwhile, the other student stood sentry at the elevator to warn if anyone was approaching. On one occasion the professor in question happened to arrive via the back stairs rather than the elevator—the shocked reaction of the "sentry" aroused the professor's suspicions and he was able to "apprehend" both culprits before they were able to escape.

themselves, as exams approach; at exam time studying no longer carries with it connotations of "sissy" or "brown-nosing."

If exams do indeed have such an influence on students then their absence ought to bring about dramatic consequences. The following natural, experimental cases make this clear. First, a social science professor, recently immigrated from an Eastern European country and still learning 'our ways', felt that he had very good rapport with his graduate class and gave them their grades three weeks prior to the termination of classes. To his dismay approximately one-half of his students stopped coming to his seminars. The more conscientious absentees phoned in to offer accounts, mostly of the role overload variety, stating that they had to prepare for exams and papers in other classes. Students who did come to class had a great deal of difficulty in keeping the seminar going. They either neglected the required readings altogether or did them in such a cursory manner that they had neither the knowledge nor motivation to maintain the previous quality of interaction. Needless to say, the professor did not issue grades "prematurely" the next year!

Second, the role of grades in student performance was highlighted in a natural "experiment" at Harvard Medical School which occurred when the traditional grading system in basic science courses was converted to a pass/fail arrangement (Goldhaber, 1973). While the last Harvard class under the old system achieved the highest scores on the National Board Exams in all basic science subjects, the first class operating under the pass/fail arrangement dropped to an overall ranking of third on all subjects, two of which were "notoriously low". Faculty members also noted an "abrupt" change in the calibre of students. As we might expect from our earlier review of exam-related behaviour, when exam pressures are no longer as compelling, students become "much more passive." Less pressure to study results in a decreased likelihood of perceiving gaps or inconsistencies in material and a concomitant decrease in number of questions to professors. The upshot of the experiment in question was that more than eighty per cent of basic science faculty members voted for a return to the more traditional grading system, while seventy-six percent of students opposed the return. The grading system was reintroduced because of faculty members' dissatisfaction with the pass/fail arrangement and the hope that reinstituting the old system would "help Harvard students compete in the national marketplace for the most prestigious internships and might encourage students to study harder" (Goldhaber, 1973:1028). In a similar vein Kwong (1983:102) notes that in China during the Cultural Revolution, especially the decade prior to 1977, the exam system was downgraded and as a result "the proper climate for learning was absent, discipline was a problem and students performed poorly." Although we are unaware of a follow-up Harvard study, the results of the present investigation lend support to its validity. As one top-ranked student states: "Despite the educational ideals that are supposed to motivate us, I, like most others, selectively attend to the grade and in the end am probably more motivated by it than by anything else. . . . I find it hard to study or even get interested in a subject if I'm not graded on it. For example, if I have tests or papers where one only received a "pass" or "fail", I put most of my effort into other courses that are graded . . . because . . . after the test or assignment is returned, I know others will ask what I got and I don't want to be embarrassed when I have to reveal my marks."

A situation similar to the one at Harvard occurred at Yale Medical School. The dean of the school, who was responsible for the return to graded exams, used himself as an example in describing the dilemma. As a student, he had a choice of attending either Yale, which did not have graded exams at the time or Columbia, which did. He chose Columbia because, "I'm a terrible procrastinator. . . . I felt I needed deadlines." This statement also describes most students in our study. During the 1930s and 1970s Yale University Medical School had a policy of no examinations in basic science courses, yet students consistently scored anywhere from first to fourth on the National Boards. This seems to indicate that formally graded exams are not necessary to ensure that students study. However, in the early 1970's, the relative ranking of Yale medical students dropped abruptly; by 1973 their performance "reached a new nadir. Out of a class of 105, 13 students flunked the National Boards" (Goldhaber, 1973:1029). Faculty members attempted to explain the shift by pointing to a change in student attitude which increasingly stressed "relevance"—presumably students felt basic science courses were not as directly applicable to their future work as were some others. At the same time, there was a change in the observability of the study role because "the faculty-student ratio declined as Yale expanded the size of its class and there was a corresponding decline in "close faculty-student contact" (Goldhaber, 1973:1029).

McMaster University medical school also has a policy of no exams. As during the forty year period at Yale and the Harvard experiment, students need only pass the National Boards at the end of their training. However, unlike Harvard and Yale, the study role at McMaster is highly observable. Students are assigned to tutorial groups consisting of five students to one tutor, where they can ask or be asked questions at any time. Consequently they must continually demonstrate their knowledge gained from studying and clinical experience. "The emphasis is on frequent assessment of the student and continuous feedback by tutors, peers, faculty and staff" (Haas, et al., 1981:112). The high degree of observability is reflected in the following statements by students: "The biggest difference for me, here, is that you have to reveal more of yourself. You can't hide yourself. You're open to scrutiny and you expose yourself in the tutorial as part of your education." ". . . its really like pulling down your pants" (Haas, et al., 1981:112). Since students are continually assessed in face-to-face conditions, anxiety is high and individuals cope by intensive, private studying[3]. Thus it is not so much the formal machinery associated with exams which motivates study as it is the observability which is inherent in them. Exams make the study role observable, and observability is a continuum. The study role is most highly observable when students are open to daily evaluation in face-to-face contexts, moderately observable when given scheduled exams that are graded to produce a distribution, less observable when only a dichotomous grade (i.e., pass-fail) is awarded, and least observable when no means of evaluation are present, as with "auditors". Given this information, and all other things being equal, we would expect the intensity of studying to vary directly with the degree of observability.

E. "Exams Generate Anxiety and Stress"

Perhaps the greatest number of objections to exams revolve around the anxiety and stress they generate and the observable psycho-physical symptoms we described earlier, such as nightmares, lack of sleep, irritability, upset stomach, headaches, sore back, eye-strain, and constipation. Stress levels may be so high that they actually interfere with the process of writing; students make silly mistakes, forget important points they knew just before the exam (and can remember after the exam is over), and some even experience complete blank-outs. Psychiatric literature describes some extreme cases of students who are "obsessively terrified" by exams. Malleson (1959:225) describes one student who, the night before a critical exam, had the following symptoms: "He was feverish, his temperature was 102 degrees F. He was shivery, and his teeth were chattering. But his symptoms otherwise were not those of a high fever; they were those of high panic. He was sobbing and tearful, bewailing his fate, terrified of the impending examination, desperate that the 'fever' wold stop his getting there. . . . Careful clinical examination failed to reveal anything suggestive of organic disease." Such severe symptoms tend to occur in students who employ denial mechanisms to blot out the approaching exams. When their reality is finally forced upon these students, they are overwhelmed by "examination panic."

While most students do get keyed up for exams, the ones who are least well prepared are more likely to experience the most debilitating effects. The students feel more pressure because their knowledge is insecure and they are motivated by fear of failure, in contrast to their better prepared counterparts

---

3. Unlike most medical training programs, "this school supports and encourages students to learn individually" during free study times. However, in "insulating themselves from each other, they create a new source of anxiety and insecurity" (Haas, et al., 1981:115). Also, without traditional exams, students lack clearly identified shared sources of danger which enhance group formation. Thus, as we would expect, when McMaster students reach the final leg of their studies and begin to prepare for licensing exams, self-organized study groups spontaneously emerge.

who feel more secure and are principally motivated by a desire to excel.[4] Also, pressure enhances performance or lowers it depending on the degree of preparedness (Yerkes and Dodson, 1913; Zajonc, 1965).

For students who have a firm hold on the subject matter the added pressures associated with exams tend to enhance performance beyond its usual levels. However, students who lack a firm grip on the subject matter are more likely to lose their composure altogether. Students who engage in last minute cramming tend to have the weakest hold on the subject matter; they experience more stress in preparing for, and writing, exams. When these students finally do get down to studying they are frequently faced with learning what seems to be an overwhelming amount of material in a very limited time. Pressures are compounded by the fact that major assignments are usually due close to exam time. Role overload can become extreme, for those who procrastinate on their studying tend to do likewise on their assignments. Such students are now forced to make a radical break with their world of everyday routines which results in "withdrawal-like symptoms." In addition, the remaining study time may be so short that students begin to cut into regular sleeping and eating times. Irregular meals, altered diets, and inadequate sleep lead to problems of concentration which are frequently "solved" by drinking more coffee. And those persons who smoke attempt to calm their nerves with more cigarettes. Given the radical changes in routine, the adoption of unhealthy practices, and the frantic last minute cramming, it is small wonder that psycho-physical disturbances become evident.

On the other hand, students who distribute their study time over the whole term are largely spared from many of these strains. Even though they may devote more time to study just before exams, the change for them is not as drastic since studying is already a part of their routine world. Their clearly established schedules also insure fewer competing relationships from which to negotiate release. Studying involves a review rather than learning the material for the first time, and such students can feel more in control of the situation. Relearning is faster and easier since most of the "trouble spots" have already been ironed out. Given fewer problems of role conflict and role overload, these students can afford to take regular meals and maintain regular sleep patterns. The result is less pressure from the studying role itself as well as from friends and acquaintances.

In short, some of the more severe stresses associated with exams are not inevitable and can be greatly ameliorated by an internal tightening of the study role that comes with regular and disciplined study. Even the absence of grades does not necessarily mean an absence of anxiety. As Haas and Shaffir

---

4. McKeachie, et al., (1955) offer experimental evidence obtained from students in exam situations to support this proposition. These assertions are also consistent with McClelland, et al., (1953) who found that students with high achievement needs feel more secure than students with low achievement needs in competitive situations, and do achieve better results.

(1982:138) note in their study of McMaster medical students, one of the greatest "sources of uncertainty is the absence of tests and grades . . . students have no clear benchmarks of progress." A McMaster student states: "I think a lot of people would like to have tests and grades and then they would be able to measure themselves and also they would feel confident they are done with an area and they could leave it behind. . . . This is one of the problems we have—never knowing if we've learned enough" (Haas and Shaffir, 1982:143). The Merton, et al., (1957:67–8) study of medical students also emphasizes the importance of exams by noting that "when the pattern of periodically reporting their grades to students is curtailed or eliminated, there apparently develops a marked concern to find a substitute basis for answering the institutionally generated question: 'How am I making out'?"

2. Some Functions of Exams

Beyond the functions mentioned in the previous section, exams also have several additional benefits associated with them. A most important socialization function is that each exam can be regarded as a "mini" rite of passage which ceremonially marks significant moments in students' careers: "Once you've written the exam, you know you've gone through a certain step in your studies."[5] The tangible evidence of progress is not only obtained from one's grade but also from the rituals associated with preparing for, taking, and "getting over" exams. The importance of this function becomes more evident when, for some reason, rituals are absent. For example, a student who missed a regularly scheduled exam and was allowed to write it at a later date, notes: "I arrived at the professor's office alone and was immediately handed an exam paper . . . he told me to sit at his desk and write until I was finished, and not worry about time. . . . I returned an hour after I had finished to receive my grade. Because I had been so comfortable in writing the exam, I felt no after-exam anxiety, nor ecstacy, for that matter. I felt like there was something missing . . . that I had not written an exam. I also did not feel entirely deserving of the grade I got."[6] As Becker, et al., (1968:31) note, these "markings" are especially important for younger students because they see "college as a place in which one grows up and achieves the status of a mature adult . . . to manage one's college life properly . . . and shows that one has what it takes to be a mature adult." Since exams are highly ritualized and form the primary basis

5. Exams, beyond offering some measure of closure, also inform students of the effectiveness of their work and thereby provide opportunities to better learn the requirements of their role. That is, exams are objective records of mistakes and deficiencies which suggest possibilities for improvement.

6. Aronson and Mills (1959) experimentally investigated the effects of rites of passage. Severity of initiation into a discussion group made the initiates more keen to join it. The ritual ordeal of exams may have the comparable effect of attaching value for students to the courses they take, the degree they obtain, and finally the institution from which the degree comes.

for grade assignment, they become significant ways to demonstrate one's growing sense of maturity: "Exams seem to alter how we view our true selves . . . how mature persons are supposed to act. . . . Drinking, partying, or just plain having fun are now viewed as childish." "Exams connote pressure and maturity . . . its your day of judgment, and others respect you for coping with exams."

If exams are indeed rites of passage, they ought to exhibit the universal three stage process identified by Van Gennup (1960). The first stage separates individuals who are about to change their activities and relationships. Secondly, there is a period of transition where individuals are in a kind of limbo, not fully knowing whether they will be capable of making the transition. Finally, they are ceremonially reincorporated into society but this time in a new status. Van Gennup also indicates any given rite of passage will tend to place more emphasis on one or two of the stages to the relative neglect of the other. In the case of exams, the second, or transition phase, is dominant. As students approach the exam, they wonder whether they "will be student enough to make it." While the consequences of failing an exam may not be as devastating as in some preliterate societies where "those who fail are killed out-right" (Weiss, 1979:274), failing an important exam can mean death to a dream or identity. One can be prevented "from attaining goals, such as admission to graduate professional training, the prestige of college graduation, or of Phi Beta Kappa, and the advantages of good grades in securing a job" (McKeachie, et. al. 1955:97). In most rites of passage which emphasize the transition phase, individuals cope with anxiety through acts of magic and increased acts of affiliation with others undergoing the same ordeal. For students, these expressive strategies are supplemented by instrumental ones such as intensive study which result in withdrawals from the usual round of activities and relationships. The separation phase of the rite is especially pronounced in the exam situation itself; initiates are tightly sealed away from the larger world and each other. However, post-exam interactions re-introduce students to each other and ease the transition back to everyday roles and routines. After completing a vast number of exams associated with the requisite courses which "must be" taken, students are finally incorporated into the graduate community. The climax of the incorporation phase comes with the ritual of Graduation Day where family, friends, and significant figures gather to honor and acknowledge the new initiates. Thus exams may be regarded as significant ceremonial pieces fitting into a ceremonial whole which culminates on graduation day.

Exams also serve more specific functions for students. Exams allow students "an opportunity to be heard" since insights they may have had but never shared may now be transmitted. In a situation where classes are frequently large and students do not have an opportunity to speak or are too shy to do so, exams provide an opportunity for one-to-one interaction with the professor.

Exams also allow students, without the aid of external props like books, to "make individual statements that separate them from the rest of the class."

Exams are also functional for professors. If students who do not regularly attend class perform as well as those who do, then lecturers may begin to ask questions about their own effectiveness. Likewise, the relative quality of answers can serve as a more direct monitor of performance and be used as a constructive guide in re-writing and clarifying lectures. In sum, exams constitute one means of letting professors know how effectively they have mastered their role.

As we noted earlier, exams make lecturing easier because reluctant "learners" are more likely to attend and even take an active part in lectures when they will be examined on them. Exams may also add flexibility to student-professor relations. Over time, in the give and take of everyday interaction, the formal characteristics of the student-professor role tend to recede and be followed by a set of more personal and informal relationships which result in a certain amount of levelling in the status relations. This reduction in the formal authority of the professor may increase teaching effectiveness if students feel freer to ask questions. However, if the trend toward informality were to continue, it could create difficulties in maintaining order and objectivity, especially when grading exams. It is interesting to note that formal relationships tend regularly to reassert themselves as exams approach, thereby recharging the authority of the professor role just at the time of grading when it is needed most.[7] When exams have been returned, relationships once again tend to become more informal until the arrival of the next set of exams.

Exams have also become a legitimate means of awarding grades. The legitimation of grades, in turn, becomes the basis for the legitimation of many other decisions, such as giving out awards, bursaries, student loans, admission to professional faculties, and even the decisions of employers who want to screen potential employees. In the eyes of the larger society, graduates are perceived to have acquired a particular range of skills. Since members of the larger society pay for most education costs, they expect some kind of assurance that these skills have been acquired: "It's one thing to enroll in a class, but it's quite another to really have to master the material in it." Thus exams are relatively convenient, inexpensive, and traditional ways of testing to ensure at least some minimum standard has been achieved. Exams are also comforting to the larger society because they give expressive support to many of its values, especially the work ethic. Since exams force students to work hard, they prevent "university from becoming a joy ride . . . or an escape from having to take a job." When students study they also demonstrate that "they are concerned about the future and will take a responsible place in it." Thus exams help to legitimate the huge expenditures borne by society at large.

7. Professors, frequently unaware of the structural and functional dynamics of the situation, sometimes complain that "exams destroy the class atmosphere I've worked so hard at achieving."

We have looked at the common criticisms directed against exams and have found them to be wanting in several respects. At best they accurately reflect only partial aspects of the "reality" they attempt to criticize. Such criticisms will persist because, as most educators would agree, exams only offer imprecise records of the amount of "knowledge" students accumulate in any one course. But at the same time, most would agree that within the conditions of the current educational system exams are the best yardsticks for measurement we have. This factor became especially evident during the mid 1960's and early 1970's when many professors attempted other methods of grading such as allowing students to assign their own grades or assigning grades solely on the basis of class attendance or participation but found them to be even more wanting than exams. Consequently, most professors have returned to the exam format for assigning grades. It is hoped that future discussions concerned with altering the evaluation of students will be informed of the factors mentioned here. On the other hand, it means that students, at least for the present, must learn to cope with exams.

The best prepared students are most likely to benefit not only from the more specific functions just mentioned but from the exam experience as a whole. Better prepared students tend to suffer fewer stresses and strains, and are less likely to suffer feelings of doom when exams are announced. Indeed, some students even look forward to exams and consider them as rewards for work already accomplished. Better prepared students are also in a position to enjoy the gratification that comes from the "less regimented social atmosphere." Less well prepared students frequently approach them for assistance and generally "open up" more opportunities for interaction. For the best prepared students the pre-exam phase, where students wait around with each other for the exam to begin, brings fewer fears about the "calibre" of others they might be "caught up with" because the chances are good that they will compare favourably. Most importantly, these advantages carry over to the actual writing of the exam. Better prepared students are more likely to "lose themselves" in answering the questions, thereby blocking out noises such as approaching footsteps or a sniffling neighbour which frequently "rattle" their less well prepared counterparts. Since the best students are frequently amongst the first ones finished, they can immediately enjoy post-exam encounters. There is no need for them to feel intimidated and escape at the first possible opportunity or "desperately" seek out others who also found the exam difficult. Instead, better prepared students can afford to be "cosmopolitans" and feel free to circulate through the various groupings, comparing answers and opinions as well as giving comfort to those who need it. The better prepared students also tend to be the ones most in the mood to celebrate. Given the advantages that come with being prepared, but keeping in mind the difficulties students face in reaching this happy state, we will attempt to offer some recommendations.

3. Strategies to Combat Fritters and Study Role Strain

At this point we turn to a more specific discussion of how the theoretical and empirical aspects of our study relate to the practical tasks of studying and preparing for exams. Accordingly the following sections are directed specifically to the student reader.

A. Problem Awareness and Study Role Salience

The first step, which we have already taken, is to identify explicitly study strains and indicate mechanisms used to neutralize the guilt which occurs when studying is postponed and ideals are compromised. Naming the strains and neutralizing mechanisms gives form to what was previously experienced in vague, discomforting ways. This new level of awareness can have implications for action. For example, a knowledge of strains and their consequences places students in a better position to make choices; they can decide whether to continue their current lifestyle or engage in more distributed studying. Where to this point our focus has been on current life-styles, it might now be profitable to consider a lifestyle which emphasizes distributed studying. The following points may be regarded as practical recommendations.

B. Debunking Study Myths

First, developing a more effective lifestyle would involve seeing through and abandoning many myths and practices perpetuated by the nonstudying subculture. For example, fritters should be "seen for what they are—excuses that save our consciences but don't help us improve our study habits." Ideas associated with the "genius myth" have to be abandoned. Also to be purged are romantic notions about it being "gutsy" to postpone study "until it's almost too late and then save the day by giving it all you've got," or that "studying early is like conceding that I don't have the mental capacity or brains to absorb it all in a few days."

If engaging in distributed studying is against the norms of one's membership grouping ("If I start studying early, my friends will laugh at me"), then consider searching for different friends. While initially this may seem unpalatable, the results can be rewarding. Consider this opinion expressed by a very socially oriented freshman: "Initially, when I began to change my study practices, I felt I couldn't like those 'suckholes' who were studying around me, but as I spent more time with them I found I liked them just as much as the anti-studying types. As a matter of fact, they were even more satisfying companions, because meeting my social needs was no longer at odds with my career prospects."

C. Schedules: Study Role Observability and Compartmentalization

Since the study role tends to be "loose," students have the opportunity to structure it through judicious scheduling in a manner that incorporates the multiple facets of their selves (i.e., educational, family, recreational, friendship, work, etc.). Since the student identity tends to be a master status and very problematic, a good idea is to begin the schedule by blocking out required academic activities such as classes and laboratory periods and then adding on all other required activities such as part-time jobs and commuting times. Also include housekeeping, and health necessities such as eating, and sleeping. When fixed activities are accounted for, block off study and recreational times in a way that fits personal dispositions and the schedules of significant others: "One's agenda is not altogether a personal matter but must be interactively determined" (McCall and Simmons, 1978:243). Some students are under the illusion that drawing up a schedule and following it means they must eliminate all other social diversions from their lives. This is not the case at all: "I was pleasantly surprised to learn that drawing up a schedule and following it did not involve trading fun for constant work." "Having fun" and nurturing social relationships are important components of a balanced personality and an overall education. To the extent that balance is achieved, individuals tend to become more effective studiers. As a rule of thumb, most study guides recommend two hours of study for every hour of class time. Researchers (Robinson, 1970) also recommend scheduling study periods just before recitation sessions and immediately after lectures. As the school year progresses, schedules can be adjusted to allow more than two hours per hour of class time for difficult courses and perhaps a little less for easier ones. Another very important point is not to overpack a schedule because chances of following it are slim, and the time it takes to compose the schedule transforms it into a frittering device rather than a solution to studying. Furthermore, students not in the habit of studying should be realistic and adjust themselves gradually as they become more disciplined.

Schedules are particularly helpful in coping with both problems of inadequate socialization to the looseness of the student role and of role competition. As we pointed out, the study role is largely unobserved and therefore easy to neglect. A well-defined and prominently displayed schedule makes study obligations more observable and frittering so much more apparent: "Drawing up a schedule forced me to give thought to how I actually spent my time. I was amazed to see how much time I wasted that could have been put to more constructive use." The greatest problem faced by students is that of "getting started." "Once I get into studying, it really isn't that bad." Since schedules dictate study at particular times, they provide an additional spur "to get on with it" rather than relying on the more prevalent practice of "waiting until I'm in the mood." In particular, schedules discipline one to make effective use of "free time" before, between, or after classes. For example, students who finish one class at 10:30 A.M. and don't have another one until 11:40 often find their planned ten minute coffee break extended to a full hour, especially if they are with friends. A well-defined schedule makes time spent on breaks much more apparent and so facilitates its control. Furthermore, short periods of time can be very effective for studying, because we tend to invest ourselves more heavily in tasks we know will soon be over. Such short "chunks" of time are particularly valuable for personality types who experience rapid buildups of reactive inhibition as study time proceeds. Schedules can also serve as external agents to appeal to when negotiating competing demands on your time.

Schedules effectively compartmentalize roles so that studying is not intermixed with other activities and vice versa: "Once I started to follow my schedule, I got rid of the guilty feelings I used to experience at parties and sporting events. Before I couldn't lose myself in the fun because I knew I ought to be doing schoolwork." Adherence to a schedule helps separate such incompatible roles, so that the benefits of each can be maximized in their "proper" time and place. It's only when schedules are absent that studying becomes an "all your waking hours concern." As schedules become routinized, they're easier to follow: "It's something like having to go to work at a certain time everyday. Once you get used to it, you don't have to struggle anymore." And once friends and relatives become aware of the schedule, they're less likely to intrude upon study time.

With routinization students can avoid wasting time and mental energy deciding when and what to study; scheduling helps prevent the negative associations which go along with vacillation and indecision. In addition, it ensures that students come to class with the appropriate equipment and don't fritter away time trying to borrow it. Finally, schedules provide students with a check on their tendency to avoid subjects they dislike and spend excessive time on subjects they enjoy.

D. Role-Enabling Environments for Study

Environments should be chosen and arranged with the aim of generating a study "self". As many non-study related stimuli as possible should be removed—including reminders of other identities such as pictures of 'good times' or family, which may lead one to daydream and break the study frame. Choose the proper equipment and props—sofas and beds are conducive to relaxation, not studying. Probably the most efficient place to study is at a table or desk which faces a bare wall. The bare wall makes what one is reading more interesting by comparison, makes distractions less likely, and makes it easier to give the appearance of being unavailable for interaction due to uninviting body orientation and lower potential for eye contact. Others get the impression of an individual "hard at work" and are less likely to interrupt.

Pauk's (1974:39) review of the effects of music on studying indicates that background music has either mixed or negative effects.[8] In seven experiments, students who had no background music performed at a higher level than did students who did. Five experiments showed no significant differences between the groups. Pauk concludes: "five ties and seven losses. A very poor record." For most students, then, music can be considered just another distraction. However, some of our more extroverted students did indicate that music helped them get into the study role and remain in it longer "because it makes me feel less lonely." Perhaps the moral of the story is that it's better to study inefficiently than not to study at all.

Students who live in residence indicate that it's very difficult to create ideal study conditions due to the fact that the pressures towards socializing are high and there are so many competing stimuli: "You come to recognize almost everybody's voice and footsteps—it's hard not to attend to them." Similarly, students who study at home "hear things like the doorbell ring. You want to know who it is—it's your uncle, so you start talking, and before you know it the study time for that night is gone." Besides doorbells and telephones,[9] there are a wide variety of highly accessible temptations like television, radio, the fridge, and one's bed. Because of the competing attractions at home, libraries are probably the most role-enabling environments for studying. They are designed for study and reading and have enforceable rules against talking. The quiet and bright environment enhances the studying atmosphere: "you almost feel embarrassed to be caught not studying." Students who have sampled a variety of settings tend to concur: "The best place to study is the library. There are fewer distractions . . . you're also surrounded by other people who want to study . . . it gives you an extra push." Since libraries are not totally homogeneous environments, it is best to choose a location with the fewest distractions possible, such as those away from doors and windows. Find a study carrel or table that faces the wall and colonize it by regular use. Over time, the public space will become a home territory and the "comfortable" ambience will be conducive to study. Earlier we noted that memory is at its best when conditions at the time of recall closely approximate those at the time of learning. For example, study carrels are walled in on both sides and are quite similar to exam tables with their "cheat partitions." Choosing the library as a study area is a good strategy because the large number of people, their arrangement in space, and the general study atmosphere closely approximates examination conditions.

---

8. This refers to music without words. In all experiments, music containing words produced negative effects on students' ability to concentrate.

9. Some students unplug their telephones when they study. One student went so far as to loan his T.V. set to a friend "so I could concentrate on my studying."

E. Study Role Embracement

Study role-enabling environments and schedules are structuring devices for the activity of studying. Studying is a special type of learning that is highly active and systematic. As Morris (1973:21) indicates: "Learning is something that goes on inevitably, continually, and almost accidentally, whereas studying is directed learning that requires a degree of motivation and skill." However, students who have well-planned schedules may go into an ideal study environment and, on occasion, not be able to get themselves into a studying frame of mind. One solution, consistent with role theory, is to act out the behaviours that go with the role and, in the process, the appropriate self will be manufactured.[10] Opening books at the appropriate page, taking pen in hand, sitting erect with an angular tilt towards books as if they are objects of interest, keeping muscles reasonably toned, and beginning to read should produce concentration. "Concentration is a process that is psychologically a good deal like sleep. Neither will come in response to a conscious effort, but both will occur naturally when conditions are favorable" (Morgan and Deese, 1957).

A most important factor related to study concentration is interest in the subject matter. Once again, if interest is not immediately present, it must be manufactured. Subjects tend to be interesting because they relate to things we already know or want to know. In an honest effort to learn, the residue of learning can serve as the foundation to make future learning more interesting. Interest can also be enhanced by trying to find some practical use for the material, therefore, a good suggestion is to try to apply what you learn to your everyday experiences. Try substituting everyday illustrations for general principles found in assigned readings; not only does it force you take a more active part in learning, it helps to ensure an understanding of the principles. Also, consistent with Marks' (1977) energy producing theory, clarification of vocational aims usually adds interest and energy, because students can specifically relate what they are learning to something to which they are committed.

A particularly effective study strategy to increase interest as well as effort in a subject matter is to search out others with whom to discuss it. It is even a good idea to set up a specific appointment because, as Marks' (1977) suggests, we tend to find the energy necessary to meet our group commitments: "I'm much more motivated to study material well when I know I'll be discussing it with someone else." "When you have to present a lecture as it were, you learn the material extra well." Participants sometimes call these study groups "mutual aid societies"; they are structured around norms of rec-

10. Roles not only function as regulatory patterns for externally visible actions, they also shape the inner worlds of moods and selves of their actors. "Each role has its inner discipline or what Catholic monastics would call its 'formation' " (Berger, 1963:98). For example, if one is not in an affectionate, romantic mood but one's mate is, it can be manufactured in the process of reciprocating the other's affectionate displays. "The kiss [a role activity] not only expresses ardor but manufactures it" (Berger, 1963:96). It is the same with studying, as students go through the motions associated with the role, a mood of concentration will tend to follow.

iprocity and individuals "must be willing to give, not just receive." Participants who have little to offer are frequently excluded from future sessions. While these expectations may seem harsh, they do serve the purpose of motivation: "By making study a group affair I feel more obligated to perform, because I'm no longer responsible only to myself but to others as well."

Study groups accelerate the learning process by providing an opportunity actually to discuss the material, and the give and take of discussion emphasizes understanding as opposed to mere memorization (Jones, 1981). These groups may actually be referred to as "brain trusts" because "there's always somebody who knows the answer or who knows somebody else who knows it." And, "unlike many professors, students can explain things in language you can understand." Students who can answer questions gain status in the eyes of their peers and learn in the process due to the fact that the questions frequently force them to think about the material "from a new angle." Since study groups facilitate knowledge, they make studying less problematic. The vicious circle concerning studying revolves around the fact that when we know little about an area we tend to have less interest in it. However, learning more increases our interest. There may also be a role-modelling effect in study groups where the enthusiasm of some wears off on others. Once students develop an interest in an area, they can overcome some of the mood problems related to study, especially the "sleepy feeling that comes over you when you want to avoid something boring."

Study groups serve not only the task-related functions mentioned earlier, but also expressive ones, in that they help to control anxiety which interferes with learning. As a summer school student who was enrolled in a history and sociology course states: "I only made use of group study for my history class. Even though I gave each subject about equal preparation time, I entered my history exam with much more confidence. The feeling of togetherness and the shared opinions as to what the professor might want on the exam were reassuring." Thus students who belong to study groups may well find that their interest in the subject area is heightened, that they actually understand the material better, and that their levels of anxiety are reduced.

F. Textbook Study Tactics: Survey Q3R

There are other methods besides drawing up a schedule and selecting a role-enabling environment that can serve to enhance study effectiveness. The first systematic approach to studying textbooks comes from Robinson (1956;1970). He draws on relevant research literature and supplements it with his own work to formulate a method he labels Survey Q 3R. The program has been thoroughly tested and can be considered a safe guide to improving study effectiveness. As the formula suggests, students should first of all survey their texts. This suggestion is designed to counter the usual impulse of people to plunge immediately into the words without first getting a map of the territory they will be travelling through. First, read the preface of the book to see why it was written and what the author is attempting to achieve; then go through the table of contents slowly and thoughtfully. Do the same for each chapter—read the introduction, go through the headings, and read the final paragraph. Finally, read the conclusion of the text.

As you move into the first chapter, once again, survey it. Try to locate it, mentally, in terms of the book's overall perspective. Look closely at the chapter headings, and read the first and last sentences of each paragraph because they generally contain the topic and summarizing sentences. Next, read the chapter summary. Beyond obtaining a sense of perspective, a quick review can also aid individuals in getting into the study mood, that is, surveying doesn't seem to be as demanding as concentrated reading, so it can serve to ease one into the rigours of the role.

The "Q" in Survey Q 3R means "question," and is designed to make reading (the first of the 3 R's) an active quest for something specific. We get more involved and remember things better when we read to answer questions (rather than attempting to absorb everything like a sponge). Take each heading and transform it into a question; for example, the heading "basic aspects of memory" could be transformed into "what are the basic aspects of memory?" When you're finished reading the section subsumed under a heading, use it as a basis to recite (the second of the 3 R's) the specific answers to questions. The use of headings as both orientational devices and checks on recall ability is especially important; it prevents students from deceiving themselves with the comfortable notion that as long as they're reading it they remember and understand it.

Preferably, answers are written out as if it were an examination situation. Students become acclimatized to exam conditions so that the "real thing" is less stressful. Also, mistakes are clearly exposed and problem areas can be pinpointed and corrected before they become costly. Such a strategy involves a further self-tightening of the study role because surveillance now originates from within self rather than from some external agent of social control. Immediate recitation has the added advantage of slowing down the forgetting process. For example, experiments have been carried out where one group was tested immediately after reading a passage while another group was tested the next day. The net effect was that "more is forgotten in one day when recitation is avoided than is forgotten in 63 days when retention is aided by [immediate] recall" (Robinson, 1970:25).

Since forgetting over time is inevitable, the only way to return learned material to its original freshness is through review, the third of the 3 R's. Ideally one or two reviews should be scheduled between the first learning session and the final review that precedes the exam (Robinson, 1970). This strategy of distributed study contrasts greatly with the cramming that most students do just before the exam. While studying under the pressure of an immediate deadline does speed up the absorption of the material, its cost is that the material is more quickly forgotten. Further, the material frequently is not mastered to the point where it permits manipulation to answer the analytic type of questions, especially ones that call for creative combination of the material. Thus well-spaced reviews provide a more effective and less stressful way to study.

In this chapter we have endeavoured to show—on the basis of social and psychological theory, borne out by the stated attitudes and observed behaviour of hundreds of students—that effective study and exam writing can be achieved by any normally intelligent student who faithfully follows a few reliable guidelines. Briefly stated these guidelines are as follows: use your time and energy resources wisely rather than becoming an academic risk-taker who lives dangerously. Plan your studies carefully as would the "organization person" rather than as the "mad hatter." Your study area should resemble the cell of the monk rather than a salon of distracting artifacts. Address yourself to the content of your study with a ritual akin to that of a monk at prayer and by now you of course realize that, in so doing, you are being scientific not magical; and that your eventual success will not have been stumbled upon but achieved.

Appendix A
Methodology

1. Participant Observation: Strengths and Weakness

Probably the most appropriate methodology available for the study of a variety of social and psychological processes (self, interaction, emerging group perspectives, and their relation to each other within formal organizations such as universities) is participant observation. This technique allows the investigator to take the role of participant and record the unfolding interactions. Since the recorded meaning and behaviours are occurring in the real world, there should be fewer problems about whether they do indeed reflect what is happening. On the other hand, participant observation, like all methodologies, has its potential weaknesses, and when employed incorrectly it can be almost the weakest of research strategies. Fortunately, however, the gravest weaknesses of participant observation are the greatest strengths of experimental strategies. This happy circumstance allows one to take advantage of the strategy of triangulation (Webb, et al., 1966) which, in essence, combines different methodological strategies to confirm one another even though each has certain weaknesses. Webb, et. al., go a step further and state that more than one method should be brought to bear on any given research problem. While the weaknesses of one strategy may be compensated for by the strengths of another, Webb and his colleagues are quick to point out that every attempt should be made to minimize the errors associated with any approach. We attempt to follow this advice by noting the strengths and weaknesses of both participant observational and experimental designs.

2. The Natural Experiment

While experimental research in laboratory settings may permit the establishment of relatively clear cause and effect relationships between specified variables, this strength comes at a cost. That is, the introduction of controls creates a somewhat unnatural "thinned out" situation with little direct connection to the "real" world. The question then arises as to whether or not the predicted behaviour would actually occur in everyday life. The answer to this question calls for a sacrifice of many of the controls possible in the laboratory and a reliance on more naturalistic approaches. Fortunately, the segment of the social world chosen for this study has many characteristics of a laboratory-like situation. Indeed, exams present a setting akin to that of a natural experiment—the major manipulation (giving an exam) occurs without intervention of the investigator. Also, the manipulation is sufficiently strong to produce powerful effects on the behaviour of the subjects in question and so offers valuable information about the direction of causality. An additional advantage of exams over most natural experiments (such as natural disasters) is that exams give advance warning of their arrival and they repeat themselves from class to class and year to year—somewhat like a series of runs of a given experimental condition in a small group laboratory.[1]

Whenever possible throughout the study we attempted to introduce quasi-experimental controls on our observation. For example, we employed interactions associated with the regular classroom as a form of "control group" against which we compared exam related interactions, since the intense forms of interaction observed following final exams could possibly be due to a number of simultaneously varying factors. Final exams have many unique features differentiating them from regular classes: (1) they are held in a much larger setting (typically a gymnasium); (2) they encompass greater numbers of students from a variety of disciplines and faculties; (3) they are almost always longer in duration than regular classes, and (4) they frequently represent the last gathering of a particular group, so interactions would be expected to vary somewhat in form and content. In other words, it would be very difficult to determine which factor (the exam itself or something else) was producing changes in behaviour. Evening classes offered an opportunity to exert some quasi-experimental forms of control over these variables. Specifically, evening classes last for three hours with a fifteen minute break half-way through. Thus, we designed mid-term tests to last for an hour and one-half and, then, after a fifteen-minute break, had the classes resume as usual. Behaviour during regular breaks was then compared to behaviour after mid-term tests. Interestingly enough, behaviours after mid-term tests were very similar to behaviours after the final exams. Observations such as these allowed for less ambiguous interpretation of casual influences (from mere simultaneous co-variations) on behaviour.

---

1. Scheflen, a communication theorist, uses a somewhat similar procedure. However, instead of observing a vast number of behavioural sequences, he films or videotapes one sequence and then plays and replays the film to discover the underlying organizational structure or "program." While this approach is methodologically rigorous, it does have the disadvantage that it involves only one event. Thus, it is not possible to determine whether or not the observed sequences of interaction are unique to a particular occasion.

3. Techniques for Studying the Exam: A Case of Triangulation

A. Observations, Interviews, Exam Logs

The data were gathered over the past eleven years from our own and other classes. We observed and interacted with students as they studied in libraries, took study breaks, and consulted each other on problems. Also, we observed as students prepared for their exams, gathered outside the exam centres, and when they entered, chose their seats, and wrote the exams. Finally, we monitored students as they again congregated outside the exam site and even as they gathered in pubs or local eating establishments for the traditional post-mortem of the occasion.

In the early phase of the study, we observed all of the interactions we could. Observations were either recorded as they occurred or at the first available opportunity. They were interspersed with participation and on the spot interviewing. Notes were reviewed and attempts made to identify recurrent patterns of interaction (i.e., who interacted with whom, how, when, and where). Using the logic of analytic induction, we tentatively inferred a set of propositional statements (of varying degrees of abstractness) which might account for the behavioural regularities observed. Future observations served as tests of these propositions and deviant cases were carefully noted. For example, we did not merely assume that norms were responsible for many of the regularities observed, but (in accordance with our definition) paid close attention to deviants to see if they were sanctioned (or at least if they broke the sense of social rapport).[2] Deviant cases resulted in further reformulation of propositions and the development of a taxonomy of submodes of adaptation on the part of the students.

Interviews with participants (both in and outside of exam-related contexts) filled gaps in our knowledge and aided us in uncovering the meanings that students attached to observed regularities in behaviour. A source of data whch proved rich in subjective detail was to ask students to write descriptions of their behaviours and sentiments as these pertained to the total examination phenomena (i.e., from announcement of the test to interaction after it). Over time, such exam "logs" describing experiences as they occurred were obtained from approximately three hundred university students of all ages (freshmen to mature students), all achievement levels (failure to straight A's), and many social locations (single, married, divorced, and single parents). These records served as a valuable source of information about the accompanying inner life

---

2. The search for a grammar of interaction, in the form of an ongoing set of norms or rules, necessarily involves the making of an assumption that this grammar actually exists. However, there are good reasons for assuming that exam- related behaviours are rule governed because when participants are questioned they reveal awareness of the rules, especially when these are stated in the negative. Furthermore, students tend to monitor their own behaviour to conform to them.

(thoughts and feelings) of students as they went through their exam-related activities. As well, the logs provided information about activities we were in no position to observe, thereby allowing for a more complete understanding of how exams affect, or are affected by, interactions outside the university setting. The logs also provided an additional base against which data obtained from other methods could be cross-checked.

We made every effort to produce minimal changes in the interactions we were recording.[3] During initial exam observations we felt students were so involved in answering the questions that there was no need to shield our note-taking activities. However, it soon became evident that they did notice. They also provided interesting interpretations of our behaviour. Some thought we were gathering information on "cheaters" so as to strengthen our case should the guilty party decide to appeal, while others stated that stopping beside them and writing notes in their presence constituted a violation of their personal space. Consequently, our "deviant" behaviours provided valuable insights into the social organization of exams (norms are not visible until broken) and also resulted in more careful notetaking. Specifically, we changed to jotting down key movements, words, phrases, sentences, and then removing ourselves from direct observation to make detailed notes. We had ample opportunity for these activities when involved in the "invigilator" role. For pre- and post-exam interactions, we were forced mainly to observe classes other than our own, simply because we were not "known" as evaluators by them and would not prove as disruptive to their activities. For example, in our role as invigilators we would occasionally be required to leave the exam room and sanction (e.g., "Please keep down the noise level") students who finished early and congregated in the hallway. Inevitably, we encountered our own students, who, when they recognized us, would bring their talk to a halt (often mid-way through a sentence). Though our presence, in this case, was experienced as somewhat of a "breach", the situation nevertheless also offered valuable insights into the social organization of post-exam interactions (Garfinkle, 1967).

Recording notes just outside the exam room preceding and following the exam was facilitated generally by the large number of students in the environment and also by the fact that the interactions tended to have a loose, fluid quality (with persons regularly changing conversational circles). The impact of our presence for pre- and post-exam observations was further minimized because we were frequently able to position ourselves along the walls—a "safe region" from which to observe encounters. These areas were "safe" because we were able to adopt a stance much like some students who stand by themselves (i.e., not interacting with others) with their backs against the wall observing and listening to the various verbal interchanges that happen to catch their interest. Furthermore, some students also check their notes while getting

---

3. The effect an observer or observation has on the phenomenon under study is termed the "Hawthorne effect."

161

whatever feedback they can from the exchange of questions and answers around them. Thus, while keeping notebook in hand and recording the interactions, we were able to "fit-in" as a natural part of the scene and minimize the influence of our presence upon the phenomena under study.

B. Unobtrusive Measures

While an attempt was made to minimize the disturbance of natural processes under observation, we went a step futher and employed various unobtrusive measures—devices which do not require the cooperation of a respondent and that do not themselves contaminate the response (Webb, et al., 1966). Whenever possible we noted physical traces left by students which might indicate their activities and mental states. For example, as exam time approached, various hand-written signs demanding silence appeared just outside unofficial study areas. As well, since libraries are popular study areas, we noted the significant increase in their usage via objective turnstyle counts. We were also able to record, with minimal reactancy effects, the change in students' appearances as exam time approached. It was easy to observe the increased frequency of large dark circles around sunken eyes and the number of torn, tattered fingernails which reflected the accompanying change in mental state. Photos obtained from university archives and taken while students were writing exams provided an opportunity for extended inspection without disturbance. Triangulation[4] of these various measures (direct observation and participation by researchers who had undergone similar rituals years before, supplemented with quasi-experimental controls, exam logs from students, interviews, unobtrusive measures, incorporation of other pertinent research findings, and inviting students—for whom the exam experience is fresh in their minds—to read, comment on, and discuss earlier drafts) hopefully enabled us to develop a cumulative and credible set of research findings. Data gathering activities ended when information replicated itself (cf. Cuber and Harroff, 1960).

Overall, the aim of the report is to shed light on how people cope with stress and uncertainty[5] (with particular emphasis placed on conditions relating to accuracy versus self-enhancement motives) and to offer a meaningful description of the exam—an important but empirically neglected aspect of the educational process. In essence, we attempted to observe the recurrent patterns of behaviour that characterize exams as social occasions and to "get inside" the students' perspective to understand the situation as they view it.

4. This study employed theoretical (sociological, anthropological and psychological perspectives), methodological, and investigator triangulation. Investigator triangulation occurs with the use of more than one observer in the field. In this study the observers were male and female, which allowed for observation of students in more "private" areas (i.e. cloakrooms, washrooms, etc.) than would have been possible had there only been one observer or two observers of the same sex.

5. The statements people make about their experiences are, for social scientists, methodologically comparable to the microscope used by biologists for penetrating the world of their specimens.

For this reason, extensive use is made here of quotes: using the students' own words[6] brings a reality and a subtle insight to the exam experience (Sapir, 1960).

6. Whenever possible the quotes are exact. In some instances there were minor grammatical changes and editing when the total statement was too long to be included.

References

Abernethy, E.
    1940   "The effect of changed environmental conditions upon the results of college examinations." The Journal of Psychology 10:293–301.

Albas, C. and D. Albas
    1981   'The exam as a social occasion.' In B. Mercer and S. Hey (eds.) People in Schools: A Reader in the Sociology of Learning and Teaching. Cambridge, Mass. Schenkman.

Argyle, M.
    1975   Bodily Communications. New York: International Universities Press.

Argyle, M. and J. Dean
    1965   "Eye contact, distance and affiliation." Sociometry 28:289–304.

Argyle, M. and M. Williams
    1969   "Observer or observed? A reversible perspective in person perception". Sociometry 32:396–412.

Aronson, E. and J. Mills
    1959   "Effect of severity of initiation on liking for a group." The Journal of Abnormal and Social Psychology 59:177–181.

Back, W. and M. Bogdonoff
    1964   "Plasma lipid responses to leadership, conformity, and deviation." In P. Leiderman and D. Shapir (eds.) Psychobiological Approaches to Social Behaviour. Stanford, Calif.: Stanford University Press pp. 36–39.

Barefoot, J. H. Hoople and D. McClay
    1972   "Avoidance of an act which violates personal space." Psychonomic Science 28:205–206.

Barzun, J.
    1969   The American University: How It Runs, Where It Is Going. London: Oxford University Press.

Becker, H., E. Hughes and B. Greer
    1968   Making the Grade: The Academic Side of College Life. New York: Wiley.
    1961   Boys in White: Student Culture in Medical School. Chicago: University of Chicago Press.

Berger, P.
    1963   Invitation to Sociology. Garden City, N.Y.: Doubleday—Anchor.

Berger, P. and H. Kellner
    1964   "Marriage and the construction of reality: An exercise in the microsociology of knowledge." Diogenes 46 (Summer): 1–24.

Berger, P. and T. Luckmann
    1967   The Social Construction of Reality: A Treatise in the Sociology of Knowledge. New York. Anchor.

Berscheid, E. and E. Walster
    1978   Interpersonal Attraction. Reading, Massachusetts: Addison-Wesley.

Beriter, C.
    1977   "IQ and elitism." In A. Himelfarb and C. Richardson (eds.): People, Power and Process: A Reader. Toronto: McGraw-Hill.

Bernstein, S.
    1976   'Getting it done: Notes on student fritters.' In J. Nash and J. Spradley (eds.) Sociology: A Descriptive Approach. Chicago: Rand McNally.

Birdwhistle, R.
    1970   Kinesics and Context. Philadelphia: University of Pennsylvania Press.

Blau, P.
    1964   Exchange and Power in Social Life. New York: Wiley.

Blumer, H.
    1969   Symbolic Interactionism: Perspective and Method. Englewood Cliffs, N.J.: Prentice-Hall.

Boldt, E.
    1978   "Structural tightness, autonomy, and observability: An analysis of Hutterite conformity and orderliness." Canadian Journal of Sociology 3(3): 349–362.

Bovard, E.
    1959   "The effects of social stimuli on the response of stress." Psychological Review 66:267–277.

Bushnell, J.
    1962   "Student Culture at Vassar." In N. Sanford (ed.) The American College. New York: Wiley.

Bustamante, J., A. Jordan, M. Vila, A. Gonzolez and A. Insula
    1970   "State dependent learning in humans." Physiological Behavior 5(7): 793–696.

Cohen, A.
    1955   Delinquent Boys: The Culture of the Gang. Glencoe, Illinois: Free Press.

Coleman, J.
    1961   The Adolescent Society. New York: Free Press.

Coser, L. and R. Coser
    1979   "The housewife and her 'greedy family'." In H. Robboy , S. Greenblatt and C. Clark (eds.) Social Interaction: Introductory Readings in Sociology. New York: St. Matin's Press.

Coser, R.
    1961   "Insulation from observability and types of social conformity." American Sociological Review 26:28–39.

Cuber, J. F. and P. B. Harroff
    1960   The Significant Americans. New York: Appleton-Century.

Deutscher, I.
    1973   What We Say/What We Do: Sentiments and Acts. Glenview: Scott, Foresman and Company.

Durkheim, E.
    1956   Education and Sociology. Glencoe, Illinois: Free Press.
    1954   The Elementary Forms of Religious Life. Translated by J. W. Swain. New York: Free Press.
    1951   Suicide: A Study of Sociology. Translated by J. Spaulding and G. Simpson. New York: Free Press.

Ebbinghause, H.
    1913   Memory. New York: Columbia University Education Reprints.

Entwhistle, N. J. and D. Entwhistle
    1970   "The relationship between personality, study methods and academic performance." British Journal of Educational Psychology 40 (Feb.): 132–141.

Eysenck, H.
    1960   Experiments in Personality. London: Routledge.

Festinger, L.
    1962   "Cognitive dissonance." Scientific American (October): 1–9.
    1954   "A theory of social comparison processes." Human Relations 7:117–140.
    1953   "An analysis of compliant behavior." In M. Sherif and M. Wilson (eds.) Group Relations at the Crossroads. New York: Harper.

Freedman, N. and I. Steingart
    1976   "Kinesic internalization and language construction." In D. Spence (ed.) Psychoanalysis and Contemporary Science, pp. 335–403.

Freud, S.
    1930   Civilization and Its Discontent. New York: Cape and Smith.

Friedenberg, E.
    1980   "Education for passivity in a branch-plant society." In A. Himelfarb and J. Richardson (eds.) People, Power and Process: A Reader. Toronto: McGraw-Hill.

Furneaux, W. D.
    1957   "Report to Imperial College of Science and Technology." reported in N. Entwhistle and D. Entwhistle "The relationship between personality, study methods, and academic performance." British Journal of Educational Psychology 40(Feb.): 131:140.

Garfinkel, H.
    1967   Studies in Ethnomethodology. Englewood Cliffs, N.J.: Prentice-Hall.

Glaser, B. and A. Strauss
    1967   "Awareness contexts and social interaction." In G. Stone and H. Farberman (eds.) Social Psychology Through Symbolic Interaction. Toronto: Ginn-Blaisdell.

Gmelch, G.
    1971   "Baseball magic." Transaction June: 39–43.

Goffman, E.
    1974   Frame Analysis: An Essay on the Organization of Experience. New York: Harper Colophon.
    1969   Strategic Interaction. Philadelphia: University of Pennsylvania Press.
    1971   Relations in Public. New York: Basic Books.
    1967   Interaction Ritual: Essays on Face-to-Face Behavior. Garden City, N.Y.: Doubleday Anchor.
    1963   Behavior in Public Places: Notes on the Social Organization of Gatherings. Glencoe, Ill.: Free Press of Glencoe.
    1961a   Encounters: Two studies in the Sociology of Interaction. Indianapolis: Bobbs-Merrill.
    1961b   Asylums. New York: Doubleday Anchor.
    1959   The Presentation of Self in Everyday Life. Garden City, N.Y.: Doubleday Anchor.
    1952   "On cooling the mark out: some aspects of adaptation to failure." Psychiatry, 15:451–463.

Goldhaber, S.
    1973   "Medical education: Harvard reverts to tradition." Science 181:1027–1032.

Goode, W.
    1960   "A theory of role strain." American Sociological Review 25:483–96.

Gouldner, A.
1960   "The norm of reciprocity: A preliminary statement." American Sociological Review 25:161–178.
Gross, E. and G. Stone
1970   "Embarrassment and the analysis of role requirements." In: G. Stone and H. Farberman (eds.) Social Psychology through Symbolic Interaction. Toronto: Ginn-Blaisdell.
Haas, J., V. Marshall, and W. Shaffir
1981   "Initiation into medicine: Neophyte uncertainty and the ritual ordeal of professionalization." In: B. Warme and K. Lundy (eds.) Canadian Studies in Work and Occupations. Toronto: Butterworth.
Haas, J. and W. Shaffir
1982   "Ritual evaluation of competence: The hidden curriculum of professionalization in an innovative medical school program." Work and Occupations 9(2): 131–154.
Hakmiller, K.
1966   "Threat as a determinant of downward comparison." Journal of Experimental Social Psychology Supplement 1:27–31.
Hall, E.
1966   The Hidden Dimension. New York: Doubleday.
Handel, W.
1979   "Normative expectations and the emergence of meaning as solutions to problems: Convergence of structural and interactionist views." American Journal of Sociology 84:855–881.
Henry, J.
1963   Culture Against Man. New York: Random House.
Hewitt, J.
1979   Self and Society. Revised Edition. Boston: Allyn and Bacon.
Homans, G.
1961   Social Behaviour: Its Elementary Forms. Boston: Harcourt, Brace and World.
Hollander, E. and R. Willis
1964   "Conformity, independence and anti-conformity as determiners of perceived influence and attraction." In E. Hollander Leaders, Groups, and Influence. New York: Oxford University Press.
Hopkins, J., N. Malleson and I. Sarnoff
1958   "Some non-intellectual correlates of success and failure among university students." British Journal of Educational Psychology 28:25–36.
House, I.
1974   "Occupation, stress, and coronary heart disease: A review and theoretical integration." Journal of Health and Social Behaviour 15(March): 12–27.
Hughes, E.
1945   "Dilemmas and contradictions of status." American Journal of Sociology 50:353–359.
Hurn, C.
1978   The Limits and Possibilities of Schooling: An Introduction to the Sociology of Education. Boston: Allyn and Bacon.
Jackson, E.
1962   "Status consistency and symptoms of stress." American Sociological Review 27:469–480.

Jenkins, C.
1971 "Psychologic and social precursors of coronary disease: I." New England Journal of Medicine 284(6): 244–255.
Jones, S., D. Barnlund, and F. Haiman
1981 The Dynamics of Discussion: Communication in Small Groups. New York: Harper & Row.
Jones, S.
1979 "The study of relationships between verbal and nonverbal communicative behaviors." In M. Asante, E. Newmark, and E. Blake (eds.) Handbook of Inter-cultural Communication: Theories, Research and Applications. Beverley Hills, Calif.: Sage.
Kahn, R., D. Wolfe, R. Quinn, and H. Snock
1964 Organizational Stress. New York: Wiley.
Kelman, H.
1961 "Processes of opinion change." Public Opinion Quarterly 25:57–68.
Kerckhoff, A. and K. Black
1968 The June Bug: A Study of Hysterical Contagion. New York: Appleton-Century-Crofts.
Killian, L.
1957 "The significance of multiple-group membership in disasters." In R. Turner and L. Killian Collective Behavior. Englewood Cliffs, N.J.: Prentice-Hall pp. 45–48.
Kuhn, M. and T. McPortland
1954 "An empirical investigation of self-attitudes." American Sociological Review 19(Feb.): 68–76.
Kwong, J.
1983 "Is everyone equal before the system of grades: social background and opportunities in China." The British Journal of Sociology 34(1): 93–108.
Lipset, S.
1963 "Canada and the U.S.—A comparative view." Canadian Review of Sociology and Anthropology 1(6): 173.
Lofland, J.
1976 Doing Social Life. New York: Wiley-Interscience.
Lyman, S. and M. Scott
1970 A Sociology of the Absurd. New York: Appleton-Century-Crofts.
1967 "Territoriality: A neglected sociological dimension." Social Problems 15:235–249.
Malinowski,
1954 Magic, Science, and Religion. New York: Doubleday.
Malleson, N.
1959 "Panic and phobia". Lancet 1:225.
Mandlebaum, D.
1952 Soldier Groups and Negro Soldiers. Berkeley: University of California Press.
Manis, M.
1965 "Social interaction and self-concept." Journal of Abnormal and Social Psychology 51(Nov.): 362–370.
Manis, J. and B. Meltzer
1978 Symbolic Interaction: A Reader in Social Psychology. 3rd Ed. Toronto: Allyn and Bacon.
Marshall, S.
1951 Men Against Fire. Washington, D.C.: Combat Forces Press.

Marks, S.
> 1977   "Multiple roles and role strain: Some notes on human energy, time, and commitment." American Sociological Review 42(6): 921–936.

Matza, D.
> 1964   Delinquency and Drift. New York: Wiley.

McCall, G. and J. Simmons
> 1978   Identities and Interactions: An Examination of Human Associations in Everyday Life. New York: MacMillan.

McClelland, D., J. Atkinson, R. Clark and E. Lowell.
> 1953   The Achievement Motive. New York: Appleton Century.

MacDonald, A.
> 1970   "Anxiety, affiliation, and social isolation." Developmental Psychology 3:242–254.

McKeachie, W., D. Pollie, and J. Speisman
> 1955   "Relieving anxiety in classroom examinations." Journal of Abnormal Social Psychology 50:93–98.

Mead, G.
> 1934   Mind, Self, and Society. Chicago: The University of Chicago Press.

Merton, R.
> 1959   "Conformity, deviation and opportunity structures." American Sociological Review 24:177–188.
> 1957a   "The role-set: Problems in sociological theory." British Journal of Sociology 8:106–120.
> 1957b   Social Theory and Social Structure (rev. and enl. ed.); New York: Free Press of Glencoe.

Merton, R., G. Reader, and P. Kendall (eds.)
> 1957   The Student Physician. Cambridge, MA: Harvard University Press.

Monroe, P.
> 1918   A Text-Book in the History of Education. London: MacMillan Co. Ltd.

Mills, C.
> 1940   "Situated actions and vocabularies of motive." American Sociological Review 5:904–913.

Miner, H.
> 1956   "Body ritual among the Nacirema." The American Anthropologist 58: 503–507.

Morgan, C. and J. Deese
> 1957   How to Study. New York: McGraw-Hill.

Morris, J.
> 1973   Learning to learn. Toronto: University of Toronto Press.

Nolan, P.
> 1981   " 'Role distance' is suicide: A cumulative development in theory." Sociology and Social Research 64(1): 99–104.

Orth, C.
> 1963   Social Structure and Learning Climate: The First Year at the Harvard Business School. Boston: Graduate School of Business Administration, Harvard University.

Parsons, T.
> 1951   "Illness and the role of the physician." American Journal of Orthopsychiatry 21:452–460.

Pauk, W.
> 1974   How to Study in College. Boston: Houghton Mifflin.

Reed, H.
    1931   "The influence of a change of conditions upon the amount recalled." Journal of Experimental Psychology 14:632–649.

Roach, J.
    1971   Public Examinations in England. London: Cambridge University Press.

Robinson, F.
    1970   Effective Study. New York: Harper and Row.

Roethlisberger, F. and W. Dickson
    1939   Management and the Worker. Cambridge: Harvard University Press.

Ryan, W.
    1971   Blaming the Victim. New York: Pantheon.

Sacks, H.
    1973   "UCLA Lectures," No. 2, Spring quarter. In M. Speier How to observe Face-to-Face Communication: A Sociological Introduction. New York: Prentice-Hall.

Sapir, E.
    1960   Culture, Language, and Personality. Berkeley: University of California Press.

Sarbin, T. and V. Allen
    1969   "Role Theory." In G. Lindzey and E. Aronson (eds.) The Handbook of Social Psychology. Reading, Mass.: Addison-Wesley.

Schachter, S.
    1959   The Psychology of Affiliation. Stanford, Calif.: Stanford University Press.

Scheflen, A.
    1972   Body Language and the Social Order: Communication as Behavioral Control. Englewood Cliffs, N.J.: Prentice-Hall.
    1964   "The significance of posture in communications systems." Psychiatry 27:316–331.

Schulz, R. and B. Hanusa
    1979   Environmental influences on the effectiveness of control and competence-enhancing interventions. In L. Perlmutter and R. Monty (eds.) Choice and Perceived Control. Hillsdale, N.J.: Lawrence Erlbaum.

Schwartz, B.
    1974   "Notes on the sociology of sleep." Sociological Quarterly 11:485–499.

Scott, C.
    1908   "On how to write an examination." The Western School Journal 6:208–209.

Scott, M. and S. Lyman
    1968   "Accounts." American Sociological Review 33(Feb.): 46–62.

Seligman, M.
    1975   Helplessness: On Depression, Development, and Death. San Francisco: Freeman.

Sieber, S.
    1974   "Toward a theory of role accumulation." American Sociological Review 39:467–478.

Simmel, G.
    1969   The Sociology of Georg Simmel. Translated by K. Wolff. New York: Free Press.

Simon, S.
    1971   "Grades must go." In A. Shostak (ed.) Sociology and Student Life: Toward A New Campus. New York: David McKay.

Smith, S., A. Glenberg and R. Bjork
    1978   "Environmental context and human memory." Memory and Cognition 6(4): 342–353.

Sommer, R.
    1969   Personal Space. Englewood Cliffs, N.J.: Prentice-Hall.

Stone, G. and H. Farberman
    1970   Social Psychology Through Symbolic Interaction. Toronto: Ginn & Blaisdell.

Smollet, E.
    1975   "Different enculturation and social class in Canadian schools." In Adam Kendon, Richard M. Harris, and Mary Ritchie Key (eds.) Organization of Behavior in Face-to-Face Interaction. The Hague: Mouton.

Sprinthall, R. and N. Sprinthall
    1981   Educational Psychology. Reading: Addison-Wesley.

Stinchcomb, A.
    1964   Rebellion in High School. Chicago: Quadrangle.

Stokes, R. and J. Hewitt
    1976   "Aligning Actions." American Sociological Review 41:838–49.

Sykes G. and D. Matza
    1957   "Techniques of neutralizations: a theory of delinquency." American Sociological Review 22(Dec.): 664–670.

Turner, R.
    1962   "Role taking: process vs. conformity." In Arnold M. Rose (ed.) Human Behavior and Social Process: An Interactionist Approach. Boston: Houghton-Mifflin.

Van Gennup, A.
    1960   The Rites of Passage. London, England: Routledge and Kegan Paul.

Webb, E., R. Schwartz and L. Sechrest
    1966   Unobtrusive Measures: Nonreactive Research in the Social Sciences. Chicago: Rand-McNally.

Weinstein, E. and P. Deutschberger
    1963   "Some dimensions of altercasting." Sociometry 26:454–466.

Weiss, M.
    1979   "Rebirth in the airborne." In Peter Rose (ed.) Socialization and the Life Cycle. New York: St. Martin's Press.

Wheeler, L.
    1966   "Motivation as a determinant of upward comparison." Journal of Experimental Social Psychology Supplement 1:27–31.

Whyte, W.
    1949   "The social structure of the restaurant." American Journal of Sociology 54:302–308.

Wittgenstein, L.
    1958   Philosophical Investigations. Translated by G. E. N. Anscombe in E. Goffman, Frame Analysis: An Essay on the Organization of Experience. New York: Colophon.

Wrightsman, L.
    1975   "The presence of others does make a difference—sometimes." Psychological Bulletin 82(6): 884–885.
    1960   "Effects of waiting with others on changes in level of felt anxiety." Journal of Abnormal and Social Psychology 61:216–222.

Yerkes, R., and J. Dodson
    1908   "The relation of strength of stimulus to rapidity of habit formation."
            Journal of Comparative and Neurological Psychology 18:459–482.
Zajonc, R.
    1965   "Social facilitation." Science 149:269–274.

Name Index

Abernethy, E., 66
Albas, C., 10
Albas, D., 10
Allen, V., 57, 58
Argyle, M., 88, 106, 110
Arnason, E., 146
Atkinson, J., 145

Back, K., 57
Back, W., 16
Barefoot, K., 113
Barzun, J., 140
Becker, H., 31, 140, 146
Berger, P., 3, 154
Beriter, C., 5
Berne, E., 65
Berscheid, E., 139
Bernstein, S., 9, 23, 25, 35, 58, 65
Birdwhistle, R., 95
Bjork, R., 70
Blau, P., 53
Blumer, H., 9, 94
Bogdenoff, M., 16
Boldt, E., 10
Borlund, D., 67
Bovard, E., 16
Bushnell, J., 30
Bustamante, J., 70

Clark, R., 145
Cohen, A., 28
Coleman, J., 32
Coser, L., 47
Coser, R., 10, 31, 35
Cuber, J., 162

Dean, J., 106
Deese, J., 154
Deutschberger, P., 56
Deutscher, I., 82, 136
Dickson, W., 32
Dodson, J., 24, 75, 145
Durkheim, E., 6, 64

Ebbinghouse, H., 24
Entwhistle, D., 26
Entwhistle, N., 26
Eysenck, H., 26

Festinger, L., 10, 17, 63, 76, 85, 119
Freud, S., 65
Friedenberg, E., 112
Furneaux, W., 26

Garfinkel, H., 141, 161
Glaser, B., 67, 87, 93
Glenberg, A., 70
Gmelch, A., 17, 77
Goffman, E., 10, 18, 31, 56, 71, 85, 92,
    98, 109, 114, 119, 125
Goldhaber, S., 138, 140, 142
Goode, W., 65
Gouldner, A., 122
Greer, B., 31, 146
Gross, E., 80, 118

Haas, J., 143, 145
Haiman, F., 67
Hakmiller, K., 85
Hall, E., 89, 105, 111
Handel, W., 11
Harroff, P., 162
Henry, J., 68
Hewitt, J., 11, 23, 44, 89
Hollander, E., 43
Homans, G., 53, 140
Hoople, H., 113
Hopkins, J., 27
House, I., 57
Hughes, E., 31, 47, 146
Hurn, C., 4, 5

Jackson, E., 57
Jenkins, C., 57
Jones, S., 67
Jones, S., 155

Kahn, R., 57
Kelman, H., 42
Kelner, H., 3
Kendall, P., 146
Kerckhoff, A., 57
Killian, L., 61
Kuhn, M., 8
Kwong, J., 5, 142

175

Subject Index

Accounts, 9, 23, 71, 72, 125–130
Accuracy of comparison motive, 17–18, 82–85, 121–125
Altercast, 56, 69, 70
Analytic induction,
Anxiety, 13, 17, 85, 87, 91, 121, 144

Civil inattention, 86
Classroom interaction, 67–69
Cognitive dissonance, 76
Compartmentalization, 30, 31, 35, 47, 151
Compliance, 42, 43
Contextual effects, 70, 78
Conversational preserve, 62
Coping mechanisms, 13, 15

Distributive justice, 140
Dramatic realization, 71

Etc. assumption, 141

Family, 44–52
Friends, 54–57
Fritters, 23, 150

Hawthorne effect, 161

"I", 26, 27
Identification, 42, 43
Identity, 8
Internalization, 42

Macro world, 1
"Me", 26, 27
Micro world, 1
Motive talk, 9

Natural experiment, 158
Negotiations, 69
Norm
    definition of, 7
    looseness, 10
    tightness, 10

Occasions, 10

Participant observation, 158
Personality, 25, 27
Positions, 7, 8
Psycho-physical symptoms, 57

Reference group, 27, 62
Religion, 54
Residual conflict, 49
Role
    competition, 15, 33–36, 53
    concentration, 69, 75
    conflict, 14, 28, 34, 49
    contraction, 47
    definition of, 7
    distance, 64
    overload, 15, 34, 46, 49
    personality, 24
    sector, 8, 62, 67
    set, 8, 62
    strain, 13
    withdrawal, 47, 48, 53

Safe supplies, 86
Self, 26, 27, 64
Self-enhancement motive, 18, 82–85, 121–125
Status set, 8, 37, 62
Stigma, 30
Stress, 13
Structural approach, 7
Study role, 21
Symbolic interactional approach, 9

Triangulation, 160, 162

Unobtrusive measures, 162

Yerkes-Dodson law, 75, 118

177